RESIDENTIAL APPRAISER SITE VALUATION

&

COST APPROACH

SECOND EDITION

WILLIAM G. WILLSON

This publication is designed to provide accurate and current information regarding the subject matter covered. The principles and conclusions presented are subject to local, state and federal laws and regulations, court cases and revisions of same. If legal advice or other expert assistance is required, the reader is urged to consult a competent professional in the field.

Real Estate Publisher
Leigh Conway

Academic Information Analyst
Laura King

Writers
Nicole Thome, Senior Technical Writer
Ben Hernandez, Technical Writer
Sue Carlson, Technical Writer

Copyeditor
Emily Kazmierski

Graphic Designer
Susan Mackessy

Published by
Ashley Crown Systems, Inc.
22952 Alcalde Drive
Laguna Hills, California 92653

Printed in the United States of America

ISBN 978-0-934772-00-6

TABLE OF CONTENTS

Preface. . . . .*v*

About the Author. . . . .*v*

Acknowledgments. . . . .*vi*

Unit 1: Fundamentals: Real Estate and Value **1**

    Introduction 1

    Real Estate 2

    Property. 4

    Value 18

    Economic Principles 24

    Summary. 33

    Unit 1 Review 34

Unit 2: Importance of the Appraisal Process **39**

    Introduction 39

    The Appraisal Process 40

    Summary. 62

    Unit 2 Review 63

Unit 3: Depreciation. **69**

    Introduction 69

    Depreciation: Accounting vs. Appraisal 70

    Types of Accrued Depreciation 73

    Measuring Accrued Depreciation 78

    Summary. 87

    Unit 3 Review 89

Unit 4: Site Valuation: Theory **95**

    Introduction 95

    Separate Site Valuation. 96

    Elements that Affect Land Value 98

    Site Valuation Methods – Theory. 100

    Summary. 112

    Unit 4 Review 113

Unit 5: Site Valuation: Practice **119**

    Introduction 119

    Sales Comparison Method 120

    Allocation Method 122

    Abstraction Method 123

    Subdivision Method 124

    Ground Rent Capitalization Method 127

    Land Residual Method 127

    Summary 130

    Unit 5 Review 131

Unit 6: Estimating Improvement Costs **137**

    Introduction 137

    Estimating Improvement Costs 138

    Methods Used to Estimate Costs 145

    Summary 152

    Unit 6 Review 154

Unit 7: Cost Approach: Application **159**

    Introduction 159

    Components of a House 160

    The Inspection 166

    Applying the Cost Approach 170

    Summary 176

    Unit 7 Review 177

Unit 8: Cost Approach: Summation **183**

    Introduction 183

    Completing the URAR Cost Section 184

    Final Opinion of Value 187

    Case Study 188

    Summary 204

    Unit 8 Review 205

Appendix A: Uniform Residential Appraisal Report 209

Appendix B: Detailed Inspection Checklist 215

Appendix C: Answer Key 219

Glossary 231

Index 261

PREFACE

Residential Appraiser Site Valuation and Cost Approach covers required topics established by the Appraiser Qualifications Board of The Appraisal Foundation. Although written for the beginning appraiser, anyone—consumers and investors alike—will find detailed answers to his or her questions about the value and condition of property.

The entire real estate transaction is constantly evolving; therefore, the professional real estate appraiser must keep up with the changing marketplace. Although a large portion of the marketplace information is available through technology, it is important for an appraiser to know how to interpret and apply this data correctly. To obtain the competency required in real estate appraisal, a basic knowledge of appraisal fundamentals is essential.

This textbook specifies the reasons why site valuation is used. Replacement cost and reproduction cost are discussed. In addition, depreciation and methods used to estimate accrued depreciation is presented. Finally, these concepts are illustrated with multiple examples and case studies.

Each unit in this textbook has been divided into topics. Topic content is reinforced through real-life examples, photographs, illustrations, charts, and tables. Important terms are highlighted in **bold** in each unit. Each unit ends with a summary. Review exercises, featuring appraisal terminology and multiple-choice questions, have been designed for each unit. These challenging questions were designed to test comprehension of the learning objectives and material presented in the units. Answers with complete rationales are provided in the Answer Key in the Appendix.

ABOUT THE AUTHOR

WILLIAM G. WILLSON

William G. Willson brings a rich background in real estate appraisal to the creation and production of this textbook. He is a licensed residential real estate appraiser in California and specializes in residential, small apartment, and vacant land appraisal. In 2003, Mr. Willson established Advance Real Estate Appraisal. His company provides appraisal services for 10 Southern California counties.

For several years, Mr. Willson has taught the 75-hour required core curriculum for the appraiser license. His classroom and field experience contributed to the practical case studies included in this textbook.

Mr. Willson has a Bachelor's Degree in Economics and a Masters Degree in Accounting/Finance from the University of California at Los Angeles (UCLA).

ACKNOWLEDGMENTS

The authors would like to thank the following reviewers for their feedback and suggestions. Their experience and expertise assisted us in putting together this textbook.

Timothy C. Andersen – Palm Beach Gardens, Florida
>   Certified General Appraiser
>   MAI - Appraisal Institute
>   MRA, MSA - National Association of Master Appraisers
>   AQB Certified USPAP Instructor
>   Appraisal Author and Instructor

Linda E. Bemis – San Clemente, California
>   Certified Residential Appraiser

Anthony S. Cangelosi – Santa Maria, California
>   Certified General Appraiser
>   California Real Estate Broker
>   MSA - National Association of Master Appraisers
>   CVA - National Association of Certified Valuation Analysts

Randall E. Grapner – Celina, Ohio
>   Certified Residential Appraiser
>   MRA, MFLA, MSA - National Association of Master Appraisers
>   Instructor

Samuel P. Martin – Schaumberg, Illinois
>   Certified Residential Appraiser
>   IFA - National Association of Independent Fee Appraisers
>   AQB Certified USPAP Instructor and Author

Fundamentals: Real Estate and Value

Unit 1

INTRODUCTION

Real estate is, in addition to a topic of conversation in almost every social circle, a multifaceted career that requires an in-depth understanding of the vocabulary and terminology. This unit provides the basic real estate concepts and definitions that will be used not only throughout this text, but also throughout the appraiser's career.

Real estate appraisal is about money, or more specifically, the monetary value of real estate. As such, the appraiser must be able to identify the real estate being appraised, the interests owned, and all factors affecting the property. The appraiser must present the client with an analysis of existing market conditions and understand the underlying economic principles. Careful study of the material presented in this unit will prepare the appraiser for those tasks.

LEARNING OBJECTIVES

After reading this unit, you should be able to:

- define real estate and real property.
- differentiate between real and personal property.
- list the types of value.
- describe the factors that affect real estate value.
- identify the real estate interests being appraised.
- express the underlying economic principles.

REAL ESTATE

Real estate has been a source of wealth and security since the beginning of time. Real estate was of paramount importance because it was the source of food and water. Whether an economy was based on agriculture or hunting, land was required, and people fought wars to control land (real estate). Real estate is no less important today. Real property provides the resources necessary to sustain daily life and provides us with the security of having a place to live and call home. The importance of owning one's own home was recognized early on in the United States, and the government has taken significant steps to insure that the laws and support mechanisms are in place allowing an orderly exchange of real estate.

Real estate appraisers, who are licensed or certified by their respective states, can appraise only real estate. It is imperative that we understand what real estate is and therefore what we can appraise. **Real estate** is defined in USPAP as "an identified parcel or tract of land, including improvements, if any."

The theory of appraisal separates these two concepts but in many jurisdictions, the terms real estate and real property are used interchangeably. The distinction between the two is important from a theoretical perspective as real estate deals only with the land, while real property deals with the rights associated with ownership. Real estate is an identified parcel or piece of land, and any attached improvements and anything appurtenant to the land.

LAND

Land has certain characteristics that are the foundation of real estate value. In general, land unlike personal property can be considered indestructible. In any discussion of real estate, do not take every word literally for it is evident that under some circumstances land can be destroyed, such as by an earthquake.

Land is unique. Gazing down the street of a residential tract development, most of the properties look similar, but each parcel does have its unique characteristics that allow us to identify and value it separately from the surrounding parcels.

Land is unique.

Characteristics of Land

- Each parcel of land is unique as to its physical attributes and location.

- The parcels of land cannot be moved.

- Land is durable and remains over time—it is indestructible.

- There is a limited supply of land.

- Land is useful to people.

- Theoretically, land extends from a point at the center of the earth outward into space.

More must be said about the verticality of real estate. Land includes much more than the surface of the Earth—it includes airspace and subsurface rights. Included is ownership of all that is underneath the land (**subsurface rights**) and rights to the airspace above the parcel (**air rights**). There are limits to each, but practically, it is important to consider what is beneath the surface as well as air rights.

AIR SPACE

SURFACE RIGHTS

MINERAL & WATER RIGHTS

SUBSURFACE RIGHTS

There are situations in which the air rights are worth more than the physical land itself. For instance, the air rights of a condominium are the principal part of the property being bought or sold. The rights to anything under the property can be equally important, specifically in the case of minerals like water or oil. Frequently,

Subsurface rights

owners of large parcels reserve the mineral rights when they sell their property. If the holder of the mineral rights has the right of surface entry, then the property can be mined at any time, making it almost useless for any other use.

IMPROVEMENTS AND ANYTHING APPURTENANT TO THE LAND

Real estate is more than just the land. It includes all that is built on it and items that may permanently affect its use. This definition is important for the appraiser to understand, because these items can affect the value of the real estate. All must be considered when identifying the real estate to be appraised and the rights being appraised.

The definition of real estate includes improvements attached to the land and anything appurtenant thereto. That definition still leaves a lot of room for question, so the definition will be further refined to eliminate as much ambiguity as possible.

Improvements are structures that are built on the land. These can include all types of buildings, driveways, sidewalks, wells, pools, athletic fields, and almost anything built on the land and designed to remain a part of it.

Improvements include buildings, driveways, and sidewalks.

Appurtenant means to go with. Anything that goes with the land, that is not attached or personal property, would be appurtenant to it. The best example is an easement. An easement gives a third party, not the landowner, the right to use a portion of the land. An easement can be created in several ways, but once created, stays with the land. Another good example is a deed restriction, such as the exclusion of mineral rights in the transfer of the land. Once the restriction is created, it continues with the land.

PROPERTY

Property is anything that may be owned and gained lawfully. Property can be real or personal.

REAL PROPERTY

Real property is defined in USPAP as "the interests, benefits, and rights inherent in the ownership of real estate."

Real property deals with the rights and interests associated with ownership of real estate. These rights are known as the **bundle of rights**. The bundle of rights includes the right to use, possess, transfer, encumber, and enjoy. This full bundle of rights is associated with free and clear ownership of fee simple estates. A **fee simple estate** is the greatest interest that one can have in real property, an estate that is unqualified, of indefinite duration, freely transferable, and inheritable.

Use:	The right use of property, within the law in any way, or for any purpose.
Possession:	The right to live on the property and the right to keep others out.
Transfer:	The right to sell the property, give it as a gift, or dispose of it in any way permitted by law.
Encumber:	The right to borrow money and use property as security for the loan.
Enjoyment:	The right to peace and quiet enjoyment without aggravation by others.

Bundle of Rights: Property rights are the rights someone has in something. Remember the mnemonic "UPTEE"– Use, Possession, Transfer, Encumber, and Enjoyment.

The owner of the real estate has all of the above rights. The owner has the right to use his or her property in any way as long as it is a lawful purpose.

The owner has possession of the property and can refuse admittance to anyone.

The owner has possession of the property and can refuse admittance to anyone. In plain English, it is the right to tell anyone to get off the property. In the United States, this means that the owner may demand that anyone who does not have a court order of special circumstances must leave the property. That includes police, government officials, or just the person down the street. This very important right helps to provide the security that is part of real estate ownership.

The property can be sold or transferred. Only the owner may grant or give the property. **Grant** is a legal term in a deed of conveyance giving an interest in real property to another. The owner may grant a partial interest in the real estate or all interests. The type of deed used in this process depends on the circumstances of the granting and the desired outcome.

An owner can lease his or her property.

An owner can lease his or her property. Note that in this case, the owner of the real estate is trading the use of the property for money. Under a lease agreement, the lessee is guaranteed quiet enjoyment of the property. **Quiet enjoyment** means the lessee gets to enjoy the use of that property free of unwarranted interruptions from the lessor. This is the basis for most landlord/tenant law.

PERSONAL PROPERTY

Personal property refers to those items not permanently attached to land, and are usually moveable and portable. Personal property does not have many of the rights and interests of real property. Personal property appraisal is a separate discipline, which some real estate appraisers incorporate into their practice. Real estate appraisers are licensed or certified to appraise real—not personal property under their state appraisal licenses. Therefore, it is necessary to understand the differences between real and personal property and under what circumstances personal property can become fixtures.

A **fixture** is personal property affixed to real property that meets certain tests. An item of personal property that meets one or more of these tests can be called a fixture and is part of the real property.

> **Tests of a Fixture**
> **Mnemonic = MARIA**
> **M**ethod of attachment
> **A**daptation
> **R**elationship of the parties
> **I**ntention
> **A**greement of the parties

Method of attachment is the most important of these tests. The attachment has to be permanent. An example would be the installation of a microwave in the kitchen cabinetry. Normally, it is attached with screws and not easily removed.

Adaptability addresses whether the personal property is consistent with the real property. The microwave installed in the kitchen cabinetry is certainly consistent with the property and is deemed adaptable.

Two parties involved in a transaction can agree that a piece of personal property is permanently attached and is a fixture. This is one of the weaker tests and used often as additional support of the determination as a fixture. When there is an **agreement between two parties**, the **relationship between them** must be reviewed. In circumstances in which the parties have a less than an arm's-length relationship, their agreement may not support the determination of a fixture. An **arm's-length relationship** is a relationship between parties who are not related or in a confidential relationship and have equal bargaining power.

An installed microwave is an example of method of attachment.

The **intention** of the party installing the piece of property should be considered. This is an important test, especially if the method of attachment leaves room for doubt. An example might be the installation of a spa. In some circumstances, the spa is installed in a structure, with plumbing and electrical placed underground. This method of attachment would insure that the spa is considered a fixture. In other circumstances, a portable spa is placed on a cement slab. This leaves doubt about the permanency of the installation. Here, the intent of the party installing the spa could be the differential test.

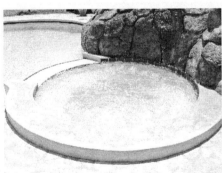

An in-ground spa is a fixture.

A portable hot tub placed on a cement slab is not a fixture.

A piece of personal property installed by a tenant operating a business under a lease is considered a **trade fixture**. Trade fixtures are owned by the tenant and can be removed at the termination of the lease.

Trade fixtures owned by the tenant, can be removed at the end of the lease.

INTERESTS IN REAL PROPERTY

An **interest** is the legal portion of the property and rights that are owned. Interests can describe the physical real estate, the property rights, or a combination of both. Again, the clear description of the interest is required in any appraisal.

TYPES OF INTERESTS

An owner of real property may have a fee simple interest in that property or something less. Fee simple is ownership of all the rights to the property. An owner may purchase less than fee simple interest or have an interest that is limited or partial. A **partial interest** is an interest in real estate that represents less than the fee simple estate. Some examples of partial interests are condominium ownership, easements, leasehold interests, and reversionary interests.

Condominium Ownership. The owner of a **condominium** does not own the entire real estate. He or she owns the airspace between the walls of the condominium and a partial interest in the common areas.

Easement. An **easement** is a partial interest. It is the right to use a portion of a property.

Leasehold Interest. A **leasehold interest** is a partial interest and is the right to use the real estate for a defined period for a specific payment. A **leasehold estate** is the tenant's interest in the leased property during the term of the lease. The owner of the property (**lessor**) would have a leased fee interest in the real estate while the renter (**lessee**) would have a leasehold

A leasehold estate is the tenant's interest in the leased property during the term of the lease.

interest. This type of estate has value if the agreed-on rent is less than the market rent or if the lessee can sublease the property for a higher rent than what he or she is paying. An appraiser may be asked to appraise either the leased fee or leasehold interest in a property.

Reversionary Interest. A **reversionary interest** is a future interest—the interest a person has in property, upon the termination of the preceding estate. The owner of a reversionary interest has granted or leased property for a period, at the end of which the interest transferred returns to the owner. The main feature of reversionary interests is the time limit upon the initial transfer of rights and interests. At the end of that time, the rights and interest revert to the grantor. The real estate appraiser can receive an assignment to appraise either interest, the one transferred or the reversionary interest. The full and complete terms of the transferred interest must be analyzed before any valuation can occur. Typical reversionary interests include leased fee estates and some life estates.

Leased Fee. A leased fee is the reversionary interest owned by a lessor. The lessor has limited or no use of the real estate until the end of the lease, at which time he or she again has a fee simple interest. This can be critical in cases of long-term land leases in which any improvements made to the property by the tenant revert to the property owner at the end of the lease.

Life Estate. A life estate is one that is limited in duration to the life of its owner or the life of another designated person. The term used to describe a life estate created on the life of a designated person is **pur autre vie**, meaning for another's life.

Reserving a Life Estate. An elderly couple sell their property to a developer reserving the right to live on the property until their death when the developer will be able to take possession of the property. This is called reserving a life estate.

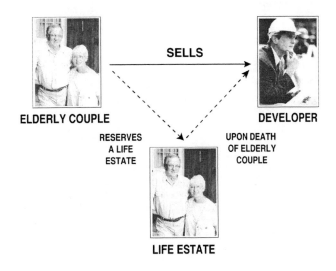

ELDERLY COUPLE   SELLS   DEVELOPER

RESERVES A LIFE ESTATE   UPON DEATH OF ELDERLY COUPLE

LIFE ESTATE

Estate in Reversion. Amy grants Bob a life estate with the provision that upon Bob's death, the property reverts to Amy. Bob is then the life tenant, or the designated party on whom the life estate is based. Amy holds an estate in reversion.

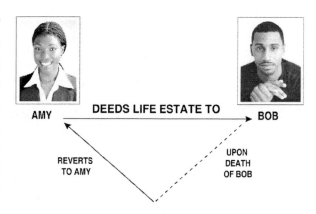

Pur Autre Vie. Tom grants a life estate to Susan for the life of Elizabeth, with the provision that it goes to Laura when Elizabeth dies. Susan may enjoy the benefits of the life estate as long as Elizabeth is alive. Upon Elizabeth's death, the estate goes to Laura or her heirs. That is known as reserving a life estate.

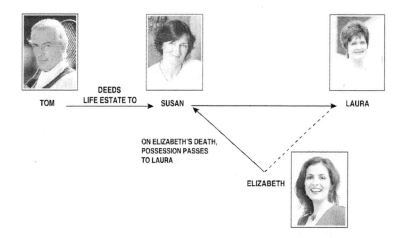

Estate in Remainder. Greg grants a life estate to Linda, with the provision that upon Linda's death, the property goes to a third party, Charles. The interest that Charles holds is known as an estate in remainder.

OWNERSHIP OF REAL PROPERTY

All property has an owner—the government, an institution, or an individual. Most governmental authorities hold title to some real property. The U.S. government property holdings are vast and include federal parks and armed forces bases. States, counties, and cities also hold title to real property for the benefit of their citizens.

Ownership is the right of one or more people to possess and use property to the exclusion of all others. **Tenancy** refers to the method of owner-ship of holding title to property. The word **title** is the term used to describe the combination of the manner in which a property is held, and the interests in the real property. Title is the legal link between the person who owns property and the property itself.

> **Types of Ownership**
> **Sole Ownership**
> **Concurrent Ownership**
>> Tenancy in Common
>> Joint Tenancy
>> Tenancy by the Entirety
>> Community Property

Title can be held in a number of different ways, depending on the needs and goals of the owner(s). Separate (sole) ownership and concurrent ownership are the two ways a person or other entities can take title to or own real estate.

SOLE OWNERSHIP

When one person or entity holds title to the entire parcel of real estate, it is called **tenancy in severalty** or **ownership in severalty**.

CONCURRENT OWNERSHIP

When property is owned by two or more persons or entities at the same time, it is known as **concurrent ownership**, or co-ownership. The title is held jointly and severally. Concurrent ownership has several forms, such as tenancy in common, joint tenancy, tenancy by the entirety, or community property.

Tenancy in common allows two or more people to hold unequal percentages. Each co-owner has an **undivided interest**, which means that each owner has a certain equitable interest in the property, but has the right to use the whole property.

Joint tenancy allows two or more people to hold equal percentages with the right of survivorship. **Right of survivorship** means that if one of the joint tenants dies, the surviving joint tenant automatically becomes sole owner of the property. In order to have a joint tenancy, four unities must be in existence: (1) time, (2) title, (3) interest, and (4) possession. If any one of the unities is missing, a tenancy in common is created.

The Four Unities of Joint Tenancy
Mnemonic = T-TIP

Time	All parties must become joint tenants at the same time.
Title	All parties must take title on the same deed.
Interest	All parties must have an equal undivided interest in the property.
Possession	All parties have equal right of possession.

Tenancy by the entirety is a type of joint tenancy between husband and wife in which each have an equal, undivided interest in the entire property. If either one dies, the title is passed to the surviving spouse, who owns the property without probate. The tenancy may be severed only by joint conveyance or divorce. When a marriage is dissolved, the tenancy becomes a tenancy in common.

Community property is property acquired by a husband and wife during a valid marriage—except for certain separate property. Each spouse has an equal (50/50), undivided interest in the property. Nine states—Arizona, California, Idaho, Louisiana, Nevada, New Mexico, Texas, Washington, and Wisconsin—use the community property system to determine the interest of a husband and wife in property acquired during marriage.

Each spouse has an equal (50/50), undivided interest in community property.

Ownership Table					
Ownership	Number of People	Percentage of Ownership	Use of Property	Ability to Sell	Disposition Upon Death
Separate Property	One person or entity	100%	Full use	No restrictions	Can be willed or passed to heirs.
Tenants in Common	Two or more	Equal or unequal	Equal right of possession	Each party can sell his or her interest separately	Each party can will or pass to heirs. No survivorship.
Joint Tenancy	Two or more	Must be equal	Equal right of possession	All owners must sign	Always goes to surviving tenant. Right of survivorship.
Tenancy by the Entirety	Two – husband and wife	Equal 50% each	Equal right of possession	Each spouse must sign Divorce – becomes tenancy in common	Goes to spouse.
Community Property	Two – husband and wife	Equal 50% each	Equal right of possession	Each spouse must sign Divorce – becomes tenancy in common	Each can will to heirs. If intestate, goes to surviving spouse.

LIMITATIONS ON OWNERSHIP

The use of real property is limited by encumbrances. An **encumbrance** is an interest in real property that is held by someone who is not the owner. Anything that burdens or affects the title or the use of the property is an encumbrance. Most buyers purchase encumbered property. The categories of encumbrances include financial encumbrances and non-financial encumbrances. **Financial encumbrances** affect the title, and **non-financial encumbrances** affect the use of the property.

The financial encumbrances that create a legal obligation to pay are known as liens. Common types of liens are mortgages or deeds of trust, mechanic's liens, tax liens, and special assessments, attachments, and judgments. The types of non-financial encumbrances that affect the physical use of property are easements, building restrictions, zoning requirements and encroachments.

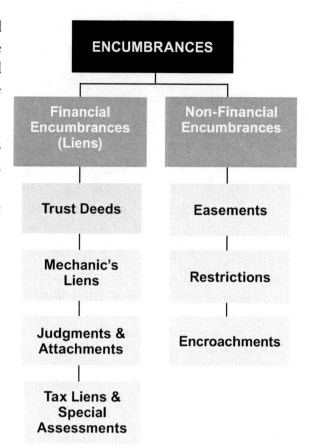

FINANCIAL ENCUMBRANCES

The majority of encumbrances that affect real estate are financial. These are known as liens or security interests. Specifically, a **lien** is a perfected security interest in the real estate.

Liens may be voluntary or involuntary. Typical **voluntary liens** include mortgages and deeds of trust. For example, a voluntary lien is created when an owner borrows against the real estate and uses the real estate as security for the loan.

Involuntary liens are those that are a result of court action or operation of law. Typical involuntary liens include mechanic's liens, judgments, tax liens, and attachments. For example, if the owner does not pay taxes or a debt, an involuntary lien may be placed against his or her property without permission. A **judgment lien** can be created only after a judgment is issued by the court at the conclusion of a suit. This is true for all except tax liens. The Internal Revenue Service can create a tax lien without due process. In addition, a lien for property taxes is the first lien on almost all real estate. The state or county collecting property taxes will have that lien created and appurtenant to every parcel of real estate.

NON-FINANCIAL ENCUMBRANCES

A non-financial encumbrance is one that affects the use of property, such as easements, profit-à-prendres, and restrictions.

EASEMENTS

An **easement** is the non-exclusive right to use a portion of a piece of real estate. Easements are created for the benefit of at least one party, at the expense of the property owner. The party benefiting from the creation of the easement is the **dominant tenement**. The property that is subject to the easement is the **servient tenement**. The dominant tenement is usually the only party that can abandon an easement.

Servient Tenement

The owner may create an easement or give the right to use a portion of the real estate to a person or group of people. For example, owner Sam grants an easement to pass over a portion of his property to next-door neighbor Donna, who needs access to her property. In granting that easement to the neighbor, the easement will continue until abandoned by the neighbor. Sam is called the **servient tenant** because he owns the property burdened by the easement.

Paths are often adverse easements.

Donna, who benefits from the easement, is called the **dominant tenant**. The dominant tenant is the party who must abandon the easement.

Easements can be created with the approval of the servient tenement or in rare cases, against the wishes and desires of the servient tenement. Such an easement is called an **adverse easement** and is created by continuous use against the wishes of the servient tenement. An example of this type of easement would be a path used by pedestrians to the beach over private property. This can become an adverse easement after all the requirements are met.

Another type of easement is an **easement in gross**. In this case, the easement benefits an individual or organization, not a particular parcel of real estate. Utility easements are examples of easements in gross. They are created to allow employees of the utility company to gain access to the property for the installation and maintenance of utility equipment. In many cases, the utility company has an easement for the equipment and an easement in gross to allow access to that equipment.

Utility easements are examples of easements in gross.

PROFIT-À-PRENDRE

The right to enter another's land to remove soil or substances of the soil (water, minerals, timber, fruit, game, or other resource) is known as **profit-à-prendre**. An example would be the right to harvest timber on land owned by someone else.

It is created by the owner granting the profit-à-prendre to the profit-à-prendre holder in writing. It differs from an easement because an easement only gives the right to use the land, whereas, a profit-à-prendre gives the right to remove the soil or products of the soil. A profit-à-prendre can last indefinitely. If an owner grants a profit-à-prendre to someone and then sells the property, the new owner will still have to abide by the terms of the profit-à-prendre. The profit holder can sell, lease, give away, or bequeath the profit-à-prendre to someone else.

RESTRICTIONS

The use of property is limited by restrictions. Restrictions may be placed on property to assure that land use is consistent and uniform within a certain area. They may be placed by a private owner, a developer, or the government. Public restrictions are used primarily to promote the general public welfare. Private restrictions placed by a present or past owner, affect only a specific property or development.

Public Restrictions

Public restrictions on real estate are those associated with government intervention. All private ownership of real estate is subject to the legitimate powers of government, which includes police power, eminent domain, taxation, and escheat. Three of the four powers deal with specific situations while the fourth, police power, is used by government to support the enactment of laws and regulations and the enforcement of these for the benefit and protection of the public health, safety, and welfare.

Police power is the most important of the four powers of the government and the one under which most governmental regulation is promulgated. This power allows the government to make and enforce laws and regulations for the safety, health, and welfare of the public. Zoning regulations, building codes, and fire codes are all enacted under the government's police power.

Eminent domain is the power given government to take private property for public use or purpose. It requires that just compensation be paid the private property owner. There are a couple of issues with this power, now more than ever in the news. The definition of public purpose or use is up to the municipality, but the Supreme Court has upheld that increasing tax revenue is a public purpose. The payment of just compensation is required and an appraisal is usually necessary. The final point is that government is given the right to take private property. The owner has nothing to say as to the **taking**, only the amount of compensation that may be considered just.

Taxation is the right of the government to tax the owners of private property to raise revenue for both general purposes and special assessments, which have a defined purpose. Most property taxes are based on value and are known as **ad valorem taxes**. Each state has its own laws that determine how real property is to be taxed and how the revenue will be shared with the different levels of government. The federal government does not tax real property directly.

Escheat is the process by which private property reverts to the government when the owner dies without heirs and without a will (**intestate**). The **will** is the legal instrument that allows an individual to establish the division of his or her property, personal and real, upon death. The property will revert to the state only if the deceased has neither a will nor an heir.

> **Review – Public Restrictions**
> **Mnemonic = PETE**
> Police Power
> Eminent Domain
> Taxation
> Escheat

Private Restrictions

Usually **private restrictions** are created in the deed at the time of sale or in the general plan of a subdivision by the developer. Private restrictions on ownership of real estate include deed restrictions, encumbrances, and easements. All of these items restrict the use or title to the real estate in some way. In almost every case, except one, restrictions require the agreement of the owner of the real estate before they can be created.

Deed Restrictions

Deed restrictions are commonly known as conditions, covenants, and restrictions (CC&Rs). **CC&Rs** are the rules and regulations established for a parcel of land and accepted by the owner when the property is purchased or transferred. The CC&Rs for a new subdivision are listed in a recorded **Declaration of Restrictions**, which gives each owner the right to enforce the CC&Rs. These regulations are often more restrictive than municipal zoning but are not enforced by the municipality. A private entity, such as a homeowners' association is responsible for enforcement.

Another example of a deed restriction is the reservation of mineral rights by a previous owner. This type of restriction must be carefully reviewed because it can include the right of surface entry. The holder of the mineral rights can mine for those minerals at any time without regard to any improvements on the property. That situation would make building on the property extremely difficult.

VALUE

Value is the monetary worth of property, goods, or services to buyers and sellers (the market). The concept of value includes the benefits received from or related to a property, product, or service. The value today is the present value (or worth) of the future benefits.

This series of concepts appears simple, but it is the basis of the profession of real estate appraisal. Appraisers express an opinion of value, usually market value. Remember, the market establishes value as evidenced by the price an item brings in the open market. The oversupply of a product will have a negative impact on its market value. An enhancement made to a product increasing its utility will have a positive impact on its value.

Price is the best evidence of market value. **Price** is the amount of money actually paid for a property. The amount paid in an open market sale and an arm's-length transaction is real. The opinion of value that the appraiser develops is an approximation based on facts and information, which is analyzed using verifiable appraisal techniques.

TYPES OF VALUE

The majority of appraisal assignments will be to determine the market value of a property. Of the following types of value, many represent different appraisal assignments. Other types of value—scrap value and going concern value—are accounting concepts, which have limited applicability in real estate appraisal.

Types of Value

Annuity	Interim
Assessed	Lease
Book	Listing
Capitalized	Loan
Cash	Market
Court	Replacement
Depreciated	Scrap
Easement	Square Foot
Front Foot	In Use
Going Concern	

MARKET VALUE

USPAP defines **market value** as a type of value, stated as an opinion, that presumes the transfer of a property (i.e., a right of ownership or a bundle of such rights), as of a certain date, under specific conditions set forth in the definition of the term identified by the appraiser as applicable in an appraisal. Market value, or **value in exchange**, represents the value of a property as determined by the open market.

The market value definition used in most standard form reports today is that offered by the Federal Register, V55, No. 251, December 31, 1990, Washington, D.C.

"The most probable price which a property should bring in a competitive and open market under all conditions requisite to a fair sale, the buyer and seller each acting prudently and knowledgeably, and assuming the price is not affected by undue stimulus. Implicit in the definition is the consummation of a sale as of a specified date and the passing of title from seller to buyer under conditions whereby:

1. the buyer and seller are typically motivated;

2. both parties are well informed or well advised, and acting in what they consider their best interests;

3. a reasonable time is allowed for exposure in the open market;

4. payment is made in terms of cash in United States dollars or in terms of financial arrangements comparable thereto; and

5. the price represents the normal consideration for the property sold unaffected by special or creative financing or sales concessions granted by anyone associated with the sale."

ARM'S-LENGTH TRANSACTION

Market value is the most likely amount of money paid for a property in cash or cash equivalents under a fair and open market transaction on a particular date. The term often used for this type of fair transaction is **arm's-length**.

Requirements for an Arm's-Length Transaction

1. Both the buyer and seller must be typically well informed as to the conditions of the market and the subject property.

2. Both the buyer and seller must be acting reasonably, in their own best self-interest, and without undue duress.

3. The property must be exposed to the market for a reasonable time.

4. No extraordinary circumstances, such as liberal financing or concessions, are involved.

It is important to understand the circumstances of a sale before accepting an appraisal assignment and before using a sale as a comparable property. Any sale that does not meet the standards of an arm's-length transaction should not be used as a comparable. A sale that is not arm's-length is not representative of market value and is of little use to an appraiser using the sales comparison approach. Sales that were not exposed to the market for a reasonable amount of time through an accepted forum, usually the multiple listing service (MLS) do not qualify as open market sales. A foreclosure sale is equally unsuited as a comparable as the seller was certainly under duress. The application of this definition of market value and application of the arm's-length transaction conditions to every appraisal helps to standardize the appraisal and improve credibility in the market.

ELEMENTS THAT CREATE VALUE

There are four elements required to be present for an item to have a value. The four factors that contribute to **value** are **demand**, **utility**, **scarcity**, and **transferability—DUST** for short. If any of the elements are missing, the product cannot have value in the marketplace.

DEMAND

An item must be in demand if it is to have value, and that demand must be real or effective. **Effective demand** is demand or desire coupled with purchasing power. The market must want a product before it has any value.

UTILITY

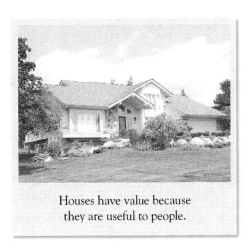

An item must have some use to the market or at least the portion of the market considering purchasing the item. The key is that it is the opinion of the market, not the opinion of one individual. Both a car and a home have significant utility to the purchaser and their utility contributes to their value.

Houses have value because they are useful to people.

SCARCITY

A product must be scarce in order for it to be of value. An example often used in class is the relative value of a grain of sand to someone sitting on the beach. If a grain of sand were put up for auction on the beach, there probably would be no bidding as it was not a scarce resource and the potential market could obtain sufficient amounts of sand for no cost. Diamonds are a good example of a product whose scarcity is strictly monitored by the diamond cartel, thereby helping to maintain their value.

TRANSFERABILITY

Owners must be able to transfer their title.

The ability to transfer title to a product is an essential element of value. Something that cannot be sold or transferred cannot have a value. Real estate, while not being moveable, is certainly transferable and therefore has value. The real estate market has made great progress over the years in identifying the real property interest, any appurtenances, and liens against the property allowing title to be transferred with relative ease.

FACTORS IMPACTING REAL ESTATE

An appraiser must be able to define and identify the real estate. In addition, he or she should understand all the factors that affect real estate and be conversant with their impact on market value.

> **Review – Four Elements of Value**
> **Mnemonic = DUST**
> **D**emand
> **U**tility
> **S**carcity
> **T**ransferability

The four basic factors that affect real estate are physical factors, economic conditions, political considerations, and social influences.

PHYSICAL FACTORS

Physical factors that affect real estate include size, topography, and location. Everyone has heard the admonition in real estate that the three most important things about a property are location, location, location. While that is not entirely true, it certainly is extremely important. The location of a property, relative to negative factors like a freeway or positive factors like a lake or the ocean have a significant impact on its value.

A beach house will have more value than the same house by the freeway.

ECONOMIC FACTORS

Economic factors can have real and immediate impact on real estate values. The single most important economic factor is employment or job availability. There is a direct connection between the job market and the real estate market. In areas of high unemployment, real estate values will be depressed. As unemployment rises, people who lose their jobs may eventually have to sell their homes, increasing the supply on the market. That will have the effect of depressing prices. The opposite is true in areas experiencing job growth.

Employment or job availability affects real estate value.

To a lesser extent, interest rates have an impact on real estate. Historically, real estate has sold at a faster rate in a low interest rate environment, but in 1988, when the average mortgage rates exceeded 10%, the real estate market was still strong. Typically, when residential mortgage rates rise there may be a negative impact on real estate sales.

Analyzing the economic environment includes a thorough review of the present and predicted job market, the types of industry and employment available in an area, the dominance of any particular industry or company, and the financial markets and availability of mortgage and equity monies.

POLITICAL FACTORS

Restrictive building permits limit the supply of real estate.

Political or government factors include planning, zoning, building and fire codes, and taxes. The government can restrict the supply of real estate by limiting building permits, restricting access to utilities, or creating restrictive zoning. All of these factors can have an impact on the value of real estate.

SOCIAL FACTORS

School test scores and crime rates affect real estate values.

Social factors can also influence real estate values. The social factors that are included are schools, crime rates, age restrictions, and any other factors that may affect value other than race. Race is never a factor that affects value of real estate. Schools and crime appear to be the most significant social factors that affect real estate values. A home in a great public school district sells for significantly more than a home that is literally across the street, but in an un-favorable school district. Areas with higher crime rates will see their real estate values depressed. These factors change over time and it is important to stay up-to-date on research and maintain current knowledge of neighborhoods.

> **Review – Four Main Forces Influencing Value**
> **Mnemonic = PEPS**
> Physical forces
> Economic forces
> Political forces
> Social forces

ECONOMIC PRINCIPLES

Basic economic principles apply to all aspects of the real estate industry. Appraisal is no exception. The economic principles of value are the basis for all appraisal procedures and approaches. The principles frequently are interrelated.

HIGHEST AND BEST USE

USPAP states that when necessary for credible assignment results, an opinion of highest and best use is required. Therefore, an opinion of highest and best use should be incorporated into appraisals for market value, both for the land, as if vacant, and as presently improved, as a measure of property utilization as of a certain date. Before estimating a property's value, appraisers must determine its most legally profitable and physically permitted use—the highest and best use—that is, the use that will give the maximum net return or benefit.

The two criteria that determine highest and best use are demand (either existing or imminent) and police power approval (zoning, building site approval, and necessary permits). There are four tests to explore these criteria for highest and best use.

The demand (new condominium construction) and police power determine highest and best use.

Tests for Highest and Best Use

1. **Physically possible.** Is it feasible to build and maintain the intended structure on the property? The physical characteristics of land dictate and place limitations on the project.

2. **Legally permitted.** Is it likely that the use is, or could be, legally permitted? If there has been no actual approval, the appraiser can weigh the probability of receiving this approval and apply it to the estimate of value. (In cases with a possibility of a zoning change, many properties are sold contingent on the buyer being able to obtain the necessary zoning.)

3. **Economically feasible.** Is the cost of establishing the use of the property economically sound?

4. **Maximally productive.** Will the use provide the highest present value?

The highest and best use of a property may change over time, depending on zoning changes and other factors. The use providing the maximum return on investment should be determined.

Consideration of feasible alternatives for land use, without the improvements, provides the basis for land valuation. Evaluating the contribution of improvements to the land provides a complete picture of property value. If the improvements do not represent the highest and best use as if vacant, an interim use value may be estimated for the improvements. **Interim use** is a short-term and temporary use of a property until it is ready for a more productive highest and best use.

Vacant property, interim use, highest and best use.

The existing or proposed zoning, of itself, does not create value. It is a means to determine the highest and best use of a property. Some properties today are zoned for a particular purpose, such as industrial or commercial. If there is no demand for that particular use, the property value may suffer or the owner may have to wait years for demand to increase to the point that it becomes economically prudent to develop the property for that use.

Multiple-family residential units yield a higher net return.

SUPPLY AND DEMAND

The **principle of supply and demand** is the basis for analysis of any market economy. The price levels will change based on the relative supply of and demand for any resource. The supply of and demand for dissimilar types of property changes with the location and the timeframe. Both supply and demand must be analyzed. An analysis of one without the other is useless and incompetent. Market segments react differently to changes in the supply and demand. Not only will properties in that particular market segment be affected, but also changes in one area have a ripple effect in other market segments. An example of this is the lagging demand for apartments as prices rise with increased demand for single-family homes. As home prices rise, some of the potential homebuyers will be priced out of the market and forced to rent. This increased demand for rental units lags the home price increase but is a result of that increase.

The principle of supply and demand is the basis
for analysis of any market economy.

Appraisers are required to analyze the relationship of supply and demand for the market segment being appraised. The reason for this requirement in every summary report is to provide the theoretical and practical basis for anticipating price changes in the market. Prices will remain relatively stable when supply and demand are in balance. When demand exceeds supply by a significant amount, there will be pressure on prices to increase. The opposite is also true. In situations of over supply, there will be pressure on prices to decline. **Balance** indicates when equilibrium exists in the marketplace. Market forces often change. This creates a situation in which supply and demand are not in balance with the resulting pressure on price levels. This information is important to clients so that they can make an informed decision based on a complete perspective of the existing market conditions.

SUBSTITUTION

Substitution is one of the basic economic principles of a free market system and is the foundation for the appraisal process. The **principle of substitution** states that the maximum value of a property tends to be set by the cost of acquiring an equally desirable and valuable substitute property. Essentially, a three bedroom, two-bath 1,500 square foot (SF) ranch style home is a substitute for a similarly sized and configured home in the same neighborhood. This principle holds true in real estate markets as well as most all other efficient markets. In each of the appraisal techniques used, the appraiser bases his or her analysis on the availability of substitutes.

If two houses are similar, buyers chose the least expensive.

In this text, the cost method will be addressed. The essence of that method is that the appraiser can develop costs for a similar property that is a substitute for the property being appraised. The sales comparison method is similarly based upon the principle of substitution. In selecting comparable properties recently sold, the appraiser is substituting them for the subject. Substitution is essential to the operation of the free market system and the principle that allows appraisers to employ successfully the cost, sales comparison, and income approaches.

ANTICIPATION

The **principle of anticipation** is exactly what it says. The market believes it can foresee the future and act upon its expectation. No one is making the claim that this anticipation is perfect but it is the basis of the appraiser's use of the income approach. The appraiser, as well as the buyer, anticipates the continuation of the stream of income associated with the property and values this set of future benefits. This is an example of how part of our definition of value can be used. The value definition includes the present value of future benefits. That is exactly what the appraiser is calculating in the income approach. The appraiser anticipates the future income stream and performs calculations to develop an opinion of the present value of that stream.

CHANGE

Change is constant and it is the reason appraisers must continuously monitor and analyze the economic environment. Every portion of our world, from the global

Past and present income production suggests future property earnings.

geopolitical situation to the local economy is constantly changing. The **principle of change** states that it is the future, not the past, which is of prime importance in estimating value. The appraiser must be aware of these changes and analyze their impact on real estate. The URAR 1004-5 form has a section that requires the appraiser to describe the existing market conditions. Many appraisers use a generic paragraph that provides the reader little or no real information. This approach does not provide the reader with the information needed to make an accurate determination regarding the property. Appraisers are required to update their files in order to provide the client the most up-to-date and accurate information. That is why we recognize change as part of our principles and recognize our responsibilities to remain current.

EXTERNALITIES

Externalities are the countless influences outside the subject property that affect that property. These must be identified and their impact analyzed. For example, a home built next to a large freeway or four-lane highway would be negatively impacted. The impact of the noise, traffic, and dirt will have a negative impact on the market price when compared to a property without those influences. Externalities include physical, social, economic, and governmental influences all of which are outside the property. These

Change is constant—note the small two-story building squished between the two buildings scheduled for demolition.

influences are not always negative. The impact of a good school system is very positive. An area with a lower crime rate would have a positive impact on the property. It is important to recognize the existence of these outside influences and analyze the impact.

A freeway has a negative impact on the market price for residential property.

CONFORMITY

Conformity is not entirely limited to real estate, but is most often associated with real estate. The **principle of conformity** states that maximum value results when properties in a defined area or neighborhood are similar in size, style, quality, use, or type. A neighborhood in which the homes are similar in design, style, and utility is said to be a **conforming neighborhood**. A neighborhood in which there are varied land uses, improvements of differing ages, design, and utility is said to be a **non-conforming neighborhood**. In general, a conforming neighborhood will have stronger market appeal and therefore higher prices. Areas that have significant diversity

Homes conform when they are similar in style and lot size.

in property use and type can be difficult to value for both the appraiser and the market and are subject to the impact of outside influences. A single-family home built next to non-conforming properties, such as a large apartment building or shopping center will be negatively impacted by these improvements. This is compared and contrasted to the conforming neighborhood in which the homes have nothing other than similar homes in the surrounding area.

CONTRIBUTION

Contribution is the process of adding a permanent improvement to an existing property. The importance of this concept is that people want to improve or change their properties all the time. The type of improvements made, how they are done, and the costs associated with those improvements are factors that the appraiser must take into account. Once armed with this knowledge, the appraiser can move to the next principle and analyze the market impact of the contribution.

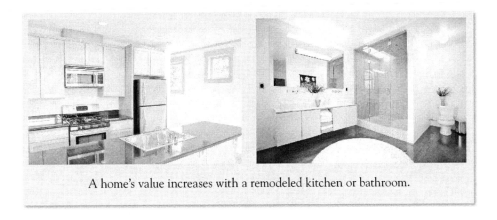

A home's value increases with a remodeled kitchen or bathroom.

INCREASING AND DECREASING RETURNS

Once a contribution has been made, the homeowner and the appraiser would like to know the market's response to that improvement. Analyzing the market's valuation of the contribution leads the appraiser, and homeowner, to evaluate whether the expense of the improvement generates a positive return or a negative return.

An **increasing return** occurs when the cost of a contribution is less than or equal to the amount the market will pay for that contribution. An example would be the addition of central air conditioning to a home. If the cost were $2,500 and the market would pay an additional $2,500 or more for the home after the addition, then the contribution would have an increasing return.

A **decreasing return** occurs when the cost of a contribution is more than the amount the market will pay for that contribution. In other words, the owner spent more than the market is willing to pay for that improvement. The best example of this situation is the addition of a swimming pool. The pool could cost between $30,000 and $100,000, but the market might not pay more

Will the remodeled sunporch cost contribute to the property's value?

than $10,000 to $20,000 for the improvement. There is little doubt that this is a decreasing return. The appraiser is not being judgmental or expressing an opinion as to whether the contribution should be undertaken, he or she is making an economic analysis of the market response to that particular contribution.

BALANCE

The **principle of balance** is also known as the theory of surplus productivity. **Surplus productivity** is the income generated by a project after the four agents of production have been paid. Each of the four agents of production has a specific cost associated with it. The real point of contention is whether management is compensated on a fixed basis or entitled to the entrepreneurial profit of the project. This analysis is useful in appraising future developments, commercial or residential, and calculating the total costs and potential profit associated with the development.

AGENTS OF PRODUCTION

The production of goods and services depends on the coordination of the four **agents (factors) of production**. The agents are labor, management (entrepreneurship) capital, and land. All four agents are essential to the success of any project.

Labor

Labor has first claim on returns from production and includes wages (except management) and operating expenses. Labor is required to operate an existing property or transform a vacant parcel to a finished, marketable product.

Management has second claim on the returns from production and includes entrepreneurial effort. The manager (entrepreneur) is responsible for coordinating the project—from choosing the land, raising capital, and constructing improvements to marketing the project.

Management

Capital

Capital covers the purchase of the land and the cost of improvements and equipment. Capital also includes the amortization of any loans to pay for capital expenditures, reserves for future depreciation, and insurance and tax expenses.

Land

Land is the last agent to have a claim on returns from production. The remaining amount, called a residual, can be used to determine the value of the land.

SUMMARY

This unit has discussed real estate, its terminology, value, and the economic principles traditionally affecting real estate. The appraiser can now identify both the physical attributes of a specific property, the interests owned, all things appurtenant to, encumbering, and restricting its use or ownership. The methods of holding title to real estate and their impact on ownership were discussed. Once the real estate has been identified and its attributes explored, then the factors that affect real estate, PEPS, physical, economic, political (government), and social factors must be identified and analyzed. Finally, all of this must be presented in a coherent, organized format consistent with USPAP standards.

UNIT 1 REVIEW

MATCHING EXERCISE

Instructions: Write the letter of the matching term on the blank line before its definition. Answers are in Appendix C.

Terms

A. ad valorem tax	J. fixture	S. principle of substitution
B. air rights	K. improvements	T. profit-à-prendre
C. appurtenant	L. joint tenancy	U. real estate
D. arm's-length	M. leasehold estate	V. reversionary interest
E. community property	N. lien	W. right of survivorship
F. easement	O. life estate	X. subsurface rights
G. encumbrance	P. market value	Y. title
H. escheat	Q. partial interest	
I. fee simple estate	R. personal property	

Definitions

1. _____   An identified parcel or tract of land, including any improvements

2. _____   Ownership of all that is underneath the land

3. _____   Structures that are built on the land

4. _____   The greatest interest that one can have in real property

5. _____   Items that are not permanently attached to land, and are usually moveable and portable

6. _____   An interest in real estate that represents less than the fee simple estate

7. _____   The tenant's interest in the leased property during the term of the lease

8. _____ An interest in real property that reverts to the owner after a period of time or the conclusion of certain conditions

9. _____ An estate or interest in real property that is limited in duration to the life of its owner or the life of another designated person

10. _____ Term used to describe the combination of the manner in which a property is held, and the interests in the real property

11. _____ Type of ownership that allows two or more people to hold equal percentages of a property with the right of survivorship

12. _____ Property acquired by a husband and wife during a valid marriage—except for certain separate property

13. _____ Anything that burdens or affects the title or the use of the property

14. _____ A perfected security interest in the real estate

15. _____ The non-exclusive right to use a portion of a piece of real estate

16. _____ The right to enter another's land to remove soil or substances of the soil (water, minerals, timber, fruit, game, or other resource) over a period of time

17. _____ A tax based on value

18. _____ The most probable price a property will sell for in an open market and under all conditions required for an arm's-length transaction

19. _____ The description of a transaction in which all parties act from equal positions, without duress

20. _____ The principle that states the maximum value of a property tends to be set by the cost of acquiring an equally desirable property of equal utility

MULTIPLE CHOICE QUESTIONS

Instructions: Circle your response and go to Appendix C to read the complete explanation for each question.

1. Which is a characteristic of land?
    a. Land is destructible
    b. There is a boundless supply of land
    c. Each parcel of land is unique as to its physical attributes and location
    d. All of the above

2. The rights associated with fee simple ownership of real estate are called the:
    a. rights of the lessee.
    b. bundle of rights.
    c. tests for a fixture.
    d. factors that affect real estate.

3. Which is not one of the tests of a fixture?
    a. Method of attachment
    b. Agreement between the parties
    c. Size of personal property
    d. Adaptability to the real estate

4. Personal property that is permanently attached to the land or improvements by a tenant under a business lease:
    a. is not removable after the lease terminates.
    b. remains with the property after the lease terminates.
    c. may be removed after the lease terminates.
    d. remains real property even if it is used for business purposes.

5. The government uses _____ to enact laws and regulations regarding building and fire codes.
    a. taxation
    b. police power
    c. escheat
    d. eminent domain

6. The process by which private property reverts to the government when the owner dies without heirs and without a will is called:

    a. eminent domain.

    b. appurtenance.

    c. anticipation.

    d. escheat.

7. Which element is not necessary for an item to have value?

    a. Demand

    b. Cost

    c. Utility

    d. Transferability

8. Which of the following is not one of the four factors affecting real estate?

    a. Scarcity

    b. Economic

    c. Social

    d. Physical

9. Which economic principle is based on the sales comparison method?

    a. Anticipation

    b. Contribution

    c. Substitution

    d. Surplus Productivity

10. Which economic principle underlies the income approach to real estate appraisal?

    a. Contribution

    b. Anticipation

    c. Substitution

    d. Conformity

11. Which economic principle describes the impact on real estate of the proximity of a freeway?

    a. Anticipation

    b. Contribution

    c. Externalities

    d. Balance

12. A neighborhood of similar houses would be an example of the economic principle of:

    a. balance.

    b. conformity.

    c. contribution.

    d. externalities.

13. The analysis of a contribution as to whether it produces an increasing or decreasing return is based on the:

    a. cost of the improvement.

    b. market's valuation of the contribution.

    c. appraiser's inexperience.

    d. owner's enjoyment of the improvement.

14. Surplus productivity measures the income generated by a project after paying the:

    a. costs associated with construction.

    b. expenses and debt service.

    c. cost of a contribution.

    d. four agents of production.

15. Which agent of production covers the purchase of an improvement on land?

    a. Land

    b. Capital

    c. Management

    d. Labor

Importance of the Appraisal Process

Unit 2

INTRODUCTION

This unit discusses the appraisal process, which is the framework for every appraisal. The approach to any appraisal problem must be systematic and thorough. The steps are addressed from the definition of the problem at the beginning to reconciliation of the value opinions at the end. This valuation process is shown in a flow chart found later in this unit. Copy this chart and place it in the front of every appraisal. The appraiser can then check off each step as it is concluded, assuring that all the elements of an appraisal are satisfied and complete. Emphasis is placed on the appraiser's ability to research the appraisal problem and verify the results of that research. Appraisal data and data sources are analyzed to ensure that the appraiser understands the source, quality, reliability, and veracity of the data. The final section of this unit addresses the analysis needed to begin the appraisal process. The "appraiser should have a meticulous, complete road map of the process and steps needed to produce a comprehensive, credible appraisal."

LEARNING OBJECTIVES

After reading this unit, you should be able to:

- list the steps in the appraisal process.
- determine appropriate data for an appraisal.
- enumerate data sources.
- analyze selected data as to its source, quality, reliability, and veracity.

THE APPRAISAL PROCESS

Appraisal is defined as the act or process of developing an opinion of value. An appraisal is not simply the result of the efforts of the appraiser. It is the sum and substance of the process that the appraiser practices to arrive at the opinion of value. The appraiser should have a good understanding of the concept of value. The other part of the definition—opinion—when used by an appraiser or attorney, has a specific legal meaning. The term **opinion** refers to the application of the professional's expert knowledge and experience as applied to the set of facts presented. Hence, the **opinion of value** developed by the appraiser is a result of first developing the set of facts surrounding the problem, and then applying his or her expert knowledge and experience to those facts. An opinion of value may be expressed as a single point value, a range in value, or a value relationship.

Appraisal of real estate is a process that uses methodology and techniques that are applied in a consistent and replicable manner. Appraisers learn the techniques that can be applied in a scientific method to develop the information on which the final opinion of value is based. This unit discusses the processes set forth in USPAP that are central to the completion of a competent appraisal. Some sections appear to be obvious. However, it is in just these areas that most beginning appraisers make their most significant errors. The discussion of each methodology and its techniques is important because they are the backbone of the appraiser's approach to any problem.

The **appraisal process** is a systematic procedure used by appraisers to arrive at an opinion or estimate of value. The process begins exactly as one would expect it to begin—with the definition of the problem. This step most often is taken for granted. That oversight can result in an appraisal that is not what the client requested or does not reflect the correct interest or value. Not only is the definition of the problem a good place to start, it establishes the path the appraiser uses to complete the process.

FLOW CHART: THE VALUATION PROCESS

1. Define the Problem

- Identify client or user
- Intended use of the appraisal
- Definition of value
- Date of the appraisal
- Identification of the property including location and interests
- Extraordinary assumptions and hypothetical conditions

2. Determine the Scope of Work

This is now one of the most important steps in the process. The appraiser must define what is needed to solve the problem before starting the data collection and analysis.

3. Collect, Verify, and Analyze the Data

Market Data:	Physical, economic, government, and social characteristics
Subject Property:	Interest held, owner, site and improvements, fixtures, personal property
Comparable Property:	Interest held, type of property, site and improvements, personal property
Highest and Best Use:	As vacant and as improved
Land/Site Value Opinion:	One or more of the six techniques is applied to develop an opinion of the land/site value

4. Apply One or More of the Three Approaches to Value

All approaches that add to the credibility of the appraisal are applied—Cost Approach, Sales Comparison Approach, and Income Approach.

5. Reconcile the Information to Arrive at a Final Opinion of Value

6. Report Appraisal Findings

Three types of reports: Restricted, Summary, and Self-Contained

DEFINE THE PROBLEM

A clear and complete definition of the problem is required before any other action may begin.

Facts Needed When Defining the Appraisal Problem

- Client and intended users of the appraisal

- Intended use of the appraisal (sale or financing transaction)

- Definition of value

- Date of the appraisal

- Property and its characteristics

- Any extraordinary assumptions or hypothetical conditions

CLIENT AND INTENDED USER

The definition of the problem must begin with the identification of the client and the intended use of the appraisal. The **client** is the owner of the appraisal and must be accurately identified. Accurate identification of the client eliminates any possible problems caused by violation of confidentiality provisions. Just as important is the intended user of the appraisal, which may include the client. USPAP defines an **intended user** as the party who uses the appraisal. The client owns the appraisal and must approve its release to any other party.

The client is the owner
of the appraisal and must
be accurately identified.

INTENDED USE

Identifying the **intended use** of the appraisal refers to the use by the client. Appraisals are used by clients as part of the information on which they base a decision. The appraiser needs to know what type of decision is being addressed as that has an effect on the appraisal assignment.

Typical Intended Uses for an Appraisal

- Sales price of a property

- Loan amount

- Terms of a lease

- Property dispute in a divorce

- Tax issues, probate

- Partial interest, easements, liens

The client has often not thought through all of the specifics of the assignment. The appraiser is responsible to obtain all of the information required to identify properly all aspects of the problem.

DEFINITION OF VALUE

Different definitions of value produce different value estimates. There are many types of value that may be identified in an appraisal assignment. Therefore, appraisers need to be aware of the kind of value they are to estimate. For example, a client may request a market valuation to support a loan request, or an investment value to support the sale to a particular investor.

A client may request a market valuation to support a loan request.

DATE OF THE APPRAISAL

The effective date of the appraisal is related to its purpose and use and must be accurately determined. The effective date may not be the same as the date the report was prepared and signed by the appraiser. An appraisal may be made as of a current date, historical date, or future date. An appraisal for a past date may be the result of a dispute or death. This would require the property to be valued at the time that the dispute or death occurred. The federal government taxes estates over a certain size, so upon death, the amount of equity the decedent has in the real estate has a direct bearing on the amount of estate tax to be paid. When the final evaluation date is for the future, it usually is because improvements need to be added to the property. Another example is a construction loan that requires an appraisal estimating the value of the property when it is completed. These situations require making a hypothetical condition, addressed later.

PROPERTY AND PROPERTY RIGHTS

The subject property must be identified and described. Most appraisals identify the property three ways: (1) street address, (2) legal description, and (3) assessor's parcel number. In addition, a description of the physical characteristics of the property is required. The client probably never sees the property, except through the eyes of the appraiser, so a thorough description is of real value to the client.

One of the most important elements of the description is the location. The old joke in real estate is "What are the three most important things about any property?" Answer? "Location, Location, and Location!" Each property is unique, and its location is the basis of part of that uniqueness.

Additional elements to consider are the size of the site, size of and condition of the improvements, and conformity with other properties in the neighborhood.

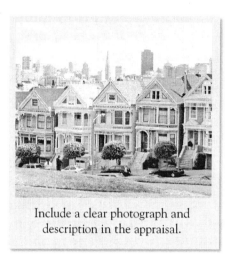

Include a clear photograph and description in the appraisal.

When appraising view properties, the appraiser may discover that some of the largest adjustments are attributable to differences in the views.

EXTRAORDINARY ASSUMPTIONS AND HYPOTHETICAL CONDITIONS

An **extraordinary assumption** is an assumption the appraiser is making, due to a lack of a piece of information, which if it proves to be false would

Appraisers do not know how the hazardous waste impacts the property.

materially affect the opinion of value. An example of this situation is evidence of hazardous waste on the property. The appraiser is not qualified to ascertain the impact of any hazardous waste on the property and may continue with the appraisal by assuming that there is no impact, if the client permits it.

A **hypothetical condition** is basing an appraisal on a condition known to be false. The appraisal of proposed improvements is a good example of a hypothetical condition. The appraisal is completed subject to the completion of the improvements. The value is based on the improvements being completed, which is a condition that both the appraiser and client know to be untrue. Now that all of the elements of the problem have been identified, it is time to address the scope of work.

SCOPE OF WORK

Under the **scope of work**, the appraiser identifies the problem to be solved, evaluates the assignment, makes the scope of work decisions, and discloses that scope of work in the report.

The scope of work should clarify . . . not confuse.

Included in the Scope of Work

- Property idenification
- Property inspection
- Type and extent of data researched
- Type and extent of analysis applied to solve the appraisal problem

Appraisers should be aware of what they are not including in the scope of work. Leaving something out of the scope of work should be a conscious decision, not an afterthought. When disclosing the scope of work in the report, it may be valuable to describe both what was included in and excluded from the scope of work. The reader should not have to guess about the approach or reasons for the scope of work decisions.

Scope of work decisions also establish the priorities and order in which tasks are performed. The appraiser can then develop a plan to complete the appraisal. It may appear to be overkill to do this much advance planning for a simple tract home appraisal. There are two reasons that this is necessary, outside the fact the client must understand the amount and type of work required to accomplish his or her task. The appraiser develops a systematic approach to each problem, which becomes more important in addressing appraisals that are more complex. Then, if the appraiser encounters an unforeseen problem during the research or application of an approach, there is a systematic methodology in place to address and resolve the problem. Finally, as the appraisals become more complex, and detailed reporting formats are used, an outline may be required to complete the report in an organized manner. Approaching the scope of work in an organized and thorough manner can make the remaining tasks much easier.

DATA COLLECTION

Proper and complete research can help make a competent appraisal. The opposite is also true. The appraiser who tries to save a little time in the research pays a large price when attempting to apply the different approaches with inferior or inaccurate data. At best, it becomes very difficult to complete the appraisal in a competent manner. At worst, significant data is missed or not properly verified and lead the appraiser to an incorrect conclusion.

The Internet has made research much easier.

The Internet has made research much easier, but not always more accurate. The amount and quality of data available grows every day, so the task of data collection actually is becoming more complex.

The appraiser needs both general data and specific data. **General data** includes information regarding social, governmental, economic, and physical factors affecting the region, and locality. **Specific data** addresses the subject property and comparable properties.

SOURCES OF DATA

Information is available from many sources and it is essential to understand the quality and veracity of that information. The depth and thoroughness of the research is the backbone of the appraisal. The appraiser must completely research the subject and comparables with all available sources of information.

The sources of this data vary depending on the type needed. Data sources include firsthand data—data from personal inspection or review, and secondhand data—data from reliable sources, which still must be verified, and the appraiser's files.

FIRSTHAND DATA

Firsthand data is data that has been observed personally by the appraiser. It requires the physical presence of the appraiser and usually includes the inspection of the subject and comparable properties. This is the best type of data available and is the data on which appraisers can base their findings. **Physical observation** is the most accurate means of verification. Most appraisals require a physical inspection including the measurement of the improvements. Appraisers measure improvements from the outside and subtract the garage, basement, and attic to obtain the **gross living area (GLA)**. This methodology is not standard for all measurements of real estate improvements. Builders or developers may include the garage, basement, or attic in the living area or may measure from the inside. The GLA figures in public records are usually taken from architectural plans, which may be different from actual GLA. Some assessors verify the information with physical inspections because the information can vary because of additions and demolitions to a property of which the assessor may be unaware.

Appraisers should physically inspect and measure the property.

The appraiser's results can vary from public records and still be accurate in this situation. The appraiser should check the GLA in the public records at the time of inspection and try to determine the reason for any discrepancy. In other words, he or she should try to identify precisely why the public records are out of date. The appraiser should attempt to identify what area may have been double counted or not counted, whether it was a basement or garage conversion, stairway, or perhaps an unpermitted addition.

Firsthand data is the most reliable data available, but that does not mean it is perfectly accurate. The appraiser can err when making observations or performing tasks like measuring. Occasionally, the appraiser has to return to a property and remeasure to make sure that the initial measurements were accurate—usually because the appraiser's measurements differed substantially from those obtained from public records. The appraiser should take thorough notes during the inspection process and record as much as possible with pictures (photographs). Simply relying on memory is a recipe for disaster.

SECONDHAND DATA

The majority of the data used in appraisals is secondhand data. **Secondhand data** is data that is obtained from someone or some other source, such as public records. Every piece of secondhand data must be verified.

The main issue with all secondhand data is its accuracy. Data not personally verified can be significantly in error. There are many reasons for this including human error inputting the data, different methods used to develop the data, data not updated, or simply the wrong data used.

Data sources include private data providers that use the public databases as their primary source of information. Typical data providers include title companies and multiple listing services. Title companies access public information daily and create their own database, which is used to support their issuance of title insurance.

Another important source of information is a multiple listing service (MLS). A **multiple listing service** is the database used by real estate brokers and sales-people to list properties being offered for sale. The broker is responsible for the accuracy of the information contained in the listing. The appraiser can access these databases (for a fee) and use the information contained in the listings as

The MLS is a good source of information.

verification of the public data. Since these listings are designed to help sell the property, the appraiser must learn to read the comments carefully as brokers usually do not discuss any negatives of the property. An appraiser must always remember the source of the information (brokers wanting to sell a property) and carefully evaluate the information in the listing.

APPRAISER'S FILES

Each time an appraisal is performed, a workfile is saved. The **workfile** is the appraiser's records that contain all the documentation necessary to support the appraiser's analyses, opinions, and conclusions conveyed in the appraisal report. The appraiser retains all of the information and verification that was done in association with that appraisal. These files must be kept at least five years (or longer in cases in which the appraisal was involved in litigation) and provide a good source of information for current appraisals. If the appraiser is lucky enough to have appraised a property that is being used as a comparable, then the appraiser has reliable firsthand detailed information on that comparable. The appraiser still needs to verify the information, and be sure that the property has not changed. The workfile information provides more verified detail than public records or multiple listing services, and gives the appraiser a more factual base from which to make adjustments. Not all of the information contained in an appraiser's files is firsthand information. All of the secondhand information (even though verified) must be reviewed and updated if necessary.

Occasionally, the appraiser contacts other appraisers for assistance with an appraisal. Those appraisers can provide firsthand information to the appraiser, as long as the confidentiality requirements of USPAP are met. This information, while normally reliable, still must be verified. It is essentially secondhand information and not to be accepted without secondary verification.

Be sure to keep your workfile for at least five years or longer.

VERIFICATION

Because unverified information has little or no value, it should not be used in an appraisal. The three areas in which an appraiser is allowed to express his or her opinion are the boundaries of the neighborhood, the effective age of the improvements, and the reconciliation of the appraisal. All other information presented in the appraisal must be factual and verified. An appraiser must **verify** (make sure) that the information he or she has is correct. This can be a heavy burden on the appraiser, but is necessary if the public is to view the appraiser's work as credible.

Information can be incorrect for many reasons. We have all heard that eyewitness testimony is usually not reliable because the eyewitnesses so often have faulty recollections. This can be true of an appraiser's firsthand information, especially if the appraiser has not taken copious notes during the inspection and taken supporting pictures. Pictures should be taken of anything that the appraiser thinks might warrant discussion. Digital cameras allow appraisers to take an unlimited number of pictures without incurring any cost, so the inspection should be well documented.

Secondhand information relies upon the diligence and integrity of the people involved in handling the information. The more people handling the information, the higher the probability that it has errors. Review appraisers are always asked to verify the accuracy of the information presented. All of these are reasons that make verification of the information essential.

DATA ANALYSIS

Collecting and verifying information is not sufficient to produce a credible appraisal. The verified data must be reviewed and analyzed. **Analysis** is the process of taking facts and ascertaining their relevance to a particular situation. The mass of data collected is almost meaningless without order and perspective. Placing facts in context and explaining their relevance is an essential part of the appraisal process.

The appraiser begins with market analysis. Market trends must be reviewed. Supply of and demand for property in the subject's market area must be evaluated and compared to other times and other geographic regions. It is through this process of comparing the raw facts that trends appear and fallacies are exposed. The news media is famous for sensationalizing information and taking it out of context. Certainly, if the news is bad, it is even more apt to be sensationalized. The appraiser must read beyond the headlines and get to the facts. Then, place those facts in context, allowing the reader to make sense of the situation.

An example of this is that most appraisers research a neighborhood before attempting to appraise property in that neighborhood. One of the social characteristics that can be factually researched is crime statistics. A particular neighborhood may have a certain number of violent crimes committed per 1,000 residents. This fact is relatively meaningless unless compared to the similar statistics for other surrounding neighborhoods. The use of comparisons

Crime affects the value of a neighborhood.

and contrasts allows the appraiser to put the facts in a context that is relevant to the reader. That particular statistic may be high or low compared to neighboring cities and provides information regarding the relative safety in this particular neighborhood.

DEFINE THE NEIGHBORHOOD

A **neighborhood** is an area whose inhabitants share some common ties or characteristics. A neighborhood may be defined by physical boundaries, a change in land use, or intangible factors like school district boundaries. The definition of the neighborhood is of critical importance to a residential appraisal as it sets the boundaries in which all of the comparable properties should reside. The establishment of these neighborhood boundaries is an opinion of the appraiser supported by the facts that have been researched and analyzed.

The physical, economic, governmental, and social factors that differentiate one neighborhood from another must be identified and reported. As can be seen in the discussion above, the facts are not sufficient, but they must be compared and contrasted to similar facts for other areas to establish the areas of similarity.

A neighborhood is similar in the majority of its physical, economic, govern-mental, and social characteristics. Defining the neighborhood establishes the area in which similar families purchase similar properties, all of which underlies the substitution principal supporting the appraisal processes.

LIFE CYCLES

Neighborhoods go through life cycles much like people or plants, except that neighborhoods can be revitalized. The neighborhood's position in the life cycle helps the appraiser understand the market dynamics and anticipate future changes in that market. The life cycle is growth, equilibrium, decline, and revitalization. All neighborhoods experience this cycle, but not at the same time. **Equilibrium** is the most stable part of the cycle while each of the other sections requires significant changes to be occurring. Change affects real estate value so it can be seen that the life cycle can have a real impact on real estate value.

Neighborhoods go through life cycles.

During reconciliation, the appraiser accounts for the neighborhood's current stage in the life cycle and anticipates what may happen in the near future.

PROPERTY IDENTIFICATION

Once properly identified, an accurate and complete description of the property is required. This is necessary so that the client, who may never see the property, understands the attributes of the property. Also, complete descriptions enable accurate comparisons with comparable properties. Appraisers must remember that they are acting as the eyes, ears, and nose of the client. The only impartial review of the property comes from the appraiser. Therefore, the quality of the property description assists both the appraiser and the client.

In most report forms, the subject property is identified using the street (**situs**) or post office address, legal description, and assessor's parcel number (APN). The three methods are required to insure that the correct piece of real estate is being appraised.

1. **Street Address.** The street address or post office address is actually provided by the post office. There are times, especially with vacant land, that a post office address is not available. In these cases, only the APN and the legal description are used. The appraiser identifies the property using the post office street address in the Letter of Transmittal in a summary report.

2. **Legal Description.** The legal description is the official description of the property on all legal documents. The property may be described by the metes and bounds system, government survey system, or the lot, block, and tract system. Regardless of the method used, it is the official description of the property and is used on legal documents, such as deeds.

3. **Assessor's Parcel Number.** The third method of identification is the assessor's parcel number, or **APN**. This number is given to each property by the county tax assessor and is found on the property tax bill. Often, it can be found on the plat map, with the last one or two digits of the APN appearing circled on the plat map in the center of the property.

Comparables are usually identified using only the post office street address and the APN. Form appraisal reports, such as the URAR, have no place for the legal descriptions of the comparable properties. The legal descriptions are still part of the appraiser's workfile and can be provided to the client upon request.

HIGHEST AND BEST USE

A highest and best use analysis is required on every appraisal. The appraiser and the client have to know the best use of the site versus the site's present use. Highest and best use is about money. The **highest and best use** is the one that is physically possible, legally permissible, and economically feasible that produces the best value. The highest and best use analysis is completed both as though the site is vacant and as improved.

Determine the highest and best use as if the site is vacant and as improved.

The appraiser begins with the vacant site analysis by determining what is possible to build on the site. The size, setbacks, and fire and building codes all limit the range of possible improvements.

The next step is to determine if the improvements that are possible, are also legally permissible. This addresses the zoning issues. Then, of the remaining physically possible and legally permissible uses, the appraiser determines which would make money (economically feasible). The final step is to choose, from the list of those that are economically feasible, which one produces the highest value (maximally productive).

The steps appear easy and for some sites, such as an interior residential lot in a tract development, only a few options make sense. Other sites, specifically those that have undergone zoning changes, present significant challenges and require the analysis to be thorough and complete. The site may be more valuable vacant than as improved.

Once the appraiser has completed the highest and best use analysis for the site as vacant, the same procedure is followed for the site, only as presently improved. This analysis is somewhat redundant for residential sites or tract homes. Commercial or industrial properties, whose improvements can have a variety of uses, require more care and diligence.

LAND OR SITE VALUE OPINION

The appraiser is ready to apply the initial valuation techniques to develop the land or site value. **Site value** is the value of the land without the improvements, including the cost of offsite improvements, utilities, and access. This is a required element of every appraisal that involves land as a component of the real estate. This is also the basis of the cost approach and can be used in paired sales analysis to establish adjustment values. This text addresses the techniques used to develop an opinion of site value. The best technique is always the sales comparison approach because it provides the most direct evidence of the market's valuation. However, sales comparisons are not always available for vacant land, so several different appraisal techniques have been created that allow the appraiser to develop a competent valuation of almost any parcel of land. More information on the sales comparison approach is available later in this unit.

APPLY APPROACHES TO VALUE

Appraisers may use three different approaches to value. USPAP requires the appraiser to use all approaches that add to the credibility of the appraisal. Stated another way, the appraiser must apply all approaches that produce an opinion of value that has substance. It also means that the appraiser should not use an approach that does not have the verifiable data available needed to produce a credible opinion.

COST APPROACH

Cost is not one of the factors that contribute to value, so the challenge is to develop an approach, which is credible using the cost of the improvements as a basis. The element that provides relevance to this approach is the application of depreciation to the cost new. The use of depreciation converts the cost of the improvements to their value today. To obtain the property value, the site value is added to the depreciated cost of the improvements.

Formula – Cost Approach

Property Value = Site Value + (Cost new of the improvements – depreciation + the as is value of the on-site improvements)

An appraiser must make a number of assumptions when using this approach to develop an opinion of value. Whenever assumptions are made, there is room for error so the resultant value has less credibility. Usually, this approach is used as a secondary support for the sales comparison and income approaches. However, it can be the primary approach if there is insufficient information to develop an opinion of value using one of the other two approaches.

A good example of the use of the cost approach alone is for a single purpose building that has no income associated with it, and no available comparable sales. The information needed to develop the income and sales comparison approaches is not available, so the only choice is to use the cost approach. A publicly owned athletic stadium would be an example of this type of property. It would be impossible to find adequate comparable sales for a mansion in the middle of an economically depressed neighborhood, so only the cost approach would be appropriate.

SALES COMPARISON APPROACH

The **sales comparison approach** is the appraisal approach that provides the most direct evidence of the market's valuation of the property. It is often referred to as the market approach because it most directly reflects the market's opinion of value. The appraiser researches public records and the MLS to locate recent sales of similar properties. The approach requires the identification of these similar properties, and the identification of the elements in which each comparable property differs from the subject. An adjustment is made for every element in which the comparable differs from the subject. The adjustments are summed and then added or subtracted from the comparable's sales price to arrive at the comparable market value. Elements of difference must be relevant or significant. At least three sales comparisons must be used. More can be used if required to produce a credible value. The appraiser may want to use more comparables if the available comparables are not truly similar, the area is non-conforming, or if the differences between the comparables and the subject are

The sales comparison approach requires the identification of similar properties.

significant so the range of value is 10% or more. **Range of value** is the difference between the highest and lowest adjusted value.

Of special note is that sales—not listing prices—must be used and the sales must be arm's-length sales. A sale that is not arm's-length is not a market sale and does not represent the market's opinion of value. It does not qualify as a comparable property for use in this approach. Properties that are listed or pending sales can be included in the appraisal as evidence of the market's current condition, and to support time adjustments, but their adjusted values cannot be used as part of the value range. The adjusted market value of each comparable property is its sales price plus or minus adjustments.

Formula – Adjusted Market Value for Comparisons
Adjusted Market Value = Sales Price + (−) Adjustments

These adjustments are a result of paired sales analysis. **Paired sales analysis** is the process of finding two nearly identical sales that differ in only one element. The difference in sales price is the market's value of that one element. This is a conceptually easy methodology, but its application is difficult and time consuming. The analysis requires research and verification. Once an element is valued, the adjustment can be used until the market changes. When the market changes, the process must be repeated. The appraiser's book of paired sales analysis supported adjustments is constantly updated and verified. The accuracy of the sales comparison approach is dependent on both the accuracy of the data and the quality of the adjustments. While this approach is the most direct evidence of the market's valuation, careless or lazy application of the approach leads to unacceptable valuations.

At a minimum, three comparable properties are used and rarely are all three adjusted market values equal. The appraiser has a range of values from which to identify one final sales comparison value. This is an application of reconciliation, which is discussed later. Reconciliation is not an objective approach, but is based on the opinion of the appraiser and yields the opinion of value.

Careful application of the sales comparison approach yields a supportable and credible market value. This approach is most useful for properties with good, recent, comparable sales. Most appraisals of residential properties employ this approach as the primary approach. The cost approach is employed as secondary support of the opinion of value. The income approach can be used successfully for properties that generate income. In these cases, a combination of the sales comparison approach and the income approach is used. Both would be required, as both add to the credibility of the opinion of value.

INCOME APPROACH

Properties that generate income are valued based on the present value of that future income. Property value can be computed using gross income or net income. The techniques primarily used by appraisers to translate future income to present value are the gross rent multiplier and direct capitalization.

GROSS RENT MULTIPLIER

Residential properties that are rented can be valued using the **gross rent multiplier (GRM).** The formula for finding value using the gross rent multiplier is **Value = Rent x Gross Rent Multiplier.**

When applying this formula for residential properties, the appraiser uses monthly rent. Market income (rent) is obtained through market research and rent surveys. Once the market income (rent) is established, a market GRM is derived from market sales comparisons. The use of market-derived GRM and market rent results in a credible estimate of market value.

Commercial and industrial properties derive their income from sources other than just rental income. These properties are valued using a **gross income multiplier (GIM).**

DIRECT CAPITALIZATION

Direct capitalization is the process of estimating the value of an income-producing property by forecasting the annual net operating income that the property is expected to generate during a specific period (usually one year) and dividing it by a capitalization rate. A capitalization rate is developed for each specific assignment using market research. The **capitalization rate** (cap rate) is a market-derived ratio reflecting the relationship between the net operating income a property generates and its value. Generally, an appraiser uses a capitalization rate provided by the client/investor for those appraisals in which investment value, rather than market value, is desired.

> **Formula – Income Approach**
>
> Property Value = Income ÷ Capitalization Rate

RECONCILE THE VALUE

The appraiser develops each of the three approaches that lend credibility to the appraisal. Usually, he or she arrives at slightly differing values for each approach. The last step in the appraisal process is the reconciliation of value. **Reconciliation** is the process of analyzing the appraisal problem, weighing the different approaches to value, and determining a final opinion of value. Reconciliation is never an average and is not used to correct errors committed elsewhere in the appraisal.

Reconciliation is a subjective—not objective—process. The appraiser completes the research, verifies and analyzes the data, and applies the approaches necessary to develop all the factual data. The appraiser applies his or her knowledge and experience to the observations and work product to develop the final opinion of value.

The appraiser develops the final opinion of value.

Appraisers must remember, when doing multi-step calculations, to keep at least one more significant digit in the intermediate results than what is needed in the final estimate of value. This prevents round-off error. There are no specific standards of practice for rounding numbers, but appraisers, in general, round their estimates of value to either two or three significant digits.

Throughout the appraisal process, one of the characteristics of a number is how many significant digits it contains. **Significant digits** are those that go from the first numeral on the left over to the last numeral on the right that is not a zero. All non-zero digits (1, 2, 3, 4, 5, 6, 7, 8, 9) are always significant. For example, 34 has two significant digits, and 34.2 has three significant digits. When zeros are added to the final value, it becomes more complicated.

a. Zeros placed before other numerals are not significant. The number 0.037 has only two significant digits.

b. Zeros placed between other numerals are always significant. There are four significant digits in 2001.

c. Zeros placed after other numerals, but behind a decimal point are significant. There are three significant digits in 4.50.

d. Zeros at the end of a number are significant only if they are behind a decimal point (see c. above). In an amount such as $4,500, it is impossible to determine if the zeros are significant or not. Without a decimal point, there are at least two significant digits. With a decimal point followed by two zeros ($4,500.00), there are four significant digits.

e. When adding or subtracting quantities, the number of decimal places (not significant digits) in the answer should be the same as the least number of decimal places in any of the numbers being added or subtracted.

> Example: A number calculated in an appraisal may contain all significant digits, for example, $344,637.17. However, a final value estimate made using one technique and the available data may result in a value conclusion of two significant digits—$340,000, and another technique may result in a value of $344,637 or six significant digits. This difference implies that the second value is more accurate, but both may be equally accurate.

There are two instances regarding significant digits that always should be avoided.

1. Do not write more digits in an answer (either intermediate or final) that is justified by the number of digits in the data.

2. Do not round off to two digits in an intermediate answer, and then write three digits in the final answer.

The reconciliation process can be very simple when all approaches used arrive at similar results. The difficulty comes when the three approaches do not arrive at similar results. The appraiser must consider the reliability of the data and the relative applicability of each approach. The appraiser must go back to the beginning—define the problem—and insure that the final opinion of value is the solution to the defined problem. Once the final opinion of value is developed, all that remains is to prepare the report.

REPORT THE APPRAISAL RESULTS

The data to support an estimate of value is placed on an appraisal report. An **appraisal report** is a written statement in which an appraiser gives his or her opinion of value. Reports must be written in such a way as to provide the reader sufficient information without being misleading in any manner. Omitting relevant facts, or choosing comps for their sales price rather than their similarity are examples of being misleading. It is never acceptable to write a report that misleads the reader.

The completion of these reports is a synopsis of the appraiser's work product. The supporting data, analysis, and development of approaches are fully supported and documented in the appraiser's workfile. The workfile is the appraiser's record that contain all the documentation necessary to support the appraiser's analyses, opinions, and conclusions conveyed in the appraisal report. Completing these reports in a competent and thorough manner helps maintain the appraiser's credibility, and supports the efficient working of the real estate market.

In fact, Statement 2 in USPAP fully describes the essential elements of each report and the required certifications of that appraiser. All reports must meet all requirements of USPAP, including the certifications and assumptions and limiting conditions associated with the appraisal. Statement 2 in USPAP sets forth all of the reporting requirements for real estate appraisal reports. A complete workfile must be developed and maintained in accordance with the provisions of USPAP.

TYPES OF APPRAISAL REPORTS

According to USPAP, reporting standards for appraisals require that the report must clearly and accurately set forth the appraisal in a manner that is not misleading, and the report must contain sufficient information to enable the intended users of the appraisal to understand the report properly.

Three Types of Appraisal Reports

1. Summary Appraisal Report

2. Self-Contained Appraisal Report

3. Restricted-Use Appraisal Report

The choice of report type goes back to the beginning, when the problem was defined. The client's needs were identified and the type of report was selected to meet those needs. The choice of report type does not affect the amount of work done to complete the appraisal. The client needs determine the report type, but the entire appraisal process must be completed prior to preparing the report.

SUMMARY APPRAISAL REPORT

The **summary report** is usually known as a form report. Forms have been developed by users and appraisal groups to make the reporting uniform and consistent. A **Summary Appraisal Report** is the most commonly used appraisal report, which fulfills the minimum requirements for lenders to process loans. The standardization of these forms has gone a long way toward facilitating the secondary market in real estate loans.

The **Uniform Residential Appraisal Report (URAR)** is probably the most widely used summary report. The URAR is used to report the results of single-family residential appraisals. It allows for all three approaches, but emphasizes the sales comparison approach. The cost approach is located on the third page, below an area designed for the appraiser's comments regarding the appraisal. The results of all three approaches are reported on page two, which has room for reconciliation. The abbreviated format presented on the form reflects the relative importance of the cost approach in most single-family residential reports.

SELF-CONTAINED REPORT

The **Self-Contained Appraisal Report** is the most detailed of the three types of reports. The report is exactly what the name implies, a complete rendering of the entire appraisal process. The appraiser provides all of the data analyzed, his or her reasoning, the complete review of the techniques applied, and finally the results of his or her work product.

RESTRICTED-USE REPORT

A **Restricted-Use Appraisal Report** is the briefest presentation of an appraisal and contains the least detail. It is called restricted-use because the client is the only intended user of the report. It can be oral or written, one or multiple pages, a range, or just a single number. The amount of detail in the report depends upon the client needs and the problem being addressed by the appraisal. Here, as in the summary report, the amount of work completed before preparing the report has nothing to do with the report type, but the scope of work defined earlier in the process.

SUMMARY

A significant amount of time and energy has been spent describing the **appraisal process**. The process is the most significant aspect of the appraisal. The use of the complete process every time assures both the appraiser and the client of a credible result. That process always begins with the **definition of the problem**—a definition that the appraiser looks back to during the entire process to guide the remaining steps. Once the problem is defined, the **scope of work** required to resolve the appraisal problem could be expanded. The scope of work can be thought of as an outline of the remaining steps necessary to develop fully the solution of the appraisal problem. The appraiser now has a road map describing exactly what must be accomplished to obtain a credible result.

It is only after the scope of work has been completely defined, that the appraiser can actually start researching and selecting the data to analyze. Then the appraiser **analyzes the data**, using the appropriate techniques and approaches, and then **reconciles** the approaches to finalize the **opinion of value**. There is no shortcut. Every appraisal must be completed using this process. Many appraisers use the appraisal process flow chart as the first page in their **workfile**. They then check off each completed item until the entire process is completed leaving nothing unfinished. This may seem a little pedantic, but can often help the appraiser avoid costly errors.

UNIT 2 REVIEW

MATCHING EXERCISE

Instructions: Write the letter of the matching term on the blank line before its definition. Answers are in Appendix C.

Terms

A. APN

B. appraisal process

C. capitalization rate

D. client

E. equilibrium

F. firsthand data

G. general data

H. GLA

I. highest and best use

J. hypothetical condition

K. intended use

L. multiple listing service

M. opinion

N. paired sales analysis

O. range of value

P. reconciliation

Q. sales comparison approach

R. scope of work

S. secondhand data

T. Self-Contained Appraisal Report

U. site value

V. specific data

W. Summary Appraisal Report

X. workfile

Definitions

1. _____ A systematic procedure used by appraisers to arrive at an opinion or estimate of value

2. _____ The owner of the appraisal who must be accurately identified

3. _____ The detailed outline or road map describing all the steps required to produce a complete and credible appraisal resolving the identified problem

4. _____ The data that includes information regarding social, governmental, economic, and physical factors affecting the region and locality

5. _____ The data that addresses the subject property and comparable properties

6. _____ Data that is developed personally and directly by the appraiser

7. _____ The living area of the improvements (house) measured from the outside, less the garage, basement, and attic

8. _____ Data from reliable sources, which still must be verified

9. _____ The database used by real estate brokers and salespeople to list properties being offered for sale

10. _____ The appraiser's records that contain all the documentation necessary to support the appraiser's analyses, opinions, and conclusions conveyed in the appraisal report

11. _____ The most stable part of the neighborhood cycle

12. _____ The identification number given a parcel of land by the tax assessor

13. _____ The physically possible, legally permissible, economically feasible, and maximally productive use for a parcel of land

14. _____ The value of the land without the improvements but including costs of offsite improvements including utilities and access

15. _____ The appraisal approach that provides the most direct evidence of the market's valuation of the property

16. _____ The difference between the highest and lowest adjusted value

17. _____ A technique used in the sales comparison approach to develop the value of adjustments

18. _____ A market-derived ratio reflecting the relationship between the net operating income a property generates and its value

19. _____ The most commonly used appraisal report, which fulfills the minimum requirements for lenders to process loans

20. _____ A report type that includes all the facts researched, analysis completed, and the entire thought process of the appraiser

MULTIPLE CHOICE QUESTIONS

Instructions: Circle your response and go to Appendix C to read the complete explanation for each question.

1. The first step in the appraisal process is:
   - a. state the problem.
   - b. define the problem.
   - c. identify the property.
   - d. identify the client.

2. The scope of work is important because it establishes:
   - a. approaches the appraiser needs to use.
   - b. type of information needed.
   - c. sources to be used.
   - d. all of the above.

3. Firsthand data:
   - a. is usually the best data available because the appraiser develops it personally.
   - b. must be verified.
   - c. is part of the appraiser's workfile.
   - d. is all of the above.

4. All of the following are correct regarding secondhand data, except it:
   - a. is used in most every appraisal.
   - b. is the most accurate.
   - c. is included in appraiser's files.
   - d. needs to be verified.

5. The life cycle of the neighborhood is:
   - a. growth, stability, decline, resurgence.
   - b. growth, equilibrium, decline, revitalization.
   - c. growth, equilibrium, regrowth, revitalization.
   - d. growth, stability, declare, revitalization.

6. The most stable portion of the life cycle of a neighborhood is:
   - a. equilibrium.
   - b. growth.
   - c. decline.
   - d. revitalization.

7. The subject property is identified using the _____ in the Letter of Transmittal in a summary report.

    a. assessor's parcel number

    b. post office street address

    c. legal description

    d. legal address

8. Highest and best use is all of the below, except:

    a. maximally profitable.

    b. environmentally friendly.

    c. legally permissible.

    d. physically possible.

9. Though the sales comparison approach may be the best technique to obtain a land or site value opinion, the major drawback is that:

    a. an improvement must be present on the land.

    b. it has questionable accuracy even after careful application.

    c. there is a lot of heavy, complicated calculation involved.

    d. sales comparisons for vacant land are not always available.

10. All three appraisal approaches must be used:

    a. for every appraisal.

    b. when each approach adds to the credibility of the appraisal.

    c. only when appraising income property.

    d. for special purpose properties.

11. The cost approach is most often the best approach when appraising:

    a. income properties.

    b. residential properties.

    c. single purpose properties.

    d. condominiums.

12. A gross rent multiplier is used in the:

    a. sales comparison approach.

    b. cost approach.

    c. income approach for residential properties.

    d. income approach for large commercial properties.

13. The last step in the appraisal process is:
    a. reconciliation of value.
    b. reporting the results.
    c. applying applicable approaches.
    d. identifying the highest and best use.

14. The type of report to be completed depends on:
    a. the needs of the client.
    b. the time available to the appraiser.
    c. the writing skills of the appraiser.
    d. Standard 1 of USPAP.

15. All of the following are report types, except the:
    a. Self-Contained Appraisal Report.
    b. Summary Appraisal Report.
    c. Sales Comparable Appraisal Report.
    d. Restricted-Use Appraisal Report.

Depreciation

Unit 3

INTRODUCTION

Depreciation is the essential element in the cost equation that allows the appraiser to develop a credible opinion of value. The more accurate the estimate of depreciation, the more credible the opinion of value developed using the cost approach.

Depreciation can be calculated for an entire property or for individual components of the property. Depreciation only applies to the improvements on a property. The land does not physically depreciate even though the value of the land may decrease due to external forces.

In this unit, the theory of depreciation is evaluated first and then the three methods appraisers use to calculate depreciation are discussed. The appraiser must learn the strengths and weaknesses of each method and apply the one best suited to the circumstances of the particular appraisal. Accurate use of the vocabulary is a part of this unit and each of the key terms is identified and defined as it is presented.

LEARNING OBJECTIVES

After reading this unit, you should be able to:

- define and understand the concept of depreciation.
- identify three types of depreciation and their methods of calculation.
- describe the strengths and weaknesses of each method of calculation for depreciation.
- determine which depreciation calculation is best suited for the circumstances of an appraisal.

DEPRECIATION: ACCOUNTING VS. APPRAISAL

The concept of depreciation is the same in accounting and tax as it is in appraisal. Over time, the methods used to arrive at an estimate of depreciation have become more rigid in accounting. Appraisers approach depreciation realistically with the goal of calculating actual depreciation from all sources. **Depreciation** is the loss in value of an improvement from any cause. The purpose of depreciation for appraisers is different from that of accountants or tax preparers.

DEPRECIATION IN ACCOUNTING

Depreciation for tax purposes is designed to shelter income rather than offer a realistic estimate for the loss of value over time. The accounting concept is similar to the appraisal concept as depreciation represents the loss in value of the item for almost any reason. Accountants recognized that material items, both real and personal, experience a loss in value due to time, wear and tear, and other external factors. This loss of value had to be accounted for and several methods were developed to arrive at an estimate of depreciation. **Depreciation** is the expression of the loss of value of tangible items.

The simplest method in book accounting is the straight-line method, which is similar to the method that appraisers use to calculate physical depreciation. Other methods were developed and some adopted by the IRS, the Financial Accounting Standards Board, the Securities & Exchange Commission, and other regulating bodies. In tax accounting, accelerated depreciation methods, adopted by the IRS, do more to shelter income than reflect the actual loss in value of an item. In many cases, these calculations reflect the tax and accounting rules and principles, but often, do not present an accurate reflection of actual depreciation. Under Generally Accepted Accounting Principles (GAAP), familiar to accountants who prepare financial statements, there are methods that are based on the matching principle, which attempts to align the periodic depreciation with the specific years when the asset is used in its income-producing economic life.

DEPRECIATION IN APPRAISAL

The definition of **depreciation** in appraisal includes anything that would cause an improvement to lose value. **Accrued depreciation** is the difference between the replacement cost new of the improvements and their current market value. Once the appraiser has estimated accrued depreciation, he or she deducts the depreciation from the replacement cost of the building(s) on a property. The resulting figure is the depreciated cost of the improvements.

AGE/TIME RELATIONSHIPS

Many of the methods used to measure depreciation involve the age of the property. This makes good sense as deterioration along with wear and tear, are a result of the passage of time. These items can also be remedied with normal maintenance.

ACTUAL AGE

Because property owners generally undertake prudent care and maintenance, the actual age of the improvements may not accurately reflect the

effects of the passage of time. The **actual age** of a property is the number of years elapsed since the construction of the structure. Actual age is also called physical age, real age, or chronological age. Actual age is not used in the calculation of accrued depreciation since improvements can be updated, renovated, and improved.

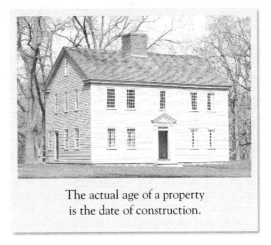

The actual age of a property
is the date of construction.

EFFECTIVE AGE

Appraisers use the effective age of the improvements as the basis for the age/life method to calculate depreciation. **Effective age** is the number of years indicated by the condition of a structure. Effective age is one of the three items in an appraisal that are opinions of the appraiser. A mathematical model to calculate effective age does not exist. Effective age takes into account a property's condition, maintenance,

Effective age is determined by the property's condition.

repair, renovation, and utility. Based on these factors, an appraiser must estimate the effective age of the improvements.

Estimating the effective age is both difficult and a major source of potential errors in any subsequent calculations. The appraiser must make the estimate as accurate as possible. Using a simple formula approach, such as effective age equals half the actual age should never be applied. It is always incorrect and misstates the effective age. An estimate of an improvement's effective age should be based on the condition of its major components including the foundation, walls, exterior material, roof, plumbing, electrical system, HVAC, utility of the plan, and significant rooms like the kitchen and bathroom(s). Interior decoration or the housekeeping skills of the owner are not relevant to this estimate. Estimates of effective age improve with knowledge of construction elements and experience. Even the beginning appraiser should estimate effective age because it is an essential element in the measurement of depreciation. Certainly, a property with an effective age of 45 years and a total economic life of 50 years can be seen to be at the end of its life cycle. A lender does not want to place a long-lived loan on a property whose improvement has only five years remaining life.

ECONOMIC LIFE

Economic life is the estimated period over which a building may be used profitably. This is not to be confused with the total life or physical life of the improvements. Improvements may last longer than their ability to add economic value to the property. If you visualize the abandoned warehouse, this concept is easier to understand. The abandoned warehouse is still standing, but no longer generates income; therefore, does not add value to the property.

Again, this is an economic analysis rather than a discussion of the physical presence of the improvements.

Economic life is also known as useful life. Useful life and economic life are similar in most situations. It can be argued that the economic life is the time in which the improvements are the highest and best use of the property. The **useful life** is the time for which the improvements have a positive contribution to the property. Whenever there is a zoning change to an existing property, the economic life may be shortened while the useful life may not be impacted. In this text, the two terms are used as though they are synonymous.

Economic life can be determined using market extraction or from estimates of contractors. There are databases with extensive construction data that appraisers use to determine the cost to replace or replicate improvements. These same databases provide estimates of the expected useful life of improvements.

Remaining economic life is the number of years between the structure's estimated economic life and its effective age. The remaining economic life is important to many clients as it represents the timeframe over which the improvements continue to provide a positive contribution. A lender wants the remaining economic life to be equal to or greater than the loan term. The lender would not be pleased if the improvements were of no significant value before the loan was paid. The collateral for the loan would have depreciated out from underneath them. Lenders carefully review the effective age and remaining life estimates.

A displeased lender

TYPES OF ACCRUED DEPRECIATION

Depreciation can be categorized by its cause and different methods have been developed to estimate each of the different types of depreciation. The types of depreciation are physical deterioration, functional obsolescence, and external obsolescence. **Physical deterioration** of a building and its equipment includes physical wear and tear, disintegration, decay or rot, or physical damage of any kind caused by the elements. **Functional obsolescence** refers to deficiencies, superadequacies, or simply undesirable features found in a building. External obsolescence is attributable to external adverse conditions that affect a property.

A property may suffer from any combination of the three types of depreciation, or it may not suffer from any depreciation at all. However, unless brand new, a building probably has incurred some degree of depreciation.

PHYSICAL DETERIORATION

Physical deterioration is a loss in value brought about by wear and tear, disintegration, use, and actions of the elements. Weather and deferred

maintenance are examples of factors that contribute to physical deterioration. The methods used to estimate physical deterioration are market extraction, age/life, and observed condition. All three methods can provide adequate estimates of real physical deterioration. These methods are evaluated later in the unit.

CURABLE AND INCURABLE DEPRECIATION

Physical deterioration can be curable or incurable. **Curable depreciation** is a type of depreciation that concerns items, which are economically feasible to repair or replace. On the other hand, **incurable depreciation** is a type of depreciation in which building defects or problems cost more to repair than the anticipated value increase from such repair.

The analysis used to determine whether an item of physical deterioration is curable or incurable is economic. The appraiser must ask the question, "Is the cost to repair the depreciated item equal to or less than the improvement in market value caused by the repair?" This analysis is analogous to determining whether a contribution has an increasing return or a decreasing return. Physical deterioration caused by deferred maintenance is usually curable. The cost of painting or repairing screens or other items is less than the improvement in market value. The amount of physical deterioration can be accurately estimated as the cost of repair or restoration of these curable items.

Curable depreciation   Incurable depreciation

The depreciation estimate for curable forms of depreciation is equal to the cost of the remedy for the depreciation. This is true for all types of curable depreciation. Appraisers have to calculate the cost to cure in order to arrive at the conclusion that the depreciation is curable. The **cost to cure** is a method of estimating accrued depreciation based on the cost to repair observed building defects. Establishing the cost to cure is part of that analysis process. Once established, the cost to cure is less than the resulting increase in market value. The appraiser can then use the cost to cure as the estimate of accrued depreciation.

Not all items of physical deterioration are curable. A crack in the foundation may render the building useless and the cost to repair may exceed the improvement in market value.

SHORT-LIVED VS. LONG-LIVED ITEMS

Another way to classify improvements when estimating physical deterioration is to identify the item (component) as short-lived or long-lived.

Short-lived structural components are those that are replaced or repaired on a consistent basis throughout the life of the structure. A short-lived item is not expected to have a useful life equal to the useful life

of the structure. Carpeting and kitchen appliances have useful lives significantly shorter than the structure. This categorization is useful when applying component depreciation.

Long-lived structural components need replacement infrequently, and sometimes, never. A long-lived item is expected to have a useful life equal  to the structure. The plumbing inside the walls of a house is expected to last as long as the structure. Long-lived items usually are not replaceable or repairable. Therefore, the physical deterioration associated with such items is not curable. This is not a hard and fast rule. Plumbing in the crawlspace of a raised foundation can deteriorate and be replaced or repaired economically. The appraiser must use common sense when applying any of these methods or definitions.

FUNCTIONAL OBSOLESCENCE

Functional obsolescence is a loss of value due to adverse factors from within the structure that affect the utility value and marketability of the structure. Functional obsolescence can be either curable or incurable. The same economic analysis is used here as for physical deterioration. Functional depreciation is either the loss of value caused by a deficiency in the plan or overbuilding called **superadequacy.**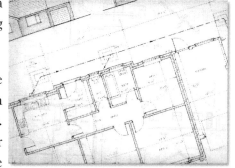

The first type of functional obsolescence is caused by a deficiency in the plan or construction of the improvements. This can be a result of a deficient floor plan, such as three bedrooms and one bathroom. Another example of a deficiency caused by a poor floor plan is a 10-foot by 10-foot room with a 20-foot ceiling. These are examples of floor plans that are not effective and the market pays less for the property that has such deficiencies.

Another type of functional obsolescence is caused by changes in the market. The houses built in the early 1950s had two bedrooms and one bathroom, which is small by today's standards. During that time, houses with this floor plan filled the needs and demands of the market. Today, houses have more bathrooms, larger kitchens, family rooms, and large master suites. These are all changes made in response to demands of the market. The houses built during the 1950s are functionally obsolete and are in less demand. This translates into a lower price. The difference in price is the loss of value associated with the obsolete style and utility.

Functional obsolescence is always associated with the improvements on the property, and does not address outside factors. Factors outside the property are addressed by external obsolescence.

TYPES OF FUNCTIONAL OBSOLESCENCE

Plan Is Not Acceptable to the Current Market

In this situation, the plan of an older house is not consistent with the newer more modern plans being built. Some renovation that can be undertaken to bring parts of the house up to current market level, specifically in the kitchen and bathrooms. Unless a new addition is built, the problem of a small master bedroom or no family room cannot be remedied. The measure of depreciation is the cost of the renovation, if applicable or the loss of market value if renovation is not economically feasible. This type of obsolescence is curable only when renovation or addition costs are less than the market value of the improvements.

House Lacks an Attribute

The market demands this additional attribute for the property to be fully competitive. For example, a four-bedroom with one bathroom needs another bathroom. The solution to the problem is the addition of a bathroom, if practical. The measure of depreciation is the cost of the addition, provided that the cost of the addition is less than its added market value.

Superadequacy

The problem of superadequacy is that the property is over-improved for the neighborhood. A classic example is the 4,000 square foot (SF) mansion built among 1,000 SF houses on small lots. **Regression** is the active economic principle stating that the lower valued properties in the neighborhood brings the subject's value down. The cost to build the house is not recovered upon sale. There is no way to remedy this situation. There is a loss of value, which can be measured. The measure of depreciation is the difference between cost new today and market value. Most cases of superadequacy are incurable.

The passage of time may allow the neighborhood to revitalize and catch up to the subject, but that cannot be determined with certainty.

EXTERNAL OBSOLESCENCE

External obsolescence is a loss of value caused by negative influences outside the specific property site. Usually external obsolescence is incurable because the property owner cannot remedy the situation. The factors causing the obsolescence may be economic or locational.

Economic obsolescence occurs when changes in the local economy affect the subject property's value. Sources of economic loss include loss of jobs, higher commuting costs, or changes in taxation policy.

Locational obsolescence is caused by the physical location of the subject property in close proximity to a negative influence. Sources of loss due to physical location include proximity to an airport, landfill, freeway, factory, or anything that produces excess noise or pollution.

External obsolescence is one of the reasons that a thorough inspection includes driving around the neighborhood. Appraisers that go directly to the subject property and then to three or four good comparable properties, may miss significant positive and negative neighborhood attributes.

Appraisers look for those items, which have a negative impact on property value since depreciation is the loss of value. Items having a positive impact reflect a higher market price compared to similar properties. The market also takes into account the impact of the negative items and a lower market value results. Rent for income properties is less when the property is impacted by external obsolescence. As a result, the landlord is not able to demand a higher market rent. A measure of the impact of external obsolescence can be the loss of rent caused by the external factor.

MEASURING ACCRUED DEPRECIATION

The reason depreciation is addressed is to develop methods to estimate the impact on market value. The remainder of this unit presents the various methods used by appraisers to measure or estimate depreciation. Depreciation accumulates over time so the total of the accumulated depreciation is identified as accrued depreciation. Appraisers estimate accrued depreciation, or the total of all depreciation that has accumulated over time, regardless of cause. The strengths and weaknesses are evaluated for each method. The application of mathematical models may insert a level of error into the final opinion of value. Models present a close, but never exact replica of reality. The type of error, source of error, and amount of error is examined. Appraisers must understand the accuracy of the methods being used so that in their final reconciliation, they are able to properly weigh the values obtained by those methods.

The basic methods used by appraisers to estimate depreciation are age/life, market extraction, observed condition, and rent loss method. Each must be applied with full knowledge of their strengths and weaknesses. The age/life, market extraction, and rent loss methods measure total accrued depreciation while the observed condition method identifies and calculates each component's depreciation. The calculation of depreciation must be completed carefully in order to include the loss in value from all sources, but not to count any depreciation twice. This becomes more of a problem in the observed condition method.

AGE/LIFE METHOD

The **age/life** or **straight-line method** is the method used most often to estimate accrued depreciation. It is based on the passage of time, employs a simple model of depreciation, and its resulting calculations are basic. As with any simplistic model, it has significant weaknesses. To calculate the depreciation percentage, simply divide the effective age by the economic life. **Straight-line depreciation** is a method of measuring depreciation based on equal annual amounts during the remaining economic life of the asset or structure. Improvements depreciate an equal amount each year in the straight-line approach. This method, despite having some built-in error, is still appealing due to its ease of calculation and the ability to apply it to almost any situation.

The age/life method requires the appraiser to estimate the effective age of the improvements and the economic life. The economic life can be obtained using the market extraction method or obtained from cost of construction databases. The effective age is the opinion of the appraiser based on the observed condition of the improvements.

Depreciation % = Effective Age / Economic Life

EXAMPLE: Appraiser John has determined that the economic life of a house being appraised is 50 years. What is the annual percentage of depreciation?

ANSWER: The annual percentage of depreciation, often called the recapture rate is found by dividing 1 by the economic life. The annual percentage of depreciation = 1/50 = 0.02 or 2%.

Accrued Depreciation = Depreciation % x Cost New of Improvements

EXAMPLE: House A has an actual age of 20 years and appraiser John estimated the effective age to be 15 years. The economic life for similar properties in the neighborhood is 60 years. He completed costing the improvements by using a cost-estimating database and found that a replacement house built today would cost $110 per SF of **gross living area (GLA)**. He measured the house and found it to contain 1,850 SF GLA. What is the percentage of accrued depreciation and what is the total accrued depreciation?

ANSWER: The actual age is of no relevance to this problem.

Percentage Depreciation	=	Effective Age / Economic Life
Percentage Depreciation	=	15/60 = 0.25 or 25%
Cost new of improvements	=	$203,500 ($110 x 1,850 SF)
Accrued Depreciation	=	$50,875 (25% x $203,500)

A variation of the method is used if an appraiser knows both the cost to cure and the positive impact it has on the effective age. Correcting the problem improves the effective age of the property. For example, by spending $15,000 to cure items of depreciation, the effective age is reduced by 5 years. The effective age before the repairs was 30 years. After the repairs, the new effective age would be 25 years.

EXAMPLE: A house has a replacement cost today of $200,000. Appraiser Sara estimates the effective age to be 25 years. She notes that there is $25,000 in curable depreciation. When the repairs are made, the effective age of the house is reduced by 5 years. The economic life of the house is 50 years. How much depreciation is there assuming the repairs are made?

ANSWER: After repairs are made, effective age is 20 yrs (25 yrs – 5 yrs)

The economic life is 50 years.

Depreciation percentage	=	Effective Age / Economic Life
Depreciation percentage	=	20 yrs/50 yrs = 0.40 or 40%
Cost to depreciate	=	Replacement cost − cost to cure
Cost to depreciate	=	$200,000 − $25,000 = $175,000
Depreciation	=	Depreciation % X Cost to depreciate
Depreciation	=	40% X $175,000 = $70,000
Total accrued depreciation	=	Cost to cure + Age/Life Depreciation
Total accrued depreciation	=	$25,000 + $70,000 = $95,000

COMPONENT DEPRECIATION

Component depreciation, a variation of the age/life method, is a method of calculating depreciation by totaling the depreciation of specific components of a property. This approach attempts to develop a more precise estimate by taking the major components of the improvements and depreciating them separately. Component depreciation is most effective for depreciation caused by physical deterioration. The method recognizes the fact that not all components that are used in construction have the same economic (useful) life. The HVAC system may have a 25-year economic life, as does a composition shingle roof, while the foundation and walls are expected to have an economic life of 50 to 70 years or more. The application is the same in theory as the age/life method. But, once a component is identified and depreciated, it must be subtracted from the cost new so that it is not depreciated twice.

Steps in the Component Depreciation Method

1. Identify the components to be individually depreciated

2. Compute the cost new today

3. Choose the appropriate depreciation method, Age/Life, Cost to Cure, Market Extraction

4. Calculate accrued depreciation on the component

5. Repeat steps 1 through 4 for all components being individually depreciated

6. Sum all individual depreciation amounts

7. Sum the Cost New of all components being individually depreciated

8. Subtract the total cost new of all the components from the total cost new of the improvements, providing the remainder that still needs to have depreciation estimated

9. The amount remaining must have estimated depreciation calculated using one of the applicable overall depreciation methods (Age/Life). Subtracting the cost new of all the individually depreciated components insures that double depreciation is not estimated

10. Add the depreciation on the remainder to the sum of the depreciation on all the individual components to arrive at the accrued depreciation for the improvements

---

EXAMPLE: This example depreciates two separate components and then the remainder of the house.

Component #1 – Roof, economic life 25 years, observed effective age 15 years, cost new today $15,000.

Component #2 – HVAC estimated life 15 years, observed effective age 10 years, cost new today $10,000.

House – 2,000 SF GLA. Cost new to replace today, $100/SF, actual age 35 years, effective age 20 years, economic life 50 years.

ANSWER: Depreciate the roof and HVAC system separately. Use age/life method to estimate depreciation on the components.

Step 1: Depreciate the roof

Roof depreciation   =   Cost New X (Effective Age / Economic Life)

Roof depreciation   = $15,000 X (15/25)

Roof depreciation   = $9,000

Step 2: Depreciate the HVAC system

HVAC depreciation   =   Cost New X (Effective Age / Economic Life)

HVAC depreciation   = $10,000 X (10/15)

HVAC depreciation   = $6,667

Step 3: Add the roof depreciation and the HVAC system depreciation

$9,000 + $6,667 = $15,667

Step 4: Add the cost new of the roof and HVAC system

$15,000 + $10,000   = $25,000

Step 5: Calculate house replacement cost new

2,000 SF X $100/SF   = $200,000

Step 6: Calculate the remainder to be depreciated

$200,000 − $25,000 = $175,000

Step 7: Estimate remainder depreciation using the age/life method

Remainder to be depreciated X (Effective Age / Economic Life)

Remainder depreciation = $175,000 X (20/50)

Remainder depreciation = $70,000

Step 8: Sum all the depreciation (the answers from Step 3 + Step 7)

$15,667 + $70,000 = $85,667 Accrued depreciation

The component approach is rarely used in residential appraisal. It is used primarily to appraise commercial and industrial properties. Each of these types of properties has components that can affect the value significantly and should have a separate evaluation.

ANNUITY METHOD

A significant departure from the straight-line age/life method is the annuity method. The **annuity method** applies depreciation on a curved basis, as it occurs naturally. This method is applied to the total improvements or it can be applied to components. It is most effective in estimating physical deterioration, as it is also a time-based model. Depreciation occurs with the passage of time and can be calculated based on the amount of time that has elapsed. The difficulty in applying this method is developing the appropriate curve, which translates into using the applicable annuity factors.

An **annuity** is a series of payments made for a period that exhaust a given starting amount (present value). This is analogous to the payments required to amortize a fixed rate mortgage loan. The portion paid to principal at the beginning of the loan is very small, like the initial physical deterioration of an improvement. At the end of the loan period, the majority of the payment is principal. This corresponds to the accelerated deterioration at the end of the life of an improvement.

The starting amount is the cost new of the improvement(s) being depreciated. The period to be used is the economic life. The only variables remaining unidentified are the interest rate and the compounding periods. In order to arrive at an annuity that reflects the real rate of deterioration, an interest rate must be chosen for the amortization.

MARKET EXTRACTION

Market extraction is a method to estimate depreciation in which building values abstracted from sales are compared to current costs new. This method requires the appraiser to estimate accrued depreciation through the application of paired sales analysis and estimate the effective age of the subject property. The actual age of the property is irrelevant.

> Example: Accrued depreciation (extracted from the market through paired sales analysis) is $45,000. The effective age of the improvement is estimated at 15 years. The average depreciation per year is $3,000 ($45,000/15 years). The cost new today of the improvements is $180,000. The economic life = 60 years ($180,000 ÷ $3,000/year).

There are several important things to note about this process. Extracting accrued depreciation from the market is easier said than done. Paired sales analysis is a difficult and time-consuming method. This method—required in all aspects of appraisal—is conceptually easy to understand, but difficult to apply. The research and statistical analysis required is intimidating but must be mastered if the appraiser is to become competent.

There are areas in which physical deterioration occurs at an accelerated rate. Houses near the ocean or in the desert experience extreme environmental forces, which accelerate physical deterioration. The use of the market extraction method to determine the economic life provides a more accurate basis for all subsequent calculation.

Paired Sales Analysis

Market extraction is often the best method as the results reflect the market's opinion of depreciation. That being said, it is often the most difficult method to apply. Application is similar to the paired sales analysis in which the appraiser finds two identical properties that differ only in one item, which in this case, is depreciation. That depreciation can be the result of physical, functional, or external sources. Competent application requires that the two properties being compared are identical with the exception of one item. If this is not the case, an advance statistical method called **multivariable statistical analysis** must be used to isolate the single differences. The research required is substantial and still leaves room for error, as limited information is available about most sold properties. The appraiser who is successful in applying this approach has a result that reflects the market's opinion and is a more accurate estimate.

Market extraction is the preferred method to be used to calculate incurable functional obsolescence and external obsolescence. There is no easily applied model that reflects the loss of value associated with certain external sources or particular deficiencies in an improvement. The market identifies the important items and adjusts market pricing accordingly.

> Example: House A is in the flight path of an airport. It sold for $450,000 after being on the market for 50 days. House B, built by the same builder, with the same floor plan and GLA but outside the flight path sold for $475,000 after being on the market for 35 days. Financing and time of sale were similar for both properties. Both properties were in similar condition. The appraiser was able to establish that the only significant difference between the two properties was location. The difference in market price can be attributed to that difference. The loss of value resulting from being in the flight path of that airport is $25,000.

RENT LOSS METHOD

The **rent loss (income capitalization) method** estimates the total accrued depreciation of an income-producing property. The theory is simple. The market differentiates between properties and pays a higher rent for those properties with less depreciation. This makes perfect sense since depreciation is a loss of value and properties of less value tend to command lower rents. The amount by which the rent is lower than a new property or a property without any depreciation is the income that is capitalized. The income capitalization equation is used.

The rent differential must be annualized, and then capitalized.

Depreciation = Annualized Rent Differential / Capitalization Rate

EXAMPLE: Apartment complex A has 10 two-bedroom units, each of which rent for $1,000 per month. Apartment complex B, also a 10-unit complex of similar two-bedroom units, is new and each unit rents for $1,200 each. The capitalization rate for small apartment complexes in this neighborhood is 10%. Using the rent loss method, find the accrued depreciation of apartment complex A.

ANSWER: The apartments in complex A rent for $200 per month less than those in complex B. There are 10 units so the monthly rent differential is $2,000. The annual rent differential is $24,000 ($2,000 x 12 months).

Depreciation = Annualized Rent Differential / Capitalization Rate
Depreciation = $24,000 / 0.10 = $240,000

The same approach can be used with a gross rent multiplier or gross income multiplier. In fact, it may be easier because the rent does not have to be annualized. Depreciation is calculated using the rent differential just as in the example above. The rent differential is the amount of rent lost due to all types of depreciation.

Accrued Depreciation = Gross Rent Multiplier X Rent Differential

EXAMPLE: Same as the above example. Apartment complex A rents its 10 units for $200 per month less than complex B. The gross rent multiplier for small apartment complexes in that neighborhood is 120. What is the accrued depreciation estimate for apartment complex A?

ANSWER: The rent differential is $200 per apartment. There are 10 apartments so the total rent differential is $2,000.

Accrued Depreciation = Gross Rent Multiplier X Rent Differential
Accrued Depreciation = 120 X $2,000 = $240,000

The rent loss method is relatively easy if the appraiser has a new complex similar to the subject. He or she can determine with a rent survey the rent associated with similar, new units. The estimated depreciation is the total accrued depreciation from all sources. The rent loss method can be used in conjunction with any or all of the other methods in the breakdown method. The largest drawback is that it can only be applied to income generating properties.

OBSERVED CONDITION (BREAKDOWN) METHOD

This approach is the most comprehensive of the methods used to estimate accrued depreciation. In the **breakdown method**, also known as the **observed condition method**, an appraiser analyzes each type of accrued depreciation separately, measures the amount of each, and totals the individual estimates to determine the total accrued depreciation. Then, the total accrued depreciation is deducted from the reproduction or replacement cost.

The first step is to separate each of the three types of depreciation: physical, functional, and external. The appraiser then further separates each into their components. Physical deterioration is broken down into curable and incurable, short-lived items and long-lived items. Functional obsolescence is broken down into curable and incurable, including both that are caused by a deficiency and by superadequacy. Since external obsolescence is nearly always incurable, only one breakdown is needed. The appraiser then applies the best estimation method to each component and then sums over the entire set of components.

This approach has the advantage that each separate component of depreciation is specified and calculated individually. The approach is both time consuming and requires extensive knowledge and research. It is rarely used for residential appraisals. The approach is appropriate for complex cost appraisals of unique or substantial houses, houses with few if any comparables, and complex commercial and industrial properties.

SUMMARY

Depreciation is the loss in value of an improvement from any cause. The definition of depreciation includes anything that would cause an improvement to lose value. Depreciation can be categorized by its cause and different methods have been developed to estimate each of the different types of depreciation.

Estimating depreciation is the most difficult and complex aspect of the cost approach. Depreciation describes the loss of value from all sources and is in both the cost approach and site valuation. Appraisers use three types of depreciation: **physical deterioration, functional obsolescence,** and **external**

obsolescence. Physical deterioration and functional obsolescence can be either **curable** or **incurable**. The analysis to determine curable or incurable is a standard economic cost/benefit analysis.

The methods appraisers can use to estimate accrued depreciation are **age/life**, **market extraction**, **rent loss**, and **observed condition**. Each of the different methods has its own strengths and weaknesses. The appraiser must understand both the theory behind the method and the application to ensure that the appropriate method is applied and that the application can be replicated. Competent estimation of depreciation provides the client detailed information about the property, its condition, utility, and location relative to externalities. Finally, for unique properties, the precise estimate of depreciation helps develop a credible opinion of value.

UNIT 3 REVIEW

MATCHING EXERCISE

Instructions: Write the letter of the matching term on the blank line before its definition. Answers are in Appendix C.

Terms

A. accrued depreciation

B. actual age

C. age/life method

D. annuity

E. annuity method

F. component depreciation

G. cost to cure

H. curable depreciation

I. depreciation

J. economic life

K. effective age

L. external obsolescence

M. functional obsolescence

N. incurable depreciation

O. long-lived item

P. market extraction

Q. multivariable statistical analysis

R. physical deterioration

S. remaining economic life

T. rent loss method

U. short-lived item

V. straight-line depreciation

W. superadequacy

X. useful life

Definitions

1. _____ The loss in value of an improvement from any cause

2. _____ The number of years elapsed since a structure's construction; also called physical age, real age, or chronological age

3. _____ The number of years indicated by the condition of a structure

4. _____ The total of the accumulated depreciation

5. _____ The estimated period over which a building may be profitably used

6. _____ The number of years between the structure's estimated economic life and its effective age

7. _____ A method to estimate accrued depreciation based on the cost to cure or repair observed building defects

8. _____ A loss in value brought about by wear and tear, disintegration, use, and actions of the elements

9. _____ A type of depreciation that concerns items, which are economically feasible to repair or replace

10. _____ A type of depreciation in which building defects or problems cost more to repair than the anticipated value increase from such repair

11. _____ An item that is not expected to have a useful life equal to the useful life of the structure

12. _____ An item that is expected to have a useful life equal to the structure

13. _____ A loss of value due to adverse factors from within the structure that affect the utility value and marketability of the structure

14. _____ A loss of value caused by negative influences outside the specific property site

15. _____ A method of measuring depreciation based on equal annual amounts during the remaining economic life of the asset or structure

16. _____ The most often used method for estimating accrued depreciation and is based on the passage of time

17. _____ A method of calculating depreciation by totaling the depreciation of specific components of a property

18. _____ A series of payments made for a period of time that exhaust a given starting amount (present value)

19. _____ A method to estimate depreciation in which building values abstracted from sales are compared to current costs new

20. _____ A method that estimates the total accrued depreciation of an income-producing property

MULTIPLE CHOICE QUESTIONS

Instructions: Circle your response and go to Appendix C to read the complete explanation for each question.

1. The word depreciation, as used by appraisers, means a loss in value due to:
    a. wear and tear.
    b. deferred maintenance.
    c. external factors.
    d. all of the above.

2. The actual age of a property is determined by:
    a. the number of years elapsed since its construction.
    b. the condition of the property.
    c. deferred maintenance.
    d. extensive repairs performed on the property.

3. The estimate of effective age comes from:
    a. a mathematical equation.
    b. a property's condition.
    c. using a cost data basis.
    d. the number of years elapsed since its construction.

4. Physical deterioration of a property can be attributed to:
    a. the particular style of a consumer.
    b. weather.
    c. a nearby airport.
    d. having four bedrooms and one bathroom.

5. Part of the analysis process to determine depreciation involves the costs involved in repairing observed defects or the _____ method.
    a. market extraction
    b. annuity
    c. component depreciation
    d. cost to cure

6. A house with four bedrooms and one bathroom would have what type of depreciation?

    a. Functional obsolescence
    b. Physical deterioration
    c. External obsolescence
    d. Accrued depreciation

7. Which is not one of the four methods that an appraiser uses to estimate depreciation?

    a. Market extraction
    b. Rent loss
    c. Unobserved condition
    d. Age/life

8. Which of the following is not true regarding the use of the age/life method?

    a. Complex calculations
    b. A simple model of depreciation is employed
    c. It is based on the passage of time
    d. Basic calculations

9. In order to calculate depreciation percentage using the age/life method, an appraiser must:

    a. add effective age to actual age.
    b. subtract the actual age from effective age.
    c. divide the economic life by the useful life.
    d. divide the effective age by the economic life.

10. In the straight-line method, the amount of depreciation calculated on improvements is based on a(n):

    a. variable amount per year.
    b. equal amount per year.
    c. equal amount every five years.
    d. variable amount every five years.

11. Mark is trying to determine the accrued depreciation for a property with a $200,000 cost for new improvements and a depreciation percentage at 20 percent. What is the amount of accrued depreciation?

    a. $4,000
    b. $40,000
    c. $45,000
    d. $400,000

12. If an appraiser uses the market extraction method to estimate depreciation, he or she would apply:

    a. a paired sales analysis.

    b. the actual age of the property.

    c. component depreciation.

    d. the cost to cure method.

13. The best method to calculate depreciation that takes into account the market's opinion, is the _____ method.

    a. rent loss

    b. market extraction

    c. observed condition

    d. the age/life

14. In the market extraction method to determine depreciation, if two properties are not identical and contain several differences, a(n) _____ could be used.

    a. multivariable statistical analysis

    b. annuity method analysis

    c. component depreciation analysis

    d. cost to cure analysis

15. One of the elements necessary to be present in a property in order to use the rent loss method is:

    a. effective age.

    b. economic life.

    c. actual age.

    d. income.

Site Valuation: Theory

Unit **4**

INTRODUCTION

Developing a credible site valuation is part of every appraisal and necessary to develop estimates of depreciation and adjustments used in the sales comparison method. The value of the land is the foundation of all real estate value. The past twenty years has seen two dramatic periods of real estate price increases and one period of significant price decrease. In all cases, these price changes were attributable to the changing land value, not to a change in the value of the improvements. The previous unit taught us that improvements depreciate rather than appreciate. In periods of high inflation, the cost to construct improvements may increase, but this is usually not a significant increase when compared to the price changes of the land. These changes in value are part of the appraiser's daily life and the appraiser's ability to understand land values as well as develop site values is required for each appraisal.

Site valuation is divided into two units so that the appraiser may grasp the big picture before focusing on the application of the different methods. Six methods can be used to develop a site value. Each method has its own strengths and weaknesses, which must be understood before the correct method(s) is chosen. The extent and importance of each weakness influences the appraisal assignment and the appraiser must understand the sources of error before determining how it affects the final opinion of value. This unit provides a complete discussion of each of the methods while the next unit addresses the application of those methods.

LEARNING OBJECTIVES

After reading this unit, you should be able to:

- describe the uses of land valuation and the methods available to the appraiser to develop these valuations.
- identify the six different methods appraisers may apply to develop their opinion of land value.
- explain the strengths and weaknesses when applying each site valuation method.

SEPARATE SITE VALUATION

One of the most significant principles underlying land valuations methods is that **land can be valued apart from the improvements.** This principle was mentioned when highest and best use was discussed, and the site's use was analyzed without regard to its present use. The same is true as site valuations are developed. The site can have more than one value, depending on whether or not its present use is its highest and best use. As with any piece of property, a site valuation can be as of the date

Land can be valued apart from the improvements.

of inspection, a date in retrospection, or a date in the future. It can also be completed "as is" or subject to completion of zoning, General Plan changes, or the recording of a tract map subdividing the property. Each of these is a separate assignment requiring a different scope of work. An appraiser approaches any site valuation as any other appraisal assignment and addresses each of the seven steps in the valuation process. The following are examples of different site valuations that an appraiser can determine.

LAND APPRAISAL

This may appear too obvious, but the methods discussed here allow the appraiser to develop an opinion of value for any piece of land and there are numerous uses for land appraisals. Land appraisals can be part of a purchase transaction, a refinance transaction, or a development transaction. A developer needs land appraised for the purchase, the land development loan, the construction loan, and finally, individual loans for each of the improvements. Land appraisals are used to establish the value of land leases and termination values.

USING THE COST APPROACH TO VALUE

The cost approach demands that the site be valued separately from the improvements. This requirement is based on the need to value improvements at today's cost and apply the appropriate depreciation. Obtaining the site value is the first step in the cost approach.

INSURANCE VALUE

The insured value of a property is usually for the improvements only. The **insurance value** is the highest reasonable value that can be placed on property for insurance purposes. There are at least two types of insurance value—replacement cost and market value. The replacement cost approach

is based on a cost to reconstruct at today's prices. The market value is the value of the improvements in the market today. This is often determined by finding the site value and subtracting it from the market value of the property. The amount remaining is the market value of the improvements today.

ASSESSED VALUE

Property tax is assessed on the combined value of the land and improvements. The tax assessor completes a separate land valuation for each assessment.

LOCATION ADJUSTMENT IN THE SALES COMPARISON METHOD

Conceptually, the difference between two identical homes is their location, such as the site value. Rarely are there two identical homes. The difference in land value is the basis for the difference in prices of similar homes. This concept is useful when forced to use comparable properties in different neighborhoods.

The difference in land value is the adjustment for location. This is only one example of the importance of site valuation to the cost approach and the sales comparison approach.

ELEMENTS THAT AFFECT LAND VALUE

The elements that affect land value include physical, economic, political, and social attributes. Changes in these elements can have an impact on site value. The property owner does have the ability to impact land value by improving the site. Two specific actions are discussed here: assemblage and subdivision. Both of these processes can have a significant and immediate impact on site value.

ASSEMBLAGE

Assemblage is the process of putting several smaller contiguous parcels together into one larger parcel. The purpose of combining the lots is to increase its value, called plottage. **Plottage** is the value added by combining two or more parcels together into one large parcel. An example may help illustrate how this can have a positive impact on value.

Individually owned vacant lots.

Assemblage creates a larger parcel for commercial use.

Example: In a particular neighborhood, the lots are 4,000 square feet (SF) each and are zoned R3, for multiple units. In addition, zoning restricts the number of units to one for each 2,500 SF of lot area. Therefore, one unit may be built on each lot and comply with zoning. A developer, who understands assemblage, purchases two contiguous lots. The total size of the new parcel is 8,000 SF. The developer may now build three units on the two lots and still comply with zoning. The value of the additional unit is the increase in value attributable to plottage.

SUBDIVISION

A **subdivision** is tract of land divided by the owner into building lots and streets by a recorded subdivision plat. The subdivider or developer splits (subdivides) larger parcels of land into several smaller, marketable lots. In order to develop the new lots, the subdivider works with an engineer to design a development plan that takes advantage of the property's physical attributes and the permitted uses. Then the subdivider submits this plan to the city or county for approval. Part of that approval process may include rezoning the area to comply with the General Plan. Once approved, the subdivider has several marketable lots/sites, which can be sold or developed.

Undeveloped land.

Subdivided lots sell for more money than the undeveloped land.

Developers are trying to do this process every day all over the country. They need the assistance of good appraisers to do feasibility studies, appraise the raw land, and provide appraisals at different intervals throughout the process. A good appraiser can be requested to do three or four assignments for the same developer for the same property, each at a different stage of development.

> Example: Developer Kate sees that an outlying area in the city is approved in the General Plan for residential development. She purchases a vacant 10-acre parcel and prepares a subdivision map with 40 new lots. Once approved by the city, she will be able to sell the lots individually, creating more value.

SITE VALUATION METHODS – THEORY

There are six distinct methods used to develop an opinion of site value. The appraiser uses one or more every time a site or land valuation is needed. The theory behind these methods must be understood so that the application is consistent and can be replicated by another appraiser. The theory supporting each of the methods is presented here.

Site Valuation Methods

- Sales Comparison Method

- Allocation Method

- Abstraction Method

- Land Residual Method

- Ground Rent Method

- Subdivision Method

The sales comparison, allocation, abstraction, and subdivision methods may be used for any type of land: residential, commercial, industrial, or agricultural. Allocation and abstraction are used to obtain a separate land value when the property has improvements. The land residual method and ground rent method are used specifically for properties that generate income.

SALES COMPARISON METHOD

The best method for developing an opinion of site value is the **sales comparison method.** That does not mean that it is the most used. In fact, it is not used often for lack of comparable properties. The sales comparison method is the most direct evidence of the market's opinion of value, which is its single largest strength. The main principle underlying the sales comparison method is substitution. The **substitution principle** states that the maximum

value of a property tends to be set by the cost of acquiring an equally desirable and valuable substitute property, assuming no costly delay is encountered in making the substitution. An appraiser must be able to identify the properties' relevant elements and locate similar properties. If the subject and the comparables have differences, adjustments must be made in the sales price of the comparable properties. Once all the adjustments are made, and added, then the three comparables have values similar to the subject. Identification of the important comparison criteria is essential to effective use of the sales comparison method.

Items Considered Important When Researching Comparables

Location. Location is the single most important attribute of real estate and is just as important in a land valuation. The comparable properties must have similar locations in the neighborhood or adjustments must be made. Consideration of subject and comparable location relative to external factors—like an airport, a lake, or the ocean—is necessary.

Size and Shape. The size of the site is important because it determines the type and size of improvements that can be constructed. A specific improvement is associated with a parcel size, which includes parking and all associated buildings. Land not required to support the existing use is defined as excess land. **Excess land** is land beyond that which is needed to support the property's highest and best use. Excess land may be used for future expansion or separated from the site. Land that is not necessary to support the highest and best use, but cannot be separated is defined as surplus land. Surplus land and excess land might not have the same value as the primary part of the site. This is the reason a home with a 5,000 SF lot does not sell for a great deal more than one with a

4,500 SF lot. The difference in land size is surplus, not necessary for the highest and best use, and cannot be used for any other purpose.

Topography. **Topography** is the land's contours, drainage, soil conditions, physical characteristics, and usefulness for development. The physical characteristics of the subject and comparables must be similar, or the differences identified and adjusted. Accurate descriptions of these characteristics are important. A description of a steep slope to one person may not be the same to another person. A more specific description is necessary to eliminate as much personal opinion as possible. Part of the topography of a site is drainage and existing flood conditions. The FEMA (Federal Emergency Management Administration) flood maps provide accurate information about flood plains. These maps are available on the FEMA website and can be purchased from several vendors.

Utilities. Access to utilities is important for all types of development. Complex improvements require complex utilities. Commercial and industrial improvements require much more access to utilities, and their availability often determines the types of improvements that can be developed.

Accessibility. Access to the property is important regardless of the type of anticipated use. An example of anticipated use is that of a flag lot in a residential development that requires an easement to insure access. Commercial or retail properties have special access requirements. Ingress and egress to a shopping center can have an impact on the center's success.

Zoning. One of the essential attributes of a site is the specific zoning or General Plan designation. Zoning answers the question, "What is legally permitted to be built on the property?" Different zoning can have a substantial impact on the value of land. In addition, as a piece of property is developed, it goes through stages, with each succeeding stage adding value. The developer who wishes to subdivide a property must file a tentative map with the city/county. This map is the government's first opportunity to comment on the developer's plan. A tentative map must be approved by the municipality at which time conditions are attached. The developer must satisfy these conditions before a final map is available for recording. It is only after the final map is filed that the property can be sold as individual lots rather than as a whole parcel. The type of map and any conditions associated with the map are factors that affect value.

STRENGTHS OF THE SALES COMPARISON METHOD

The sales comparison method is the most accurate reflection of the market and appraisers should use this method whenever possible. Quite often, sales of vacant parcels are not available. This approach produces the most accurate results when there are comparable vacant land parcels.

WEAKNESSES OF THE SALES COMPARISON METHOD

The lack of vacant land comparables is the greatest weakness of this approach. Recently sold comparables that are similar to the subject property are important to land valuation. This way, all comparables can be properly analyzed for their similarities. For those elements in which the comparable differs from the subject, an adjustment must be made. Anytime an adjustment is made, error is possible. Even in the best of situations, adjustments for differences are a source of error. The more accurate the adjustments, the fewer the errors.

The availability of land comparables, similar to the subject and in the same neighborhood, is often impossible. It can be almost impossible to find a vacant lot in a subdivision of tract homes. The developer did not sell the vacant lots, so there are no similar comparables. The same is true for the majority of improved properties. Even when valuing vacant land, there may not be recent sales of similar properties.

ALLOCATION METHOD

Allocation is the division of the property value into its two components—land and improvements. If a home has a sales price of $300,000 and the improvements are valued at $150,000, the land would be valued at $150,000 (sales price – improvements = land value). The land and improvements would each represent 50% of the sales price.

Once a land allocation has been completed in a neighborhood, the land value for a similar lot can be found by multiplying the sales price by the predetermined land allocation (percentage). This method is best used when the allocation has been predetermined either by the appraiser using one of the other land valuation methods or a source like the assessors office. The office of tax assessor not only assesses property taxes, but it separates the land value from the improvement value. A recent assessment by the assessor's office can provide a good allocation.

STRENGTHS OF THE ALLOCATION METHOD

Ease of use is the primary strength of this method. Once a reliable allocation percentage or ratio has been developed, it can be used to calculate a land value. The allocation method is also relatively consistent among similar properties in a neighborhood. It is often used as a secondary method to verify the accuracy of the primary approach. Some appraisers develop land value using the abstraction method; then verify it using the allocation method. Allocation can be used for any type of property. It is not specific to a property type or amount.

WEAKNESSES OF THE ALLOCATION METHOD

Accuracy is the most significant weakness of the allocation method. At best, it provides a good estimate. Most often, the allocation is expressed as a percentage, and has only two significant figures. The result of a calculation with one of the factors having two significant figures means that the answer can be accurate to no more than two significant figures. In the example, land is valued at $150,000, which has two significant figures. The method cannot be relied upon to produce results with any more accuracy.

ABSTRACTION METHOD

Abstraction is a method of determining the land value of a comparable property by deducting the depreciated costs of the improvements from the property's known sales price. The remaining value represents the value attributable to the land. Abstraction is the most useful of the six land valuation methods when the land is improved. It can be used only on properties with improvements.

Formula – Abstraction Method
Land Value = Sales Price – [Cost New of Improvements – Depreciation]

Even though calculations are relatively uncomplicated, there are several areas subject to significant error. This method is perfect for use in areas where the sites are similar, but all have improvements. The appraiser is abstracting (extracting) the land value from the sales price by subtracting the depreciated value of the improvements. Abstraction is used for any type of property in almost any location.

STRENGTHS OF THE ABSTRACTION METHOD

This method allows the appraiser to develop a site value for any improved property as long as there are similar, recently sold sites. This is regardless of the improvements made on those sites. Accuracy is a function of the quality of the comparable, the data used to calculate the cost of the improvements, and the precision of estimating depreciation.

Most appraisers begin with the square foot method as a first approximation when applying abstraction. The **square foot method** is a method used to calculate reproduction or replacement cost by multiplying the cost per square foot by the building's area in square feet. The square foot method provides a good estimate of the overall cost to replace the existing improvement at today's costs. Calculating cost new using the square foot method is easy and there are several quality sources of cost data available to the appraiser. The results obtained using the square foot method and even straight-line depreciation are credible. **Straight-line depreciation** is a method of measuring depreciation based on equal annual amounts during the remaining economic life of the asset or structure.

Abstraction also assists the appraiser in developing certain adjustments to be used in the sales comparison approach. The best example is appraising a home near the border of a city or school district. The values of properties in the different city or school district may be significantly different. That value difference lies within the land and not the improvements. To obtain an accurate estimate of that value difference, the appraiser abstracts the land value in the subject's neighborhood and in the neighborhood in question. The amount of adjustment is the difference in land value when adjusted for differences in size and other characteristics. This same method can be used to establish the value of different zonings and views. Abstraction is a tool used to improve the quality of the sales comparison adjustments.

WEAKNESSES OF THE ABSTRACTION METHOD

Lack of accuracy is the primary weakness of this method. A competent application of the method provides an adequate result, which is good to three significant digits.

Sources of Error

Dissimilarity of comparables – comparable sites must be as similar as possible, or adjustments need to be made. The process of making adjustment (paired sales analysis) is relatively accurate, but still leaves room for error.

Developing costs for the improvements – in most cases, the appraiser has not inspected the comparables, certainly not the interior, so the quality of the cost calculations depends on a series of assumptions about the improvements. The appraiser can use the MLS or similar services to gain some information as well as call the listing broker, selling broker, seller, or buyer. The more accurate the information, the better the cost breakdown and the more accurate the result.

Depreciation is always a difficult subject. An estimate as to the effective age of the improvements must be made before any physical depreciation can be calculated. The more research and information developed on the comparable properties, the more accurate the estimate of effective age. Most appraisers use the straight-line effective age/total economic life approach to estimate physical depreciation. Functional and external obsolescence must be noted and estimated in order to develop a credible result. The result is an estimate of depreciation that is within market tolerances.

Even with all the room for error, abstraction is one of the most effective tools the appraiser can use. When used in conjunction with one of the other methods, an accurate opinion of land value can be developed.

SUBDIVISION METHOD

The subdivision method is a special case of the abstraction method and that is why it is presented after abstraction. The **subdivision method** is a site valuation method used exclusively for finding lot value or land value in a pending subdivision. In concept, the formula is similar to abstraction.

Formula – Subdivision Method

Land Value = Total Sales Price – Total Development Costs

Once the land value is obtained, the appraiser need only divide it by the total number of lots to get a lot value. On the surface, the formula appears simple and easy to apply, however, it is often more complex.

The appraiser must estimate the sales prices and the length of time needed to sell the newly developed lots. An **absorption analysis** provides the appraiser with the rate and the total length of time in which the lots sell. The **sales analysis** establishes the projected sales price. The combination of these two provides projected sales revenue in the future. This future income stream must be discounted to today so that all analysis is completed in the same timeframe.

Similar analysis is necessary for the total cost breakdown for the project. All costs associated with the project, such as direct and indirect, on-site and off-site, and expected profit must be included in the costs. If this is a large project, construction is done over time in order to minimize the amount of standing inventory. Since these costs are also future costs, they must be discounted for today's value consistent with the income analysis. The difference between the discounted income and the discounted costs and profit is the land value.

STRENGTHS OF THE SUBDIVISION METHOD

Subdivision analysis is the best approach to develop the land and lot value resulting from a subdivision development. Application requires some familiarity with construction, cost breakdowns, and the subdivision process. The appraiser must also have a basic understanding of the time value of money and the discounting process. Builders and developers have available for the appraiser detailed cost breakdowns for the entire development, which the appraiser can use after verification. Market analysis leads to an accurate prediction of future sales prices and profit margins. Depreciation is not a part of this analysis, as the improvements are new. The lack of a depreciation component means less room for error. This combination of good information and fewer opportunities for error leads to results that are more reliable.

WEAKNESSES OF THE SUBDIVISION METHOD

Subdivision analysis requires some experience with the development process and construction costs. Any errors in the information presented can lead to erroneous results. The calculations are complex and require a significant amount of research and verification. Changing markets over time can influence current results. The information available from the developer may be biased and needs to be verified. The complexities combined with the amount of research required make this a challenging method to apply.

GROUND RENT CAPITALIZATION METHOD

Ground rent capitalization is the first of two site valuation methods that require income. The **ground rent capitalization** method determines value by obtaining the earnings of improved property credited to earnings of the ground itself after allowance has been made for earnings of improvements. This is the more basic of the two methods and has limited applicability. Use of this method is limited to properties that have identifiable land rent. The basic income capitalization formula (value = income ÷ capitalization rate) is then applied. The capitalization rate can be developed through market extraction.

> **Formula – Ground Rent Capitalization**
>
> Land Value = Income ÷ Capitalization Rate

STRENGTHS OF THE GROUND RENT METHOD

Ease of application is the primary strength of ground rent capitalization. Once the appraiser has identified the ground rent and the appropriate capitalization rate, the calculations are relatively easy. Ground rent income can be ascertained with accuracy and verified. The development of a capitalization rate can be complicated, but the most effective method is market extraction from recent sales of similar properties. This method is credible and used by many real estate practitioners.

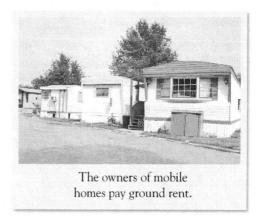

The owners of mobile homes pay ground rent.

WEAKNESSES OF THE GROUND RENT METHOD

This method is applicable to sites with income directly related or attributed to the land. This method works best when the land is leased to the owner of the improvements or the land is vacant and earns rent, such as a parking lot. As is seen in the next method, there are methods to separate total income into income attributable to the improvements and the land. There are limited applications, but the next method expands on this by identifying income attributable to the land on income property with improvements.

LAND RESIDUAL METHOD

The **land residual method** is a method for determining land value in which the net income remaining to the land (after income attributable to the building has been deducted) is capitalized into an estimate of value. The name describes the method: (1) establish the residual income, (2) calculate the income left over after determining the income attributable to the improvements, and (3) capitalize the income to estimate the value of the land.

The land residual method can be used for income-producing property.

The remaining income **(residual)** is attributable to the land. The land residual method can be applied to any income property to develop a credible land value.

Income is derived from both the land and the improvements for most income properties. In order to identify the income attributable to the land, the income attributable to the improvements must be calculated and subtracted from the total income. The application of this method requires that certain assumptions be made.

Assumptions in the Land Residual Method

- Land does not depreciate.

- The improvements do depreciate.

- The holding period is the remaining economic life of the improvements.

- The value of the land does not change over time.

- The overall rate of return for the improvements equals the capitalization rate plus the recapture rate.

- The recapture rate equals the remaining economic life of the improvements, and is the return of investment. Return of investment is necessary because the holding period is for the remaining economic life of the improvements, at which time their economic value is zero. Investors want the initial investment returned.

- No return of investment is necessary for the land because it retains its original value.

All of these assumptions become central to application of the land residual method. The total annual income generated by the property must be identified. The next step is to calculate how much of that income is attributable to the improvements. The two parts to this calculation are the return on investment (capitalization rate) and the return of investment (recapture). The **return on investment** is the percentage (capitalization rate) that shows the rate of return derived from the amount of capital invested. The return on investment is the net income or loss that an investment produces. On the other hand, the **return of investment** or recapture is the recovery of the capital invested.

A straight-line recapture rate is usually assumed, as it is the easiest to calculate. Once the recapture rate is established, it is applied to the cost of the improvements. This amount is the income attributable to return of investment for the improvements. The appraiser next applies the capitalization rate to the building cost to find the annual income attributable to return on investment for the building. The combination of return on investment and return of investment equals the total income attributable to the improvements. This amount is subtracted from the total property income and the residual is the income attributable to the land. That income is capitalized using the capitalization rate applied to the building. The result is the value of the land. This method is a little cumbersome, but useful as the appraiser now has the ability to develop the land value for any improved income property.

STRENGTHS OF THE LAND RESIDUAL METHOD

The land residual method can be applied to any improved income property and produce credible results. That is its main strength. It is a bit complex for the beginning appraiser, but after a little practice, it can yield reliable valuations. The method can be replicated by any appraiser, and can be developed in a thorough and complete manner. Each element can be independently verified and quantified allowing the appraiser an audit trail. The information required to complete the calculations is readily available and again verifiable.

WEAKNESSES OF THE LAND RESIDUAL METHOD

Weaknesses can be explored one item at a time. A key element to an accurate result is a good capitalization rate. The accuracy of the capitalization rate determines the accuracy of the valuation. Complex income-based appraisals usually develop the capitalization rate with at least two different methods. The capitalization rate can be built using the band of investment technique or through market extraction. The **band of investment technique** is a method of estimating interest and capitalization rates, based on a weighted average of the mortgage interest rate (or other cost of borrowed funds) and the rate of return on equity required.

Developing the recapture rate can be significant to the results reported. The most basic approach is to use straight-line recapture or an equal amount each year. As with physical depreciation, this is not an accurate representation of the actual deterioration in any one year. The straight-line approach overstates depreciation in the beginning years and understates it in the final years of the improvement's economic life. The use of a loan constant based on the cost of the improvements is a more accurate representation of depreciation. Consequently, there is the need for return of investment. A **loan constant** is the required cash flow needed annually to service both the principal and interest on a loan. Remember, return of investment is necessary because improvements deteriorate over time and their value decreases. That decrease in value must be returned to the investor. A loan constant is developed by calculating a monthly loan payment, at an interest rate equal to the capitalization rate, over a period equal to the remaining economic life of the improvements. The loan amount equals the cost of the improvements. The loan constant equals 12 times the monthly payment divided by the loan amount. This factor represents the overall capitalization rate for the improvements.

Finally, the accuracy of the income used in the calculations is the most basic element of any income analysis. Income can mean many things to many people. There is a significant difference between income for tax purposes and income for financial statement reporting. Certainly, a seller reports as much income as possible while the buyer would like to see either a smaller income or larger expenses. The net result is a smaller net income and therefore, a smaller value based on that income. The appraiser should verify all income and compare reported income to market income. If there is a significant difference, then more research is needed to establish the most accurate income.

SUMMARY

Site valuation is an integral and important part of every appraisal. It is the first of three steps in the cost approach to valuation and is needed to make adjustments in the sales comparison method. There are six methods available to appraisers to develop their opinion of site value. One of the more reliable methods is the **sales comparison method**. Properties that are good substitutes for the subject are researched and compared to the subject. Their sales prices are adjusted for differences between them and the subject. The value after adjustment is the market opinion of value for the subject.

The **allocation** and **abstraction methods** can be used on any improved property. Each of these methods allows the appraiser to separate the improvement value from the land value. Abstraction is used to establish the land value, after which a percentage of land and improvements can be calculated. This percentage can be used in the future, with the allocation method, given the market does not change materially. When prices go up or down, most of that change is in the land value. Therefore, when there have been large changes in market prices, historical allocation is not an accurate representation of the actual land-to-improvement ratio. Abstraction can be used in a variety of situations to assist the appraiser in developing paired sales analysis and adjustments to be used in the sales comparison method. Abstraction is the most useful generally applicable method presented.

The **subdivision method** is a version of abstraction with very limited application. Land that is used in a new subdivision is the only candidate for the subdivision method. The two remaining methods, **ground rent capitalization** and **land residual methods,** require an income-producing property. The ground rent capitalization and the land residual method have broad applicability to improved income properties of all types.

Each method has its own set of strengths and weaknesses. In most cases, thorough research and verification limit the amount and frequency of any errors. Each method has its own specific built-in errors—most of which can be minimized through competent application. The appraiser is responsible for choosing the method(s) that best suit his or her appraisal problem and then applying the methods in a manner that is transparent and repeatable.

UNIT 4 REVIEW

MATCHING EXERCISE

Instructions: Write the letter of the matching term on the blank line before its definition. Answers are in Appendix C.

Terms

A. abstraction	H. recapture rate	N. subdivision method
B. allocation	I. return of investment	O. substitution principle
C. assemblage	J. return on investment	P. surplus land
D. excess land	K. sales comparison method	Q. topography
E. ground rent capitalization		
F. insurance value	L. square foot method	
G. land residual method	M. subdivision	

Definitions

1. _____ The highest reasonable value that can be placed on property for insurance purposes

2. _____ The process of assembling more than one contiguous parcel into one larger parcel

3. _____ The process whereby larger parcels of land are split into several smaller, marketable lots

4. _____ A theory based on the idea that the maximum value of a property tends to be set by the cost of acquiring an equally desirable and valuable substitute property, assuming no costly delay is encountered in making the substitution

5. _____ Land beyond that which is needed to support the property's highest and best use

6. _____ Land that is not necessary to support the highest and best use of the property and cannot be separated or developed

7. _____ The land's contours, drainage, soil conditions, physical characteristics, and usefulness for development

8. _____ The division of the property value into land and improvements

9. _____ A method of determining the land value of a comparable property by deducting the depreciated costs of the improvements from the property's known sales price

10. _____ A method used to calculate reproduction or replacement cost by multiplying the cost per square foot by the building's area in square feet

11. _____ A site valuation method used exclusively for finding lot value or land value in a pending subdivision

12. _____ A method that determines value by obtaining the earnings of improved property credited to earnings of the ground itself after allowance has been made for earnings of improvements

MULTIPLE CHOICE QUESTIONS

Instructions: Circle your response and go to Appendix C to read the complete explanation for each question.

1. Site valuation methods for land are based on the principle that:
    a. the improvement on a land never depreciates.
    b. land and improvements can be valued separately.
    c. land and improvements are valued together, not separately.
    d. land depreciates at a rate similar to its improvement.

2. Pat, an investor, finds that he can increase the value of property he is purchasing by assembling two or more contiguous parcels. This increase in value is called:
    a. plottage.
    b. allocation.
    c. ground rent.
    d. land residuals.

3. When locating suitable comparables in the sales comparison method, an appraiser should consider:

    a. the location of the property.

    b. comparable property's size and shape.

    c. accessibility to the property.

    d. all of the above.

4. A home has a sales price of $400,000 with $200,000 attributed to the value of the improvement. The land and improvements each represent half of the sales price. Using the allocation method, what is the value of the land?

    a. $100,000

    b. $200,000

    c. $300,000

    d. $400,000

5. The main strength of the allocation method is:

    a. that it has the best available information.

    b. that it is used by the tax assessor.

    c. its ease of application.

    d. its overall accuracy.

6. Which method determines land value by deducting the depreciated costs of a property's improvement from the sales price?

    a. Ground Rent

    b. Abstraction

    c. Allocation

    d. Land Residual

7. A weakness in using the abstraction method for site valuation is lack of accuracy. This can be attributed to:

    a. incorrect income calculations.

    b. lack of education regarding real estate development and construction.

    c. determining the capitalization rate.

    d. the dissimilarity of comparable properties.

8. Sarah, a real estate broker, purchased a parcel of land in order to create 10 buildable lots. She is waiting for the local planning commission to approve her plans so she can develop the lots for sale. In the meantime, she is curious to know what the value of the new lots will be, so she hires an appraiser. The appraiser would probably use the _____ method.

   a. abstraction
   b. allocation
   c. subdivision
   d. ground rent

9. Appraisers using the subdivision method must be able to:

   a. calculate the time value of money.
   b. find comparable subdivisions.
   c. determine the recapture rate.
   d. develop a loan constant variable.

10. What is the main advantage in using the ground rent capitalization method?

   a. Ease of application
   b. Identification of capitalization rate is not necessary
   c. Simple calculations
   d. Both (a) and (c)

11. Which situation is best suited for the ground rent capitalization method?

   a. An appraiser determining the value of residential property
   b. An appraiser determining the value of commercial property
   c. An appraiser determining the value of a vacant parcel with no income
   d. An appraiser seeking the value of a paid parking lot

12. Which method is used to obtain the site value by calculating the residual income, determining the income attributed to the improvement, and capitalizing that income?

   a. Land Residual
   b. Subdivision
   c. Allocation
   d. Abstraction

13. How does an appraiser calculate the land income in the land residual method?

   a. Land income = total income x income attributable to improvements
   b. Land income = total income + income attributable to improvements
   c. Land income = total income – income attributable to improvements
   d. Land income = income attributable to improvements – total income

14. The rate of return from an investment, expressed as a percentage is the:

    a. return of investment.

    b. land residual.

    c. net income.

    d. return on investment.

15. What is the primary strength of using the land residual method?

    a. Application to any improved, income-producing property

    b. Inaccurate results

    c. Ease of use

    d. Relatively simple calculations

Site Valuation: Practice

Unit **5**

INTRODUCTION

This unit primarily deals with application of the theory presented in Unit 4. The student should become familiar with the logical process of applying each of the six methods and the math required to complete the application. The six methods are: (1) sales comparison, (2) allocation, (3) extraction, (4) subdivision development, (5) ground rent capitalization, and (6) land residual.

Examples and discussions of the limitations and sources of error for each of these six valuation methods are in this unit. The examples are from actual appraisals and represent exactly what the appraiser sees in his or her everyday practice. The solutions are not unique or absolutely correct. The application and math are accurate and the technique used is appropriate for the situation. Each example is illustrative of the thought process and actual application of these methods.

Most of the methods do not require extensive calculations or advanced math. Others, like the subdivision technique, require financial calculations, such as discounting cash flows and net present value. The student is urged to follow the examples closely and complete all the problems and case studies. A competent appraiser is conversant in all of these methods.

LEARNING OBJECTIVES

After reading this unit, you should be able to:

- name the six methods used to estimate land value.
- apply each technique.
- calculate the math required to complete the application.

SALES COMPARISON METHOD

The **sales comparison method** is based on the principle of substitution. It consistently provides the most direct evidence of the market and is, therefore, the best approach to use when good comparables are available. The strength of the approach lies in the quality and similarity of the comparables. A sufficient number of sales must be found to allow the appraiser to isolate the effect on value of the pertinent factor. Adjustments for comparable sales for land are made more difficult by the scarcity of available comparables. An appraiser must be able to find at least three similar vacant parcels to support use of this approach. All relevant differences must be identified and the market's opinion of the value of those differences must be developed and used as adjustments.

Appraisers enter information about the comparable properties on an adjustment grid. The **adjustment grid** is a table or matrix of relevant data on comparable properties. For an appraisal of a site or lot, it includes sales price, date of sale, location, view, usable land, zoning, and sales or financing concessions. The value of adjustments is developed through paired sales analysis, not the opinion of the appraiser. **Paired sales analysis** is a method of estimating the amount of adjustment for the presence or absence of any feature by pairing the sales prices of otherwise identical properties with and without that feature. The paired sales analysis is a difficult, complex task that requires research, analysis, and experience. The actual **adjustments** are a dollar amount or percentage that is added to or subtracted from the sales price of a comparable property to account for a feature that differentiates it from the subject property. Once all the adjustments have been made, the final opinion of value must be developed through reconciliation of the adjusted values of the comparable sales.

In the adjustment grid on the next page, note that the total sales price is listed at the top of each comparable and below that, a price per square foot or acre. In this example, the price is per acre. Comparisons must be made based on a comparable unit, as there are few vacant parcels exactly similar in size. The range of values is larger than with single-family homes as the differences are greater as is the distance between comparables.

The undersigned has recited three recent sales of properties most similar and proximate to the subject and has considered these in the market analysis. The description includes a dollar adjustment, reflecting market reaction to those items of significant variation between the subject and comparable properties. If a significant item in the comparable property is superior to, or more favorable than subject property, a minus (-) adjustment is made, thus reducing the indicated value of the subject. If a significant item in the comparable is inferior to or less favorable than the subject property, a plus (+) adjustment is made, thus increasing the indicated value of subject.

ITEM	SUBJECT	COMPARABLE NO. 1 DESCRIPTION	+(-) Adjustment	COMPARABLE NO. 2 DESCRIPTION	+(-) Adjustment	COMPARABLE NO. 3 DESCRIPTION	+(-) Adjustment
Address: 12345 Tiny Canyon Rd. Lake View Area		23450 Major St. Lake Town, CA 90000		26543 Sandy Ave. Lake Town, CA 90001		26781 Marsh Rd. Wetlands, CA 90002	
Proximity to subject:		8 mi NE		7.5 mi NE		9 mi E	
Sales Price	$ Refinance	$ 1,015,700		$ 1,168,960		$ 750,000	
Price $ / SF (AC)	$	$ 101,570		$ 141,864		$ 145,914	
Data Source		FARES/MLS/Loopnet		FARES/MLS/Loopnet		FARES/MLS/Loopnet	
Date of Sale and Time Adjustment		2/7/2006	20,000	8/31/2006		6/5/2006	
Location:	Suburban/Freeway	Suburban/F/W		Suburban		Suburban/track	
Site/View	Industrial site across street	Similar		Similar		Similar	
Usable Land	100%	100%		100%		100%	
Zoning	M-SC Light Indust.	Light Indust.		RR/Light Indust.	-10,000	Light Indust.	
Lot Size Net	14.2 Acres	10.00 acres	-5,000	8.24 acres	-10,000	5.14 acres	-20,000
APN		123-456-789/799		124-567-890		135-678-902	
Sales or Financing Concessions	None Observed	None Observed		None Observed		None Observed	
Net Adj. (Total)		☒+ ☐-	15,000	☐+ ☒-	20,000	☐+ ☒-	20,000
Indicated Value of Subject	Price per Acre	$ 116,570	Gross: 14.77 Net: 14.77	$ 121,864	Gross: 14.10 Net: -14.10	$ 125,914	Gross: -13.71 Net: -13.71

Comments on Market Data: Adjustments were made to time of sale and lot size. The price per acre of a lot tends to decrease as the size of the lot increases, all other things being equal. The price per acre for the comparables would be higher because they are smaller lots than the subject property. Therefore, the appraiser made negative adjustments for the lot size. The subject property value per acre ranges from $116,570 to $125,914. Subject's superior location and proximity to the freeway indicate a value at the upper end of the range - $122,000 per acre. The final opinion will be based on that value per acre multiplied by the usable area (14.2) for a final value of $1,732,400.

Comments and Conditions of Appraisal As is. This appraisal report is intended for use in a mortgage refinance transaction only. This is a complete summary appraisal report, completed in conformity with the Uniform Standards of Professional Appraisal Practice (USPAP).

Final Reconciliation The sales comparison analysis is given primary consideration since it best reflects what a typical buyer/seller would agree upon. The income approach is excluded, as these properties were not subject to ground rent.

ALLOCATION METHOD

The **allocation method** is based upon the principle of balance as well as on the concept of contributory value. In the allocation method, the appraised total value is divided between land and improvements. The principle of balance states that income is attributable to the land after the other agents of production (labor, management, and capital) have been paid. This is known as **surplus productivity.** When the agents of production are in balance, the income available to the land is maximized. The concept of **contributory value** states that the value of each agent of production is determined by its contribution to the whole.

The strength of the allocation method is its ease of application. The basic assumption of this method is that there is a typical ratio between the land value of a property and the value of its improvements. A **ratio** is the relationship between two numbers or measurements. The ratio varies by area, so the appraiser must extract the ratio from the local market. Then, he or she can apply it to other improved sales in the subject's neighborhood in order to establish the land value.

The allocation method makes use of the ratio of land to improvements or the percentage of the total sales price that land represents. Both applications are relatively easy to calculate. It must be remembered that the results cannot be stated with more significant digits than the lower of the two numbers being multiplied.

Ratio of Land to Improvement

Often, a simple land-to-improvement ratio has been developed for a neighborhood. The **land-to-improvement ratio** is a measurement of the value of the land compared to the value of its improvement. This ratio can be used to find the land value.

EXAMPLE: If the ratio of the land to improvements is 1 to 4 (1 : 4), this means that the value of the improvements is four times the value of the land. The total property value equals five times the land value. Find the land value if the land-to-improvement ratio is 1 : 4 and the total property value is $200,000. Land value equals the ratio of land value to total property value or 1/5 multiplied by the total property value.

Land Value = $200,000 x 1/5 (0.2 or 20%)
Land Value = $40,000

Percentage of the Total Sales Price that Land Represents

When the percentage of the total property value that land represents is known, the calculations are even easier.

EXAMPLE: Find the land value if the total property value is $200,000 and land is 20% of the total property value. Land value equals the percentage (expressed as a decimal) multiplied by the total property value.

$$\text{Land Value} = 0.20 \times \$200,000$$

$$\text{Land Value} = \$40,000$$

ABSTRACTION METHOD

The **abstraction method,** also known as the extraction method, is a variation on the allocation method. Using this method, appraisers derive the land value of a comparable property by deducting the depreciated costs of the improvements on that property from the property's known sale price. The remaining value represents value attributable to the land.

Applying the abstraction method is relatively easy and requires only minimal research to locate sites similar to the subject. In this case, only the site must be similar. It is not relevant what improvements are on those sites, nor is the condition of the improvements relevant. The selection of comparables must be limited to those sites that are the most similar in all relevant land elements, i.e. location, topography, view, and size. Once an acceptable comparable is located, the technique can be applied.

To calculate land value using the abstraction method, the appraiser subtracts the value of the improvements today from the sales price. The **value of improvements today** is the cost to replace an improvement today minus depreciation.

Formula - Abstraction Method

Land Value = Sale Price − Value of Improvements Today

The following example illustrates how the value of the improvements today can be calculated, and then subtracted from the sale price to find the land value. Depreciation is calculated for the entire property using the age/life method because it is reasonable and relatively easy. A complete inspection of the property might allow the use of component depreciation or, at least, a more accurate estimate of effective age. This is rarely available to the appraiser, as comparable property owners are not likely to allow unscheduled inspection. Normally, the best estimate of depreciation is physical depreciation based on the straight-line age/life method.

EXAMPLE: Calculate the land value when the sales price is $200,000. The improvements consist of a 25-year-old 2,000 square foot (SF) residence with an effective age estimated at 14 years. The total economic life is estimated at 70 years. Cost to replace the residence is $100 per SF.

Step 1. Calculate Replacement Cost Today (RCT)

Replacement cost today = 2,000 SF x $100/SF

Replacement cost today = $200,000

Step 2. Calculate Depreciation

Depreciation = (Effective Age ÷ Economic Life) x RCT

Depreciation = (14 yrs ÷ 70 yrs.) x $200,000

Depreciation = 0.2 x $200,000

Depreciation = $40,000

Step 3. Calculate Value of Improvements Today (VIT)

VIT = RCT minus Depreciation

VIT = $200,000 − $40,000

VIT = $160,000

Step 4. Calculate Land Value

Land Value = Sales Price − Value Improvement Today

Land Value = $200,000 − $160,000

Land Value = $40,000

SUBDIVISION METHOD

The **subdivision method** is a method of valuing land used for subdivision development. It relies on accurate forecasting of market demand, including both **forecast absorption** (the rate at which properties will sell) and **projected gross sales** (total income that the project will produce). It is also called the land development method.

Application of the subdivision technique can become complicated because of the amount of detailed information necessary and available.

Formula - Subdivision Method

Land Value = Total Sales Price of all Projected Units — All costs of development including expected developer profit.

The total sales price of all projected units equals the number of units to be built multiplied by their expected sales price. There are instances when the time anticipated to sell future units is expected to exceed one or two years. In these cases, the gross sales proceeds must be discounted to today's value. Discounting is not part of the beginning curriculum and is not addressed here.

All costs of development include both direct and indirect costs, plus developer profit. **Direct costs** include costs associated with the actual work completed to an improvement on-site. Examples of direct costs would be actual construction, wages for labor, supervision, and materials. **Indirect costs** are all costs for completed work on the improvement off-site. Indirect costs include plans, fees, permits, accounting, legal, and taxes. In addition, the developer expects to make a profit and that must be part of the calculation of total costs. Normally, developers expect to make 15% or more of the anticipated total sales as profit. Large projects can span several years and as evidenced by the potential sales revenue, the costs must be discounted to today's value. This example does not address discounting.

Indirect Costs   Direct Costs

EXAMPLE: The subdivision has 10 homes (units). Each home is 1,500 SF in GLA. The homes are pre-sold so they are purchased upon completion. The developer expects to make a 15% profit. Each home sells for $300,000. Direct costs of construction are $100 per SF. Indirect costs equal 15% of the total projected sales. What is the land value?

Step 1. Calculate total sales revenue

> 10 homes x $300,000 per home = $3,000,000

Step 2. Calculate total costs

> Direct costs equal $100 per SF. There are 10 homes, 1,500 SF each in the subdivision, equaling 15,000 SF of improvements
>
> Total Direct Costs = 15,000 SF x $100/SF
>
> Total Direct Costs = $1,500,000

> **Indirect costs equal 15% of the projected sales revenue.**
>
> Indirect costs = $3,000,000 x .15
>
> Indirect costs = $450,000

> **Developer profit is expected to equal 15% of the total sales proceeds**
>
> Developer Profit = $3,000,000 x .15
>
> Developer Profit = $450,000

> **Total Cost is the sum of direct and indirect costs and developer's profit**
>
> Total Costs = $1,500,000 + $450,000 + $450,000
>
> Total Costs = $2,400,000

Step 3. Calculate Land Value

> Land Value = Total Sales Revenue – Total Costs
>
> Land Value = $3,000,000 – $2,400,000
>
> Land Value = $600,000

The land value is $600,000. The value per lot is $60,000. The land-to-improvement ratio is 1 : 4 as in the first allocation example.

GROUND RENT CAPITALIZATION METHOD

The **ground rent capitalization** method determines value by obtaining the earnings of improved property credited to earnings of the ground itself after allowance has been made for earnings of improvements. Application of the ground rent technique uses the income capitalization formula with information developed or provided.

> **Formula - Ground Rent Capitalization Method**
>
> Value = Income ÷ Capitalization Rate

Income should be developed in an annual format. The choice of the capitalization rate should be consistent with the type of income used and with the type of property.

EXAMPLE: Subject property generates Net Income of $120,000 per year. The Market Capitalization Rate is 9%.

Step 1. Convert the Capitalization Rate from a percentage to a decimal

9% = 0.09

Step 2. Substitute the values given into the formula

Value = Income ÷ Capitalization Rate

Value = $120,000 ÷ 0.09

Value = $1,333,333

The land value developed here has more than two significant digits and should be rounded to no more than 2 significant digits. The Final Opinion of Land Value would be $1,300,000.

LAND RESIDUAL METHOD

The land residual method is an income capitalization technique in which the net income remaining to the land (after income attributable to the building has been deducted) is capitalized into an estimate of value for the land. This technique is often overlooked because of the perceived difficulty in its application. A rational, step-by-step approach should make the application more real and approachable. In order to apply the land residual technique, the building value today, its remaining economic life, and the market capitalization rate are needed.

Land residual is another application of the income capitalization formula. Income must be divided between the improvements and the land. Once the income is attributed to the land, that income is capitalized at the market capitalization rate.

EXAMPLE 1: Improvements on subject property are valued at $1,200,000. The remaining economic life is estimated to be 40 years. Net Income from the property is $200,000 per year. The Market Capitalization Rate is 11%. What is the value of the land?

Step 1. Calculate the Recapture Rate

Recapture rate = 1 ÷ Remaining Economic Life

Recapture rate = 1 ÷ 40 yrs = 0.025 or 2.5%

Step 2. Calculate the Dollar Amount of Recapture

Dollar Recapture = Recapture Rate x Building Value

Dollar Recapture = 0.025 x $1,200,000

Dollar Recapture = $30,000

Step 3. Calculate the Return on the Building

Return on Building = Cap Rate x Building Value

Return on Building = 0.11 x $1,200,000

Return on Building = $132,000

Step 4. Calculate the Total Income Attributable to the Building

Total Building Income = Return on Building + $ Recapture

Total Building Income = $132,000 + $30,000

Total Building Income = $162,000

Step 5. Calculate the Residual Income Attributable to the Land

Land Income = Total Income – Building Income

Land Income = $200,000 – $162,000

Land Income = $38,000

Step 6. Calculate Land Value with the Income Capitalization Formula

Land Value = Land Income ÷ Capitalization Rate

(Note: the cap rate is the same for the land and building)

Land Value = $38,000 ÷ 0.11

Land Value = $345,454.54

We are limited to three significant figures, so the answer must be rounded to **$345,000.**

EXAMPLE 2: Building value is $950,000. Total annual income is $180,000. The remaining economic life of the building is 25 years. The property recently sold for $1,400,000. What is the capitalization rate?

Step 1. Calculate the Recapture Rate

Recapture Rate = 1 ÷ Remaining Economic Life

Recapture Rate = 1 ÷ 25

Recapture Rate = 0.04 or 4%

Step 2. Calculate the Dollar Recapture

Dollar Recapture = Recapture Rate x Building Value

Dollar Recapture = 0.04 x $950,000

Dollar Recapture = $38,000

Step 3. Calculate the Income that equals the Return on Property

Return on Property = Total Income − Recapture

Return on Property = $180,000 − $38,000

Return on Property = $142,000

Step 4. Use the Income Capitalization formula to find Capitalization Rate

Capitalization Rate = Income ÷ Value of the Property

Capitalization Rate = $142,000 ÷ $1,400,000

Capitalization Rate = 0.1014 or 10.14%

Again, the accuracy is limited to the number of significant figures so the answer is rounded to **10%.**

The above examples provide some insight into the significance of these methods. This technique can be used to extract the market capitalization rate, which is then used in income approach appraisals as part of the valuation formula.

SUMMARY

Applying any of the land/site valuation methods depends on the quality of the information and an organized approach to each problem. The student should become familiar with the logical process of applying each of the six methods and the math required to complete the application.

The **sales comparison method** is based on the principle of substitution and is the best approach to use when good comparables are available. All relevant differences must be identified and the market's opinion of the value of those differences must be developed and used as adjustments. The **allocation method** is based upon the principle of balance as well as on the concept of contributory value. The allocation method makes use of the ratio of land to improvements or the percentage of the total sales price that land represents.

The **abstraction method**, also known as the extraction method, is a variation on the allocation method. Using this method, appraisers derive the land value of a comparable property by deducting the depreciated costs of the improvements on that property from the property's known sale price. To obtain land value using the **subdivision method**, the costs of development are subtracted from the total sales price of all projected homes.

Application of the **ground rent method** requires the income capitalization formula with information developed or provided. The **land residual method** is another application of the income capitalization formula. Income must be divided between the improvements and the land. Once the income is attributed to the land, that income is capitalized at the market capitalization rate.

UNIT 5 REVIEW

MATCHING EXERCISE

Instructions: Write the letter of the matching term on the blank line before its definition. Answers are in Appendix C.

Terms

A. abstraction formula

B. adjustment

C. adjustment grid

D. allocation method

E. direct costs

F. forecast absorption

G. ground rent method formula

H. indirect costs

I. land residual method

J. land-to-improvement ratio

K. paired sales analysis

L. projected gross sales

M. ratio

N. sales comparison method

O. subdivision method

P. surplus productivity

Q. value of improvements today

Definitions

1. _____ The valuation method that provides the most direct evidence of the market

2. _____ A table or matrix of relevant data on comparable properties

3. _____ A dollar amount or percentage that is added to or subtracted from the sale price of a comparable property to account for a feature that differentiates it from the subject property

4. _____ A method of estimating the amount of adjustment for the presence or absence of any feature by pairing the sales prices of otherwise identical properties with and without that feature

5. _____ Total value is divided between land and improvements

6. _____ A theory that income is attributable to the land after the other economic agents have been paid

7. _____ The relationship between two numbers or measurements

8. _____ A ratio between the value of the land and the value of its improvement

9. _____ Formula: Land Value = Sale Price – Value of Improvements Today

10. _____ The cost to replace an improvement today minus depreciation

11. _____ The rate at which properties will sell

12. _____ Costs associated with the actual work completed to an improvement on-site

13. _____ Costs associated with completed work on the improvement off-site

14. _____ Formula: Value = Income ÷ Capitalization Rate

15. _____ Income capitalization technique in which the net income remaining to the land is capitalized into an estimate of value for the land

MULTIPLE CHOICE QUESTIONS

Instructions: Circle your response and go to Appendix C to read the complete explanation or calculation for each question.

1. An appraiser is valuing a residential property that has good comparables. The best valuation method to use would be the _____ method.
   a. allocation
   b. abstraction
   c. sales comparison
   d. subdivision

2. What section on the appraisal report is used to list particular items that affect the value of a property in the sales comparison method?
   a. Adjustment grid
   b. Cost allocation table
   c. Appliances grid
   d. Tabular comparison chart

3. In the sales comparison method, when appraisers add or subtract dollar amounts or percentages from the sales price of a comparable, they are making:

    a. income calculations.
    b. cost allocations.
    c. adjustments.
    d. arrangements.

4. After an appraiser has made the appropriate adjustments, what is the final step in developing the opinion of value?

    a. Reconsideration
    b. Reconciliation
    c. Paired sales analysis
    d. Researching comparables

5. The allocation method is based on:

    a. the principle of balance.
    b. paired sales analysis.
    c. contributory value.
    d. both (a) and (c).

6. If the total value for a property is $150,000, what is the land value if it is attributed to 20% of the total property value?

    a. $15,000
    b. $25,000
    c. $30,000
    d. $35,000

7. Subtracting the value of the improvement today from the sales price calculates land value using the _____ method.

    a. allocation
    b. abstraction
    c. subdivision
    d. land residual

8. What is the amount of depreciation for a property with a replacement cost today of $350,000, an effective age of 15 years, and an economic life of 100 years?

    a. $52,500
    b. $57,000
    c. $62,500
    d. $152,500

9. Using the abstraction method, what is the land value of a property with a sales price of $420,000, a replacement cost today of $200,000, and depreciation at $50,000?

    a. $170,000
    b. $220,000
    c. $250,000
    d. $270,000

10. While trying to figure gross profit on a proposed development, a real estate developer subtracts proposed sales from construction costs and wages for labor. These costs are referred to as _____ costs.

    a. temporary
    b. direct
    c. indirect
    d. developmental

11. Using the subdivision method, what is the land value of a property with total sales revenue of $1.5 million and total direct costs, indirect costs, and developer's profit of $500,000?

    a. $1,000,000
    b. $750,000
    c. $500,000
    d. $250,000

12. A building has a total income of $175,000 a year with $100,000 of that income attributed to the building itself. What is the land value given that the capitalization rate is 12%?

    a. $1.5 million
    b. $833,000
    c. $625,000
    d. $600,000

13. In order to use the land residual technique, the appraiser:

    a. verifies current building value.
    b. determines remaining economic life.
    c. selects a market capitalization rate.
    d. does all of the preceding.

14. What is the recapture rate for a building with a remaining economic life of 50 years?

    a. 2%

    b. 20%

    c. 3.7%

    d. 30%

15. If a property generates $525,000 of annual income with a 7% capitalization rate, what is its value?

    a. $750,000

    b. $7.5 million

    c. $1.5 million

    d. $150 million

Estimating Improvement Costs

Unit 6

INTRODUCTION

The two major components in real estate are land and improvements. Estimating land value is straightforward. Land includes the ground itself and the rights inherent in the use of that ground. Estimating the value of improvements is a little more complex. Improvements are buildings or other structures that are permanently attached to the land. Houses, detached garages, barns, office, and retail buildings are all examples of improvements. Other improvements, such as sidewalks, curbs, drainage structures, retaining walls, grading, streets, and utility hook-ups are commonly called site improvements and need to be included when estimating costs.

There are two parts to applying the cost approach: (1) choosing the correct costing technique and completing the calculations and (2) the accrual inspection. This unit discusses cost estimating and the four costing techniques.

LEARNING OBJECTIVES

After reading this unit, you should be able to:

- explain replacement and reproduction cost.
- define data sources and their application to estimating costs.
- identify the methods used to estimate replacement cost.
- discuss the applications and limitations of each method.

ESTIMATING IMPROVEMENT COSTS

After estimating the land value, the next step is to determine the cost to replace or reproduce the improvements. Replacement cost and reproduction cost are calculated differently, and it is important to understand the difference.

REPLACEMENT VS. REPRODUCTION

Appraisers have to make a choice about the level of detail to include in developing the cost today (new) of improvements. **Replacement cost**, which is used most frequently, produces cost of improvements with **equal utility**. Replacement costs are produced by three out of four of the cost techniques.

The most detailed approach to developing the cost of improvements is called **reproduction cost**. It is a complete replication of the improvements.

REPLACEMENT COST

Replacement cost is the cost today, to build improvements with equal utility. To restate that, replacement cost is the cost to build new improvements today that have the same general construction quality, size, the same number of rooms, bedrooms and bathrooms, and the same finish quality. The details that are not considered include different styles, ornamentation, and anything specific to the improvement that does not affect marketability or utility. A good example of the use of replacement cost is costing a tract home. Most housing tracts have just a few basic plans, but each plan comes in several elevations and color schemes. The specific elevation or color scheme has no affect on the utility of the home. Therefore, replacement costs limit the detail to those items that affect utility and marketability. Quite often, replacement cost can be less than reproduction cost. The original materials, for which current materials are substituted, could be considerably more expensive. If the improvements have a functional obsolescence or superadequacy, they are not included in the replacement costs. For this reason, depreciation also is easier and more basic when replacement costs are used.

Replacement cost considers the significant components of an improvement when calculating the costs. Significant components start at the bottom, with the foundation. Then the type of wall structure, roof structure and covering, interior walls, and key subsystems are considered. The key subsystems include plumbing, electrical, heating and air conditioning. The appraiser then considers the number and type of bathrooms and the functional aspects of the kitchen. The number of fireplaces, bathtubs, showers, sinks, and finally the size of the garage, if any, are all additional factors that must be considered when calculating costs, even replacement costs. The materials, construction techniques and even the layout may be different as all are based on what is currently available. Even when using the square foot method, defined later in this unit, all of these factors must be considered and included in the basic calculations.

REPRODUCTION COST

Reproduction cost includes all the costs to produce an identical replica. This is the most detailed approach and leads to the most accurate result. Reproduction cost is used when it is required by the client, the property is unique in design, or the property is of historical significance. In these instances, a detailed cost analysis is the only method available to develop a credible opinion of value. The majority of these cases require a review of the original plans, or an in-depth interview with the architectural designer of the property. He or she usually can provide the firsthand knowledge of the design and structural elements necessary to make an accurate cost analysis.

The Frederic C. Robie House
designed by
Frank Lloyd Wright in 1909.

A reproduction cost appraisal requires a lot of time and effort on site, as well as significant research off site. All of the major components of the improvements must be identified accurately and the costs developed for each individually.

Once all of the major components have been priced, the work really begins. All of the detailed trim and finish items must be identified and costs developed. These include floors, wall types, finished doors, doorframes, windows and window frames, molding, trim, shutters, and any other detailed or finished features. The inspection must be thorough, with each room identified and each feature in the room identified. Research is needed when an item is not in regular use today.

> Example 1: In some homes of historical significance, it was discovered that square-headed nails were used to nail hardwood flooring. These nails do not work loose and the floors remain silent. Square-headed nails are not readily available, but an accurate cost must be obtained.

> Example 2: Moldings were used in custom high-end or older ornate homes. These included baseboards, door jams and crown moldings, all of which can be complex with several layers, or simply be much larger than those used today. The type of molding, type of wood, number of layers, and size all must be identified before an accurate cost can be obtained.

The novice appraiser needs a considerable amount of assistance to complete this type of assignment.

DATA SOURCES

The data that the appraiser collects is discussed throughout this text. When using the cost approach, the most important data to be collected by the appraiser is information on the building area and construction costs.

BUILDING AREA

The methods used in the cost approach require an accurate measurement of the improvements. Measuring the subject property is just one of the tasks performed during the property inspection. The appraiser, at the time of inspection, also identifies the other physical characteristics of the subject property including its quality, condition, effective age, physical characteristics, and other amenities

that need to be considered in all three approaches to value.

Depending upon the scope of work being performed in an assignment, the building area may be identified in a number of ways.

Ways to Obtain the Size of an Improvement

1. The size of the improvements may be estimated based upon information available from local county tax assessor's records.

2. The appraiser may be provided by the client with measurements from previous appraisals.

3. Improvement size may also be obtained from sales brochures, owner sketches, or blueprints.

4. The square footage of the building(s) being appraised may also be determined by personally inspecting and measuring the improvements.

If the appraiser relies on third party sources, such as (1), (2), or (3) above, the risk of producing a misinformed appraisal is increased. By personally measuring the improvements, the appraiser avoids the need to make an extraordinary assumption regarding the size of the improvements, and the risk of poorly appraising the property is lessened. Remember, when developing an appraisal, an appraiser must collect, verify, and analyze all information necessary for credible assignment results.

CONSTRUCTION COSTS

Appraisers need to rely upon credible and reliable cost data in order to formulate the cost approach. As such, gathering and identifying this information is essential.

Ways to Obtain Construction Costs

- Some of the best indicators of cost are construction contracts for buildings that are similar to the one being appraised. While these are not often available, they provide a very strong basis upon which to base a cost estimate.

- Data sources of construction costs include Marshall & Swift®, RSMeans, and Craftsman Book Company. Computer assisted cost estimation programs as well as Internet based cost estimator resources are available to appraisers.

- Having a discussion with builders and cost estimators is a good way to determine local building costs. These discussions can be incorporated into appraisal assignments.

- Some appraisers maintain extensive records that include costs of the various kinds of buildings they have appraised. While this method is very reliable, the appraiser needs to maintain confidentiality according to USPAP.

It is sensible for the appraiser to compare data obtained from different sources, such as contractors and cost estimators. This confirms or verifies the accuracy of the information provided. If significant discrepancies are found when comparing one data source to another, the appraiser must perform an additional investigation to determine why the discrepancy exists.

Cost estimates are comprised of extensive line item cost lists. These line item lists are similar to the line item cost budgets completed by contractors and developers when preparing to construct a project. The same amount of detail and effort that the contractor used to develop the original cost budget is repeated by the appraiser in completing his or her cost budget.

The result of developing costs for improvements using the reproduction approach looks very much like the original budget prepared by the developer for investors or financing. Financing deserves a more complete discussion as it is one of the driving factors behind the need for appraisals.

Budgets are usually divided into two categories of costs: (1) direct costs and (2) indirect costs. Each of these categories is fully developed in a reproduction cost estimate.

Direct Costs	Indirect Costs
Labor and materials on site	Engineering and architecture
Equipment on site	Plan check fees
Supervision	Permits and other fees
Contractor's profit	Financing
Workers' comp insurance	Administration
Fire and liability insurance	Legal
Performance bonds	Accounting
Security on site	Developer Overhead
Utility costs	
Sales costs	

DIRECT COSTS

Direct costs are those that include expenditures for labor and materials used in construction of the improvements. They are also known as **hard costs**. An easy way to distinguish between direct costs and indirect costs is that

Direct costs are expenditures for on-site labor and materials.

direct costs are for on-site labor and materials.

Identifying direct and indirect costs is more than an academic exercise. This division of costs allows the contractor/developer and financial partners to analyze the project and to determine where the money is spent. The identification of direct costs, line item by line item, allows all parties to determine accurately the areas that may be candidates for savings and those areas that may be under budgeted. This type of budget analysis is part of the developer's first line of defense from waste and incompetence when developing a project. The same attention to detail should be observed by a homeowner when improving his or her home.

Developers usually employ licensed contractors to construct the improvements. The contractor's mark-up or overhead and profit are usually considered direct costs of construction and are included in the direct costs estimates. These costs are the income made by the contractor for his or her efforts in building the project and are not to be confused with entrepreneurial profit. The use of a qualified licensed professional who understands all the local building codes is necessary and can save the developer money. The developer may also act as the contractor, in which case contractor profit is still part of the direct costs.

INDIRECT COSTS

Indirect costs are all the costs related to a project, other than land costs, that are not direct costs of construction and materials. These are also known as **soft costs**. Often these costs are calculated as a percentage of the direct costs, but that is rarely an accurate approach.

Just as each line item in the direct cost budget is taken off the plans and specifications prepared by the engineers and architects, the soft costs can be developed by addressing each line item individually. These costs include all the professional work needed—engineers, architects, lawyers, accountants, and any other professional services—along with all the costs associated with financing and selling the project.

Financing can be one of the most important line items in a budget and must be adequate to support the project from the beginning of construction until the last unit is sold. Sales costs are often the most ignored items in a budget but, in anything other than a booming market, a good sales program is required to achieve success.

FINANCING

Financing may be used for either a short period or the expected economic life of the improvements. Matching the type of financing and the source is often left to experts who make a living doing just that. Financing costs are a significant portion of the total budget of any construction project and the rates and terms reflect the relative risk as evaluated by the financier. An example of the use of several types of financing, and the costs associated with it, would be a small development of homes.

Construction is a high-risk undertaking even in the best markets. Both the developer and the lender have substantial risk and both are careful to analyze the market looking for any signs of change. The example given illustrates why lenders become conservative at the first indication of a slowing market. They do not want a partially completed project to go to foreclosure because they do not have the expertise required to complete and sell the project.

Example: Developer Tom purchased land for a project. Normally, he puts 50% down and borrows the other 50%, usually at a variable but relatively high rate—about 3% to 10% above the prime rate. This type of loan is normally for a term of one year or less. He must improve the land, add streets, curbs, and gutters to create home sites either to be sold or further improved with homes. A land development loan to improve the land is usually available at 75% of the appraised value of the finished lots. The costs run from prime + 3% to about prime + 6% with a fee of about 3% to 5%. The term normally is a year or less, which means the developer is on a schedule to either sell or improve the property.

The final phase of the development is the construction financing. Construction financing can be for an amount of up to 80% of the total appraised value. The amount of the loan includes an interest reserve that allows the developer to build interest into the loan. The term of this type of loan is usually 9 to 12 months at a cost of prime + 2% to 4%. The lender carefully disburses funds in accordance with the amount of construction completed. The risk is that the final product may not meet the market's demands or that the market changes during the time of construction.

When the internal interest reserve is exhausted, the developer must pay interest on the loan from his funds, reducing or eliminating any profit. Carrying the cost of the loan while selling the product can cause any project to go from profitable to a loss in a very short time. The cost to carry one $500,000 home is about $4,500 per month. Within a year, any potential profit can be exhausted.

The role of the appraiser becomes even more important in these high-risk situations. The appraiser must be able to understand construction, financing, sales, and marketing in order to complete a tract construction assignment in a competent manner. The competent appraiser is an essential element in the real estate cycle.

METHODS USED TO ESTIMATE COSTS

The choice of costing technique depends upon the information available and the purpose and scope of work of the appraisal assignment. If the appraiser has completed the research and thoroughly defined the problem and scope of work, the inspection and completion of the costing is mechanical. When the appraiser has all the necessary information to complete an accurate cost estimate, one of four different techniques can be used. These techniques or methods for estimating cost are the (1) index method, (2) square foot method, (3) unit-in-place method, and (4) quantity survey method.

The **index method** and **square foot method** are the quickest and easiest to calculate. However, they tend to be the least accurate of the methods used for cost estimation. The **unit-in-place method** is a more in-depth cost estimate that provides more detail than the square foot or index method. The **quantity survey method** is the most in-depth and detailed of the commonly used processes for estimating costs, but it also is the most time-consuming and arduous of the four. It is the method least used by appraisers because it requires the appraiser to prepare a detailed line item budget for the improvements similar to that used by a contractor.

INDEX METHOD

The index method is the easiest method to apply but the least used. It is least used, not only because it is one of the least accurate, but because the information required to use this method often is not available. To use the index method, an appraiser must know the original cost of improvements, select a relevant index, know the value of the index at the time of construction, and know the value of the index today.

Before addressing the actual calculations, it is important to discuss the index. An **index** is a measure of change of price levels between the time of construction and today. The first attribute of a good index is that it must have been prepared at the time of construction and still be active today. This actually eliminates many potential indexes and often no index can be found that was being calculated at the time the improvements were built and is still calculated today. The index must be associated with price levels. Typically, an index is scaled so that it is equal to 100 at a chosen point in time, so that all other values of the index are a percentage relative to this one. The two most prominent indexes are the Consumer Price Index and the Producers Price Index.

Definition of the Consumer Price Index from *Wikipedia*®

In economics, a **Consumer Price Index (CPI)** or **Retail Price Index (RPI)** is a statistical time-series measure of a weighted average of prices of a specified set of goods and services purchased by consumers. It is a price index that tracks the prices of a specified basket of consumer goods and services, providing a measure of inflation. The CPI is a fixed quantity price index and considered a cost-of-living index. The CPI can be used to track changes in prices of goods and services purchased for consumption by households, i.e., of the consumer basket. User fees (such as water and sewer service) and sales and excise taxes paid by the consumer are also included. Income taxes and investment items (such as stocks, bonds, life insurance, and homes) are not included.

The Consumer Price Index has data going back as far as 1964, which means that it cannot be used for properties built before 1964. The Producer Price Index (PPI) or Wholesale Price Index (WPI) is similar, but uses a different bundle of goods.

Definition of the Producer Price Index from *Wikipedia*®

The **Producer Price Index (PPI)** measures average changes in prices received by domestic producers for their output. The PPI was known as the Wholesale Price Index, or WPI, up to 1978. The PPI is one of the oldest continuous systems of statistical data published by the Bureau of Labor Statistics, as well as one of the oldest economic time series compiled by the federal government. The origins of the index can be found in an 1891 U.S. Senate resolution authorizing the Senate Committee on Finance to investigate the effects of the tariff laws upon the imports and exports, the growth, development, production, and prices of agricultural and manufactured articles at home and abroad.

While the Producer Price Index has its origins in 1891, the data dates back only to 1978. The PPI is the preferable index as it deals with prices at the producer level rather than the consumer level. Unfortunately, this index has a short lifetime with limited applicability.

Regardless of which index is used, it is important to have a basic understanding of what each index represents and applies to the index method.

Indexes are calculated monthly, quarterly, and annually. Most of the index calculations completed by appraisers use the annual numbers. All indexes start with a base year at 100 and use the changes in prices of the bundle of goods to adjust the index.

> **Formula for the Index Method**
>
> Value = (today's index value ÷ index value at time of construction)
> x (original cost of the improvements)

An easy way to remember this formula is the new index divided by old index multiplied by old cost—shortened to (N ÷ O) x O. The following example illustrates the application of the index method.

> **EXAMPLE:** John had his home built in 1991 for a cost of $123,000 plus the cost of the site. The PPI for 1991 in that region was 186. The PPI today for the same region is 246.
>
> Value = (246 ÷ 186) x $123,000
> Value = 1.32 x $123,000
> Value = $162,677 rounded to $163,000

This approach is easy to apply when the information is available. It is not the most accurate of approaches, but can be adequate for a ballpark estimate. The indexes used are usually a compilation of many types of costs. The PPI can be obtained for construction related prices and by region. This provides a more accurate estimate, but still, only an estimate. It should be noted that there are no more than three significant figures in any of the numbers used in the calculation, so the answer cannot be accurate beyond three significant figures. That is the reason the answer is rounded to $163,000.

SQUARE FOOT METHOD

The **square foot method**—sometimes called comparative unit method—is no doubt the method most often employed by appraisers to develop an estimate of improvement costs. It combines the advantages of relatively easy calculation with a good level of accuracy. This is the method used on the URAR 1004-5 form (see Appendix A), but its use is not required. Application of the square foot method has two steps: (1) measuring and identifying components of the subject's improvements, and (2) developing the costs from a cost database.

Once the property has been measured and the components identified, the cost must be developed using one of many cost databases. Several databases are available—ranging from a fee per use, such as Marshall & Swift® to free, such as Building-Cost.net. Marshall & Swift® is one of the most recognized names in building cost data and estimation—providing data in books, on CDs, and over the Internet, all at a price. Building-Cost.net is a basic cost-estimating program for residential construction provided over the Internet at no charge. Regardless of the database used, each calculates costs in a similar manner. Appraisers should understand how the costs are developed so that the database information is used accurately.

Database Websites

Marshall & Swift® (fee per use) – www.marshallswift.com
Building-Cost Estimating (no fee) – www.Building-Cost.net

Cost databases define levels of quality for different attributes of a home. Each attribute of the home has a quality class with a specific description. Building-Cost.net offers an example of a quality class characteristics page, which includes the costs for the garage in the costing process. The final estimate that is developed using this software combines both the gross living area (GLA) and the garage. A good, detailed inspection provides sufficient information to complete this type of quality class survey and the results of the survey produce a reasonable cost per square foot estimate.

Once the quality levels are established, a base price per square foot (SF) is developed. That cost per square foot must be adjusted for regional differences. A **regional multiplier** is applied to the base cost to obtain a localized cost per square foot. The regional multiplier represents the difference between the base cost and the cost to build the same improvements in a specific region.

Improvement costs vary from region to region based on local labor cost, local fees, local building codes, and the availability of materials. The base cost is multiplied by the regional multiplier to obtain the local per square foot cost. This localized square foot cost is multiplied by the gross living area to obtain today's cost to replace the improvements.

Basic Square Foot Method Formula

Value = GLA x Cost per Square Foot

EXAMPLE: John owns a home with a gross living area (GLA) measured at 1,430 square feet (SF). It has a 440 SF garage and no other accessory buildings. The cost database being used indicates that GLA for this geographic region cost $108 / SF and an unfinished garage costs $35 / SF foot.

The Cost Today of the improvements is:

GLA x Cost / SF	=	1,430 x $108	=	$154,440
Garage x Cost / SF	=	440 x $ 35	=	$15,400
		Total Cost	=	$169,840
		Rounded to		$170,000

The example of a line item cost breakdown on the next page uses information about a tract home built in Southern California. It is a 2,843 SF home with a 660 SF garage included in the total cost. The last item of the line item cost breakdown is the contractor markup, which is a part of the direct costs of construction. The cost per square foot (including the garage) is $263,233 divided by 2,843 SF equaling $92.59 / SF. This information is presented in a line item budget similar to that used in a quantity survey.

Accessory buildings, pools, hardscape, and custom features must be added as additional line items. All of this is done prior to calculating depreciation. Depreciation is based on the total costs of all improvements.

Example of a Line Item Cost Breakdown

Item Name	Material	Labor	Equipment	Total
Excavation	0.00	2,426.00	663.00	3,089.00
Foundation, Piers, Flatwork	5,497.00	8,221.00	1,349.00	15,067.00
Rough Hardware	589.00	882.00	146.00	1,617.00
Rough Carpentry	19,512.00	27,386.00	0.00	46,898.00
Insulation	3,654.00	2,375.00	0.00	6,029.00
Exterior Finish	10,387.00	5,898.00	766.00	17,051.00
Exterior Trim	704.00	1,053.00	173.00	1,930.00
Doors	1,625.00	1,296.00	0.00	2,921.00
Windows	2,798.00	1,809.00	0.00	4,607.00
Finish Hardware	271.00	216.00	0.00	487.00
Garage Door	767.00	297.00	0.00	1,064.00
Roofing, Flashing, Fascia	7,433.00	5,928.00	0.00	13,361.00
Finish Carpentry	1,083.00	5,186.00	0.00	6,269.00
Interior Wall Finish	5,197.00	7,631.00	0.00	12,828.00
Painting	3,105.00	6,894.00	0.00	9,999.00
Wiring	3,153.00	5,660.00	0.00	8,813.00
Lighting Fixtures	2,364.00	707.00	0.00	3,071.00
Flooring	2,116.00	2,855.00	0.00	4,971.00
Carpeting	4,210.00	1,428.00	0.00	5,638.00
Bath Accessories	1,043.00	611.00	0.00	1,654.00
Shower & Tub Enclosure	666.00	531.00	0.00	1,197.00
Countertops	2,014.00	1,605.00	0.00	3,619.00
Cabinets	6,620.00	1,979.00	0.00	8,599.00
Built-In Appliances	3,221.00	428.00	0.00	3,649.00
Plumbing Rough-in & Connection	3,023.00	6,980.00	437.00	10,440.00
Plumbing Fixtures	6,140.00	1,850.00	0.00	7,990.00
Heating and Cooling Systems	6,273.00	9,410.00	0.00	15,683.00
Unit Heating and Cooling	0.00	0.00	0.00	0.00
Fireplace and Chimney	1,020.00	1,530.00	0.00	2,550.00
Subtotal Direct Job Costs	**$104,485.00**	**$113,072.00**	**$3,534.00**	**$221,091.00**
Final Cleanup	0.00	947.00	0.00	947.00
Insurance	6,629.00	0.00	0.00	6,629.00
Permits & Utilities	4,025.00	0.00	0.00	4,025.00
Plans & Specs	947.00	0.00	0.00	947.00
Subtotal Indirect Job Costs	**$11,601.00**	**$947.00**	**0.00**	**$12,548.00**
Contractor Markup	29,594.00	0.00	0.00	29,594.00
Total Cost	**$145,680.00**	**$114,019.00**	**$3,534.00**	**$263,233.00**

UNIT-IN-PLACE METHOD

The **unit-in-place method** is somewhat of a mix between the quantity survey and the square foot methods. It is known also as the segregated cost method. Although it is more precise overall than the square foot method, it is also more time-consuming. Appraisers and contractors can estimate the cost to build more accurately if costs are estimated for segments of the improvement, rather than averaged for the whole improvement.

In the unit-in-place method, the costs of the various building components are calculated separately as units based on linear, area, volume, or other forms of measurement. Breaking down the building cost to more manageable parts generates a more accurate cost breakdown. Building components include such items as the foundation, exterior walls, interior walls, roof structure, ceiling, electrical system, plumbing system, kitchen cabinetry, kitchen equipment, windows, doors, mechanical systems, and stairways. The cost estimates for the individual unit components also include a proportionate share of direct costs, such as labor, materials, contractor's profit, and others. These segmented costs are then added together into a single value estimate.

> Example: An appraiser can apply the unit-in-place cost method to new homes in Southern California built with wood framed walls covered with stucco on the outside and painted wallboard in the interior. The unit cost per linear foot of exterior wall can be calculated and applied to the total number of linear feet of exterior walls in the home. This method also applies to interior walls having a certain number of electrical outlets, height, and finish.

This method breaks down the cost of a building into the cost of its component parts. Unfortunately, the market does not always reflect the value of a property using this method. This is because most cost databases do not have a lot of information segregated for use in the unit-in-place method. Appraisers with additional specialized knowledge or expertise in the specific area are needed to provide adequate data to build a good unit cost model.

QUANTITY SURVEY METHOD

The **quantity survey method** is the most thorough and accurate approach to estimating building costs or the cost of improvements. In this method, the individual costs of the quantity of all materials and all labor in all categories are estimated and reported in a line item budget, similar to the above line item cost breakdown from Building-Cost.net. Using this breakdown as a guideline, each major component is broken down to material, labor, and equipment, if any. Projects of any significant size are sent to sub-contractors to bid their portion. Each sub-contractor prepares a detailed list of materials and labor from the plans provided. The sub-contractor's final bid includes the markup and a contingency for error or changes. Each line of the final budget usually represents a sub-contractor's final bid for the work.

Once all the material and labor associated with the project have been bid, the indirect costs of the project must be added. Indirect costs include most of the work done off site, including architecture, engineering, plan check, city fees, financing costs, and builder's overhead, which also may include accounting and legal fees.

Most appraisers do not have a contractor's license or the expertise to do a detailed cost breakdown based on plans or a physical description. The preparation of a complete quantity survey usually requires the assistance of a professional cost estimator and is both time consuming and expensive. A normal inspection does not provide sufficient detailed information to facilitate a full quantity survey cost analysis. This method is normally reserved for reproduction costs of the improvements because it is more detailed and comprehensive than a replacement cost estimate requires. Significant advantages of the quantity survey method include a high level of accuracy, and the ability to use the detailed materials list to calculate physical and functional depreciation. This level of detail is not available in any other approach. This method is reserved for those appraisals that require reproduction costs and warrant the time and resources needed to accurately complete the cost estimate.

SUMMARY

The cost approach to value is not as commonly used as the sales comparison or income approaches. However, situations do arise in which the cost approach is the only reliable way to estimate a property's value. The first step in the cost approach is to determine the value of the site—the land value.

Once the appraiser has determined the land value, the next step is to estimate the **reproduction cost** or **replacement cost** of the subject property. This includes researching costs through cost estimating services or by contacting developers or contractors, and choosing an appropriate method to use.

Three of the four cost estimating methods rely heavily upon the detailed description of the improvements to develop the cost estimate. The **index method** has an advantage over the other methods in that a detailed inspection is not required to estimate the cost today. A detailed inspection is still needed to estimate depreciation, so the use of the index approach does not negate the need for a good inspection. The other three methods of estimating costs—**square foot, unit-in-place**, and **quantity survey**—all need the information from the inspection in order to build the cost breakdown. The more detailed the method, the more information is required. The square foot method is the one method that is both easy to apply and provides an adequate cost estimate. The use of either the unit-in-place method or quantity survey method requires both time and some expertise in contracting and construction to produce an adequate result. These methods are reserved for the more involved appraisals or appraisals in which the cost approach is the primary approach.

UNIT 6 REVIEW

MATCHING EXERCISE

Instructions: Write the letter of the matching term on the blank line before its definition. Answers are in Appendix C.

Terms

A. carry

B. construction financing

C. Consumer Price Index (CPI)

D. contractor's overhead

E. cost database

F. direct costs

G. gross living area (GLA)

H. index method

I. index value

J. indirect costs

K. interest reserve

L. Producer Price Index (PPI)

M. quantity survey

N. regional multiplier

O. replacement cost

P. reproduction costs

Q. square foot

R. unit-in-place

Definitions

1. _____ A complete detailed item-by-item cost analysis

2. _____ The type of cost analysis most often applied that produces the cost of improvements of equal utility

3. _____ Expenditures for the cost of material and labor on site

4. _____ Expenditures for items including engineering and architecture that are handled off site

5. _____ Funds in a construction loan available only to pay the cost of carry during construction

6. _____ A specific type of financing used by developers and contractors during the construction phase of their projects

7. _____ The cost estimating method that requires knowledge of the original cost of the improvements

8. _____ The price index based upon the cost of a bundle of goods purchased by consumers

9. _____ The index, based on the prices producers receive for their goods and services, that can be used in the index method to approximate change in wholesale price level over time

10. _____ An appraisal term used to describe the actual size of the residential improvements, not including the garage, attic, and basement

11. _____ The number used on the base cost data to allow for differences in local labor, materials, and government fee costs

12. _____ The place an appraiser would go to find basic cost models and costs for both residential and commercial improvements, as an alternative to employing a cost estimator and developing the costs from scratch

13. _____ The cost estimating method most often used by appraisers, and used in the URAR form

14. _____ The cost estimating method that is a mix of the quantity survey and square foot methods and can produce high quality accurate results

15. _____ The cost estimating method regarded as the most comprehensive, and used primarily to produce reproduction costs

MULTIPLE CHOICE QUESTIONS

Instructions: Circle your response and go to Appendix C to read the complete explanation for each question.

1. The cost of land is included in the reproduction cost estimate of improvements:
    a. when the original cost is known.
    b. when there are comparable vacant lots.
    c. in every cost estimate.
    d. in no instance.

2. Pat was hired by a homeowner to appraise a 75-year-old, 3-bedroom, 1-bath bungalow style home. Because it is located in an historic downtown district, the homeowner needs to purchase enough insurance to replicate the house in the event of loss. For this assignment, the appraiser would use _____ cost to develop the cost of the improvements.

    a. reproduction
    b. construction
    c. replacement
    d. indirect

3. Replacement cost is used in most appraisals because:

    a. appraisers are too lazy to do a complete reproduction cost estimate.
    b. it produces cost of improvements with equal utility.
    c. the cost manuals and databases do not provide detailed line item costs.
    d. depreciation is applied only in reproduction costs so replacement cost estimates are more accurate.

4. When using the cost approach, what is the most important data that the appraiser should collect?

    a. All the detailed and finish items of the property
    b. The history of the property
    c. Information on the building area and construction costs
    d. None of the above

5. Which of the following is a recognized data source of construction costs?

    a. RSMeans
    b. Craftsman Book Company
    c. Marshall & Swift®
    d. All of the above

6. Budgets are usually divided into direct costs and indirect costs. Which of the following is a soft cost?

    a. Developer overhead
    b. Contractor's profit
    c. Labor and materials on site
    d. Utility costs

7. Which of the following is not a cost estimating technique or method?

    a. Square mile method
    b. Quantity survey method
    c. Unit-in-place method
    d. Index method

8. The use of the index method depends on:

    a. knowing the site value.

    b. having detailed cost manuals available.

    c. knowing the original cost of the improvements.

    d. being able to complete a thorough inspection.

9. How many elements of information are required before an appraiser can effectively use the index method?

    a. three

    b. four

    c. five

    d. seven

10. John, an appraiser, has decided to complete a reproduction cost estimate using the most detailed approach. Which cost approach should he use?

    a. The index method

    b. Unit-in-place

    c. Quantity survey

    d. Abstraction method

11. John, an appraiser, is faced with a situation in which he has to appraise a custom home built ten years ago by the present owners. They have the original cost breakdown that reflects total construction costs (direct and indirect) of $143,000. They also tell John that they paid $75,000 for the lot. John decides that he needs only a replacement cost estimate and that this situation lends itself to the use of the index method. He researches the PPI and finds that ten years ago it was 224 and today it is 387. What is the present cost estimate for the home?

    a. $247,000

    b. $376,600

    c. $129,575

    d. $82,770

12. When using the square foot method, a _____ is applied to the base cost to obtain a localized cost per square foot.

    a line item addition

    b. county assessment

    c. regional multiplier

    d. construction surcharge

13. In the unit-in-place method, costs are calculated separately for:

    a. various building components.

    b. component parts.

    c. segments of the improvement.

    d. all of the above.

14. The _____ method is the most thorough and accurate approach to estimating building costs or the cost of improvements.

    a. index

    b. quantity survey

    c. square foot

    d. unit-in-place

15. Each of the following is an indirect cost in the quantity survey method, except:

    a. on-site labor and materials.

    b. architects' renderings.

    c. financing costs.

    d. engineering plans.

Cost Approach: Application

Unit 7

INTRODUCTION

The basic approaches to developing an opinion of value used by appraisers are the sales comparison approach, the income approach, and the cost approach. The **cost approach**, although theoretically sound, is probably the least used of the three approaches because it carries the least direct representation of the market. However, it does provide secondary support for the opinion of value developed by one of the other two approaches. It is appropriate to use this approach when appraising any property that does not generate income and for which there are few, if any, adequate comparables.

In the cost approach, depreciation analysis enables the appraiser to develop an opinion of credible value. A value estimate of a property is determined by estimating the replacement or reproduction cost of the improvements, deducting the estimated accrued depreciation, and then adding the market value of the site.

Applying the cost approach requires attention to detail and substantial research. It requires an understanding of the quality of construction as well as a detailed analysis of the components of the improvements. This allows a more accurate comparison between the subject and its comparables. To avoid making calculation errors, a deliberate and organized approach to the application is necessary.

LEARNING OBJECTIVES

After reading this unit, you should be able to:

- define the components of a house.
- describe the inspection process.
- discuss the application of the cost approach.
- summarize uses of the cost approach.

COMPONENTS OF A HOUSE

Before discussing the inspection process and application of the cost approach, it is important to identify the major components of a house, or other improvements that may affect the appraisal. Construction experience is not needed to become a competent appraiser, but a basic knowledge of the structure of a house, its major components, and the ability to be observant are necessary. The following sections discuss these major components so that they can be properly identified during an inspection. The actual inspection also is discussed later in this unit.

FOUNDATIONS

Every improvement has a foundation, and the type and materials used make a difference in the cost. The two basic types of foundations are raised and slab-on-grade.

RAISED FOUNDATIONS

Raised foundations have walls made of rock, brick, block, concrete, or other strong long-lasting material. These walls are along the entire perimeter of the improvements. Most often, a system of piers and beams is used inside the perimeter to provide support. A **pier and beam foundation** uses wood or concrete piers, which rest on support beams or girders that support the structure. The piers usually are made of the same material as the foundation walls and the beams are normally solid wood girders. This type of foundation can have several advantages. The plumbing and electrical systems that must go under the foundation are more accessible for necessary repairs. This allows repairs to be made with relative ease.

Two Main Weaknesses of a Raised Foundation

1. It is not as stable in earthquake regions.

2. It is susceptible to water and infestation damage.

During an inspection, a raised foundation must be checked for the presence of water. Structural damage and pest inspection are beyond the expertise of an appraiser. If an appraiser sees beams that are leaning or wood that looks damaged, he or she should suggest the services of a pest control expert, engineer, or general contractor.

SLAB FOUNDATIONS

Instead of walls, slab foundations have footings. These footings are dug to various depths depending on the size of the improvements and the soil conditions. Once a house is built, there is no way to ascertain the depth of a footing other than checking the plans at the city. Before the concrete slab is poured, the rough plumbing is laid in trenches that ultimately are under the slab. If the footings and slab are poured at the same time, it is called a **monolithic slab**. When the footings and slab are poured separately, it is called a **floating slab**. Also for slab foundations, there is no observation technique to determine which type of slab a house has. Slab foundations have the advantages of being stable in earthquake regions and costing less to build. A major disadvantage is that significant problems can occur if the rough plumbing under the slab needs repair.

WALL SYSTEMS

Once the foundation is complete, the walls must be constructed. There are numerous systems and materials, all of which have their advantages and disadvantages. A few of these systems are presented, but this is not a comprehensive construction primer—simply a presentation of the basics to assist in the inspection. Walls can be constructed from brick, block, concrete, hay, or framed with wood or steel, and then covered. Brick and block construction is often used in the Eastern and Midwestern areas of the United States because of insulation capacity and basic strength. However, these are not generally used in earthquake regions because they tend to crumble or split in an earthquake.

Framing is basically a wall structure built with wood or metal, and with both sides covered with different material. Wood framing is both sturdy and flexible enough to withstand moderate earthquakes.

Two Types of Framing

1. **Platform** is a type of framing in which each story is built as a unit, on top of the previous story or platform.

2. **Balloon** is a type of framing in which the studs extend the full two stories.

Framing allows plumbing and electrical to be easily placed inside the walls. Framing repairs are also relatively easy. The exterior can be covered with siding (wood, vinyl, or aluminum), brick, stone, or stucco. **Stucco** is a concrete product that is applied in three coats. Interior walls are usually made of **lath and plaster** or **drywall**. Production homes use painted wallboard because it is less expensive and requires much less labor to install.

PLUMBING

Plumbing includes water in and out as well as waste systems. Modern homes have a full complement of plumbing fixtures that have become more important in the past 20 years. Newly constructed homes have extensive plumbing systems and elaborate bathrooms, specifically the master bathrooms. Material is an important consideration here also. Older homes were built with **galvanized steel pipes** that corrode and can leak or break. Newer homes have copper piping for water lines and plastic waste lines. The plastic waste lines are noisier than the cast iron lines they replaced. The newest homes use flexible plastic water lines that reduce the installation time, and are quiet and safe. **Rough plumbing** is the installation of the water and waste lines and connections for all the fixtures. **Finish plumbing** is the installation of all the fixtures including sinks, faucets, toilets, water heaters, and any other plumbing fixtures needed for the house. The quality of these fixtures varies greatly from basic ceramic sinks to hand-painted glass bowls with glass faucets.

ELECTRICAL

Just as framing and plumbing have changed over the years, the electrical systems required to operate a new house have become more complex. The electrical panel or box is the location where the power enters the building to be distributed throughout the house. Years ago, the panel had fuses to protect the house from overloading the circuits. Now, circuit breakers are used.

The strength of the electrical current going into the electrical box is rated in **amps**. In the 1950s, homes came with 50 to 100 amp panels. Today's homes, with sophisticated heating and cooling systems and many more electric appliances, require panels with a much higher rating—usually in the 150 to 200 amp range. Older homes that have air conditioning systems added usually have to upgrade the electrical panel also. The newer homes also come with GFI (ground fault interrupter) circuits built into the wall sockets providing overload protection.

Older homes did not include smoke detectors as part of the electrical system, but they are now required in most new homes. If a house is being sold and does not have smoke

Fuses

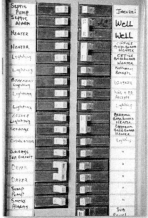

Circuit breaker

detectors, they must be added before closing. Smoke detectors were originally battery operated, then hard wired into the house circuits. They are now hard wired with battery back up. It is important to understand that the electrical panel must have a rating high enough to support the activity inside the house or the result could be a major safety hazard.

HEATING AND AIR CONDITIONING

Homes have heating requirements, and there are several different types of heating and air conditioning systems available. Heating can be supplied by a simple wall unit—gas or electric—a furnace, an air conditioning unit, or a sophisticated zoned heating and air conditioning system. A **zoned system** allows the owner to heat or cool only selected parts of a house. Zoning is especially useful where unique time and temperature control of a part of the dwelling is required, such as for a home office or granny flat. These systems require more power. In order to update the heating and cooling in a house, a new larger electrical panel with a higher rating may be needed.

ROOFING

There are many types of roofs made of many different materials. It is the responsibility of the appraiser to identify the type of roof material and estimate its condition. The two main attributes of a roof that should be addressed are

pitch and material. **Pitch**, or the slope of the roof, is more important in areas where there is snow in the winter. Due to the heavy weight of snow, the roof needs a steeper pitch so the snow does not accumulate on it. A flat roof creates a different series of problems. All flat roofs must have drainage so that water, or snow, cannot collect. When these drains get clogged, the water forms a pool that can weigh more than the roof can support. This may cause the roof to collapse. The appraiser is required to inspect the drains on a flat roof to insure they are clear at the time of the appraisal.

Roofing materials have changed over the years, as have most other parts of a house. New homes can have lightweight concrete shingles that are both decorative and fireproof. These concrete shingles have life expectancies of 25 to 50 years. Certain materials may be prohibited in areas where there is a high fire danger, and the appraiser should become familiar with the local building codes and restrictions. Some of the newer flat roofs, usually on commercial buildings, have been painted white in order to save energy.

FINISH

Interior and exterior finish contributes to the value of a house. Significant

finish items include windows, doors, appliances, countertops, cabinets, flooring, and molding. A complete inspection should identify the type, material, and quality of each of the above.

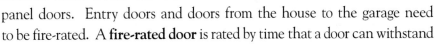

- Windows have changed dramatically in the last ten years. Newer homes have vinyl framed dual pane windows that reduce heat loss and sound.

- Doors can be simple hollow core flush doors (interior) to custom solid wood carved panel doors. Entry doors and doors from the house to the garage need to be fire-rated. A **fire-rated door** is rated by time that a door can withstand exposure to fire. It should be able to withstand fire for at least 20 minutes or more.

- Kitchen and bathroom countertops have also changed over time. Kitchen countertops can range from laminate to ceramic tile to synthetic materials such as Corian®, to granite. Each countertop has its advantages and disadvantages and the inspection should identify the material and quality.

- Cabinets used in the kitchen and bathroom can vary from laminate materials to solid hard woods and even glass. Each different material has both advantages and disadvantages.

- Finally, the flooring and moldings used can have an impact on the value of a house. There are new flooring materials being introduced all the time

and the appraiser must be able to identify the different materials. This has become more difficult with the introduction of laminate wood products that have the appearance of hard wood. These floors may be advantageous for some families, and they are not as expensive as a solid hardwood floor.

Quality materials can increase the cost of a house significantly. An accurate inspection allows the appraiser to determine the contributory value of the improvements, which produces an accurate comparison with the comparables in the sales comparison approach.

THE INSPECTION

Before going to the site for the inspection, an appraiser should bring certain tools that are necessary to complete the task.

Necessary Tools for Performing an Inspection

Camera. Most appraisers use a digital camera. The camera should have a zoom lens and enough memory for at least 30 pictures. The picture resolution or quality is not as important as the file capacity of the pictures. High-resolution pictures can make the appraisal file too large to be easily transmitted over the Internet.

Measuring device. Use a metal or cloth tape measure, laser-measuring device, or reel tape measure.

Blank or graph paper. Used to draw the outline of the house when measuring and to record information during the inspection.

Appraisal File. This should have the subject and comparable information, maps, order form, and checklist. Some appraisers carry a combination clip board/storage case to hold the file, pencils, pens, and other small items needed for the inspection.

THE INSPECTION PROCESS

Most appraisals require the appraiser to do an interior and exterior inspection of the subject and an exterior inspection of the comparables. Although some appraisals can be completed without an interior inspection by using a special form, these are exceptions to the rule. Simple steps or rules are required in an appraiser's inspection.

Steps in an Appraiser's Inspection

- Inspect the exterior. Take a minimum of three pictures (photographs) of the subject—specifically the front, rear, and street views.

- Inspect all units on a property with one to four units, even if they are identical.

- Measure every improvement.

- Inspect every room. If a room is not accessible, the inspection is not complete. The interior inspection section on the inspection report cannot be checked off.

- Include a log of the inspection in the workfile for future reference.

The inspection begins when approaching the neighborhood. The neighborhood boundaries should be identified and the physical attributes of the neighborhood should be observed. Make sure all of the comparables are within the neighborhood boundaries, as defined by the appraiser's observation.

THE EXTERIOR INSPECTION

The actual inspection of the subject begins from the street, and then requires observation and notation of the surrounding site and improvements.

THE STREET, SIDEWALKS, DRIVEWAY

What is the street type? Is it asphalt, macadam, gravel, concrete, or some other material? How many lanes are there and what is the size of each? Are curbs, gutters, drainage, storm drains, and sidewalks provided? If there is a driveway, indicate the type of material used and the number of cars that can be parked on it.

AROUND THE HOUSE

Observe the landscaping, both **softscape**—the plantings around the subject property that prevent erosion and improve aesthetic appearance, and **hardscape**—structures and features, such as pathways, pools, and retaining walls. Compare the subject property to the neighborhood comparables. Try to estimate the size of the lot relative to the other house sites in the neighborhood. Note the topography.

How much of the lot is usable and how much is excess or surplus? **Excess land** is land beyond that which is needed to support the property's highest and best use. **Surplus land** is land that is over and above what is typical for a specific property in the area. Try to communicate this information accurately to the client. A steep hillside site that requires the improvements to be cantilevered must be noted and correctly described. One appraiser almost lost his license after describing a steep hillside lot as "gently sloping."

Take a good look at how the improvements rest on the site and also describe the exterior of the improvements. Use as much detail as possible before entering the residence.

Some appraisers prefer to complete the outside work first, including the measuring. The advantage to this is that when making the interior inspection, the drawing is already completed (for at least the first story or level) and the rooms can be entered easily into the sketch. A disadvantage that often occurs when completing the outside work is the appraiser gets dirty and then must be careful not to bring that dirt into the residence.

TAKING THE MEASUREMENTS

The outside work includes observing all buildings, main residence, garage, and accessory buildings. Each must be measured from the outside. Detailed notes on construction type and materials should be made and kept. Measuring a residence is done from the outside. **GLA (gross living area)** is defined as the above-grade area of the house, measured from the outside, less the garage, attic, and basement. Appraisers do not ignore the garage, attic, and basement, but these areas are not included in the area defined as GLA. The line below the GLA on the URAR form (see Appendix A) discusses the basement. All improved areas should be included in the cost approach, but separate line items should be produced for GLA, garage, basement, attic, and accessory buildings. The second story measurements are normally taken from inside the unit, and the thickness of the walls is added to insure a correct measurement.

Measurements do not always match public records. The primary reason is that the builder or architect may not use the same definitions for GLA, as does an appraiser. Differences greater than 50 square feet (SF) should be investigated. When the appraiser arrives at a GLA larger than public records, it is often an indication that new improvements have been added. The appraiser must identify the additions and check with the municipality to insure all additions have been under permit and inspected. Keep in mind that public records are filed in bulk by clerks who can make mistakes. There are times that the GLA on public records is simply an error.

THE INTERIOR INSPECTION

The interior inspection includes detailed observations of each room in the

house. The detailed inspection checklist included in Appendix B helps to ensure that essential elements are not forgotten. Do not allow its usage to block or hamper good observation skills. Sometimes a piece of blank paper is the best way to start, insuring that the focus remains on the subject rather than the form.

Interior Components Inspected

- The flooring, types of walls, wainscoting, ceiling, crown molding, trim/finish, fireplaces, cabinets, countertops, appliances, fixtures, and any other amenities included with the house.

- All of the significant components of the house must be identified including types of windows, doors, types of heating and cooling systems, size and type of water heater, electric service panel, and any other components that may contribute to value.

Inspections are completed for several reasons, one of which is that the appraiser is the only unbiased observer in the transaction. Another reason is that the client, often a lender, never sees the property except through the appraiser's eyes and from the descriptions in the appraisal report. Information used to complete the cost approach and to compare the subject to the comparables is identified during the inspection.

A health hazard: an unfenced swimming pool covered with mold

An appraiser is not qualified to determine if there is a violation of a building code. However, observable defects or problems, such as obvious cracks in the foundation or a health hazard, should be noted. If an illegal gas line or jury-rigged hook-up has been observed, it should be noted.

The inspection of the subject property is complete when all the required information has been properly identified and recorded.

APPLYING THE COST APPROACH

The cost approach was once called the summation approach because that is exactly what the appraiser does. The costs for all of the improvement components are summed (less depreciation) and added to the site value to obtain an opinion of value. The representation in the URAR form is an accurate presentation of the application of the approach.

The economic **principle of substitution** is the theoretical basis for the cost approach. When using the principle of substitution in the cost approach, the appraiser compares the depreciated value of the subject property with the cost of building a similar property. The cost approach substitutes the value of the subject property with the cost today (new, as of the date of the appraisal) of the improvements less their depreciation.

Contribution refers to the value that an individual component adds to the property as a whole. Since the value of a contribution is based on the market's opinion, the contribution may be positive or negative. In the case of a new property, the market value of the contributions should be close to the cost of the contributions. This is the case in which the cost approach should be the most accurate and is certainly useful as a secondary support for the sales comparison approach. New construction, though, can be subject to functional or external obsolescence.

The careful observation of all three types of depreciation enables the appraiser to understand and account for any differences between cost and market value. The older the contributions, the more likely that they vary from the cost new, due to depreciation. The greater the impact of the different types of depreciation, the larger the discrepancy between the cost new and the market value.

Cost Approach Formula								
Property Value	=	Site Value	+	Replacement or Reproduction Cost of Improvements	−	Accrued Depreciation	+	"As is" Value of Improvements

This simple formula is the same for any type of property with improvements. The type of improvements and use of the property do not change the basic formula. Therefore, the cost approach is the only approach that can be used for all types of property.

Basic Steps in the Cost Approach

1. Determine the value of the site as if it is vacant and available for use.

2. Estimate the reproduction or replacement cost of the existing improvements.

3. Calculate accrued depreciation of improvements (loss in value) and deduct from the estimated reproduction or replacement cost new of the improvements.

4. Estimate the value of the "as is" site improvements. Significant improvements, such as a pool or guest house are included under the improvement section on which depreciation is specifically calculated. The value of these site improvements is "as is"—after depreciation.

5. Add the site value, the depreciated value of improvements, and the "as is" site improvements to calculate the property value.

This unit addresses the methods of calculating the cost today (new) of improvements—their accuracy, strengths, and weaknesses.

STEPS IN THE COST APPROACH

This text is structured so that most of the factors of the cost approach are presented in previous units. This unit brings all the elements together to form an organized and structured approach that provides a credible opinion of value.

DETERMINE SITE VALUE

The primary element in the formula is the site value. As you have learned, there are six techniques to develop an opinion of the site value that may be used for almost any site. The cost approach depends on many factors, but to be credible, a reliable opinion of site value is an absolute requirement. Often, more than one technique is used to obtain a reliable opinion of value. The combination of two or more of the techniques provides validation of the value and increases the credibility of the final result.

ESTIMATE COST OF IMPROVEMENTS

The cost of the improvements is often the central element in a cost approach appraisal. Although this is the step that often receives the most attention, it is not necessarily the most important element in the cost approach process.

There are a couple of reasons for this. The cost of the improvements can be less than 50% of the total value of the property, and sometimes as little as 10% of the total value. In these cases, the site valuation is much more significant. It is not difficult to develop an accurate cost estimate of the improvements based on today's costs and currently available material. There are cost data sources that make the data available, as well as maintain and update the data. A good inspection combined with an accurate cost database allows the appraiser to produce a credible cost estimate. The truly important element in this process is the estimate of depreciation, which is the element that brings the new costs of the improvements into the market range.

There are four techniques that are used to obtain the cost of the improvements today, at today's costs. They are the index method, the square foot method (the most frequently used and part of the URAR form), the unit-in-place method, and the quantity survey method.

ADD ENTREPRENEURIAL PROFIT

The motivation for starting most projects is entrepreneurial profit. **Entrepreneurial profit** is the amount that the entrepreneur expects to receive in addition to costs for the time and effort, coordination, and risk taken to create a project. Entrepreneurial profit is required to compensate the entrepreneur (developer) for both the coordination of the project and the risk associated with the project. All building projects have an element of risk, most of which is attributed to the market.

The development of a project requires the developer to make many decisions, all of which involve the interpretation of the market. These decisions include budget analysis and approval, timing, pricing, sales strategy, and product content. Every element of the project contributes to its ultimate success or failure. There is much more to being the developer than merely coordinating the project. This is illustrated by comparing a successful project to a project that fails to make a profit. A strong market that lasts for several years has the tendency to allow developers with less expertise to succeed. As soon as the market becomes more competitive, the experience and expertise of developers becomes evident. The experienced developer spends time learning and researching the market so that the product to be built is acceptable. The following episode from a televised reality show is a good example.

Example: Two teams were asked to renovate a house and prepare it for sale. One team researched the local market, noted those elements that were in highest demand, and focused on those elements. The other team did not prepare a budget and, instead of using market research, used their opinions to guide the project. Team One focused on the kitchen and bathrooms and made the remainder of the house presentable, while working with a strict budget. Team Two transformed a three-bedroom house into a two-bedroom house, severely limiting its utility and at a much higher cost. The result was that Team One presented a house that had a higher market value than Team Two's, even though Team Two spent more money. Team Two failed as a developer and the market rewarded them with a loss. Team One's project met the market's demands and the market rewarded them with a profit.

There is no doubt that it is the market that finally determines the actual amount of entrepreneurial profit. This is why the concept that there can be excess profit is unreasonable. The amount of profit almost always can be traced back to good execution, detailed follow-through, and a thorough understanding of the market. Successful entrepreneurs have these traits, and the market consistently rewards them.

Appraisers often may experience difficulty in developing an estimate of entrepreneurial profit, usually due to a lack of information. Entrepreneurs usually do not share their personal income information, but it can be extracted from market information. All of the information about the costs of a project is available from cost data services. Using the extraction method, a developer's profit can be estimated with a certain degree of accuracy. The most difficult aspect of any profit analysis is the discussion of risk, and the attributing of the appropriate risk premium to the project. The first casino built in Las Vegas was a huge risk, and became a huge success. The entrepreneurs were able to make significant profits. The same is true about development. A small in-fill project is not as risky as a large community development a good distance from an urban center. Therefore, when assessing entrepreneurial profit, not only must the actual amount be extracted, but also the appropriate risk premium must be identified. There is always a direct correlation between risk and reward and the market is accurate in its assessment.

CALCULATE ACCRUED DEPRECIATION

The three elements of depreciation were addressed in the beginning of this text, rather than at the end, because of their importance to the overall credibility of the approach. The credibility of the approach depends on the accurate calculation and application of depreciation. The definition of value specifically excludes the use of the cost of the improvements because cost does not reflect value. Rather, it is the **application of depreciation** that converts the raw cost of improvements to the market value today of those improvements.

The depreciated cost of improvements line in the summary report is a sub-total line. It is simply the cost of improvements (all lines) added together less the total of all types of depreciation.

ESTIMATE THE VALUE OF "AS IS" SITE IMPROVEMENTS

Site improvements are defined to include accessory buildings, paving, landscaping, fences, retaining walls, and patios. The URAR includes the garage as part of the improvements to be depreciated so the garage should not be included in this section. Significant improvements including a pool, spa, guest house, stables, sports courts, and other costly improvements should be included under the improvement section on which depreciation is specifically calculated. The value of the site improvements placed on this line is the value "as is", which is after depreciation.

FINAL VALUE OPINION BY COST APPROACH

The final value opinion is the sum of the site value, the depreciated cost of improvements, and the "as is" site improvements. The fact that there are a limited number of lines on the summary form does not limit the amount of research or analysis the appraiser is required to complete. The URAR (see Appendix A) is a summary report and the information presented in this section summarizes the total effort and presents it in a simple format for the benefit of the client (reader).

USES OF THE COST APPROACH

The cost approach, applied carefully, can be a credible tool and provide both the appraiser and the client detailed information not available as part of any other approach. The answer to the question, "When to use it?" is set forth in Standard 1 of USPAP: Real Property Appraisal Development.

> "In developing a real property appraisal, an appraiser must identify the problem to be solved, determine the scope of work necessary to solve the problem, and correctly complete research and analyses necessary to produce a credible appraisal."

All approaches that add to the credibility of the final opinion of value are used. The type of appraisal in which the cost approach serves as the primary approach is any appraisal in which research determines that there are few similar comparables and the property does not generate income.

Appropriate Use of the Cost Approach
- Unique or one-of-a-kind buildings
- Government-owned properties
- Properties that are significantly overbuilt for the neighborhood
- Single or special-use properties

Inappropriate Use of the Cost Approach
- Condominiums—the ownership is of air rights and a portion of the common space and improvements
- Land without improvements—the land/site valuation techniques can and should be applied, but there are not improvements to cost

The question of when to use the cost approach has been answered. The more important question is, "Why use the cost approach?" The answer lies in the underlying economic principles of substitution. A homebuyer usually does not purchase an existing house if its cost is significantly more than the cost to build a similar new house. The opposite is also true—an informed buyer purchases an existing house instead of constructing a new one if the existing house costs the same or less than a similar new one would cost to build. With the exception of a few buyers whose purchases are emotionally based, most homebuyers are motivated by economic reasons when buying property.

The full analysis and discussion of depreciation—physical, functional, and external—provides the client a full explanation of all the factors that affect the property. This explanation is much more detailed and accurate than that of the income or sales comparison approaches. The income and sales comparison approaches allow the use of similar properties, often without a detailed analysis of the factors that make these properties similar.

SUMMARY

There are three basic approaches to developing an opinion of value used by appraisers: sales comparison, income, and cost. Of the three, the cost approach has the broadest applicability, but because of its complicated application, it is often the least reliable. There are several specific instances when it is the only approach that can be used—**special purpose buildings**, and **unique** or **one-of-a-kind buildings**. Application of the cost approach requires research and meticulous effort, but the result is a verifiable opinion of value that contains specific data.

UNIT 7 REVIEW

MATCHING EXERCISE

Instructions: Write the letter of the matching term on the blank line before its definition. Answers are in Appendix C.

Terms

A. amps

B. application of depreciation

C. balloon framing

D. contribution

E. cost approach

F. entrepreneurial profit

G. excess land

H. fire-rated

I. floating slab

J. galvanized steel pipes

K. GLA (gross living area)

L. hardscape

M. monolithic slab

N. pitch

O. platform framing

P. principle of substitution

Q. raised foundation

R. reconciliation

S. site improvements

T. softscape

U. stucco

V. surplus land

Definitions

1. _____ Probably the least used of the three approaches to value

2. _____ A foundation with walls, a crawlspace, and usually a pier and beam support system

3. _____ A slab foundation for which the footings and slab are poured at separate times

4. _____ A slab foundation for which the footings and slab are poured at the same time

5. _____ Framing that completes one story at a time

6. _____ Framing that extends the full two-story height

7. _____ A concrete product applied in three coats to walls

8. _____ Newer homes have copper piping in place of these, which corrode and can leak or break

9. _____   The strength of electrical current, important in measuring the size of an electrical box

10. _____   A door that is rated by time it can withstand exposure to fire

11. _____   The plantings around the subject property that prevent erosion and improve aesthetic appearance

12. _____   Structures and features, such as pathways, pools, and retaining walls

13. _____   Land beyond that which is needed to support the property's highest and best use

14. _____   Land that is over and above what is typical for a specific property in the area

15. _____   The area of the house, measured from the outside, less the garage, attic, and basement

16. _____   The basic economic principle underlying the cost approach

17. _____   The value a component adds to real estate

18. _____   The amount a businessman expects to receive in addition to costs for the time and effort, coordination, and risk taken to create a project

19. _____   Converts the raw cost of improvements to the market value today of those improvements

20. _____   Accessory buildings, paving, landscaping, fences, walls, and patios

MULTIPLE CHOICE QUESTIONS

Instructions: Circle your response and go to Appendix C to read the complete explanation for each question.

1. Which of the following is not a method or approach of appraisal?
   a. Depreciation
   b. Cost
   c. Sales comparison
   d. Income

2. The _____ foundation is one in which the slab and footings are poured at the same time.

    a. monolithic

    b. raised

    c. floating

    d. pier and beam

3. Exterior walls can be made of many materials or systems depending on the region where the improvements are being built. In earthquake prone regions, which wall materials would not be advisable?

    a. Concrete

    b. Stucco

    c. Steel framing

    d. Brick

4. Older homes may have electrical panels smaller in capacity. That capacity is measured in:

    a. watts.

    b. volts.

    c. amps.

    d. BTUs.

5. Finish items that can influence the value of the improvements include all of the following, except the:

    a. flooring and moldings.

    b. cabinetry.

    c. interior decor.

    d. bathroom and kitchen countertops.

6. Which of the following is not usually required by an appraiser to do an inspection?

    a. Camera

    b. Voltmeter

    c. Graph or blank paper

    d. Measuring device

7. The plantings around the subject property that prevent erosion and improve aesthetic appearance are the:

    a. macadam.

    b. hardscape.

    c. softscape.

    d. wainscoting.

8. Gary accepted an assignment for a custom-built house. As part of a property inspection, he measured all of the improvements. Since this is a custom-built house, how is the GLA measured?

    a. The exterior measurements of the main house, less the garage, attic, and basement, plus the area of the guest house and accessory buildings

    b. The garage, attic, and basement, measured from the exterior, and excluding the area of the main house

    c. The area of the main house, measured room by room since this is a reproduction cost estimate

    d. The area of the main house, measured from the exterior, excluding the garage, attic, and basement

9. The basic formula for the cost approach is total property value equals:

    a. site value plus replacement or reproduction cost of improvements at the time they were built less depreciation.

    b. site value plus replacement or reproduction cost of improvements new today less depreciation plus "as is" value of site improvements.

    c. site value plus depreciated value of site improvements plus original cost of improvements.

    d. site value plus replacement or reproduction cost of improvements new divided by the effective age plus today's value of site improvements.

10. Determining depreciation affecting the subject property helps an appraiser to:

    a. address cost items not in the cost manuals.

    b. subtract all the negative factors affecting comparables and bring them to today's value.

    c. account for any differences between cost and market value.

    d. discount the impact of external forces on the value of improvements.

11. Which of the following is not a technique used to calculate the cost of improvements?

    a. Square foot method

    b. Index method

    c. Allocation

    d. Quantity survey

12. Ms. Summer is a developer who specializes in in-fill projects. For her time and effort, coordination, and risk taken to create a project, she expects to earn:

    a. a tax write-off.

    b. entrepreneurial profit.

    c. community recognition.

    d. a salary.

13. The phrase, "as is" site improvements, refers to:

    a. accessory buildings, paving and landscaping, and unique improvements such as stables or a tennis court.

    b. improvements that do not have a warranty.

    c. the accrued depreciation of the site improvements.

    d. the value of the site improvements after depreciation.

14. Ted has developed accurate estimates of value for several assignments for his current client Don Green. Don now wants Ted to appraise a large, custom-built hillside home. Even though the home is over 60 years old, Don is not interested in its historic value—just its functional utility. Due to the uniqueness of the property, there are no comparables in the city. What should Ted do?

    a. Take the assignment, look for similar properties in other cities, and complete the assignment based on the sales comparison approach.

    b. Turn down the assignment because single-family residences are valued using the sales comparison approach and there are no similar properties in the city.

    c. Take the assignment and work with an experienced contractor to develop a thorough line item cost breakdown for the house and prepare a reproduction cost estimate.

    d. Take the assignment and develop a cost estimate based on the replacement cost of a house of similar utility since single-family homes can be replaced with homes of similar utility.

15. The cost approach is not the primary approach used to appraise:

    a. land without improvements.

    b. government-owned properties.

    c. properties significantly overbuilt for the neighborhood.

    d. one-of-a kind buildings.

Cost Approach: Summation

Unit 8

INTRODUCTION

The final result is in sight. The appraiser has done extensive research, chosen the appropriate cost, applied the appropriate site valuation, and used the necessary depreciation techniques. Now, he or she is ready to reconcile the various differences to report the results of the cost approach. A great deal of the presentation thus far has been dedicated to the strengths and weaknesses in each method from a theoretical and practical perspective. Now, this understanding allows the appraiser to address those strengths and weaknesses in order to develop an opinion of value based on the best available information.

This unit focuses on the summation process and the ways appraisers report their findings. **Summation** is the arithmetic operation of calculating the sum of two or more numbers—it is the final aggregate. In appraisal, it is the assessing and reporting of information based on the cost approach to render an opinion of value. All of the techniques and methods applied in the previous units result with the simple act of summation.

At the end of the unit, a comprehensive case study incorporates many of the techniques presented in the text. This exercise is designed to challenge the reader to think about every aspect of the application of the cost approach while completing the URAR form.

LEARNING OBJECTIVES

After reading this unit, you should be able to:

- explain the summation process in appraisal.
- complete the cost section on the URAR.
- identify the procedures used to arrive at a final estimate of value.

COMPLETING THE URAR COST SECTION

Appraisers must report the results of their appraisals in one of the three approved appraisal reports required by USPAP. Most appraisers use the URAR, which is a summary report. The URAR form was created by the Federal National Mortgage Association (FNMA) and the Federal Home Loan Mortgage Corporation (FHLMC). The **Federal National Mortgage Association (FNMA)**, or Fannie Mae, is a quasi-public agency converted into a private corporation whose primary function is to buy and sell mortgages in the secondary market. The **Federal Home Loan Mortgage Corporation (FHLMC),** or Freddie Mac, is a federal agency whose primary function is to purchase residential mortgages and sell them as mortgage-backed securities. **Mortgage-backed securities** are investments with returns that are tied to pools of mortgage loans. By creating the form, a standardized method in the reporting of residential appraisals was developed. The form also helps to facilitate the sale and trading of mortgage-backed securities in the secondary market.

Regardless of the report format chosen, the basic structure of the cost approach remains unchanged. Individual line items may vary from this report form to others, including the previous URAR form.

The initial standardized URAR form, approved in June of 1993, was updated only recently, and is used solely for purchase or refinance transactions. The cost approach has always been part of the URAR (the single-family residential report) form.

The first line establishes one of the most significant differences between the current and previous cost sections. The appraiser must provide adequate information in each section, so that an independent reviewer is able to verify and replicate the figures and calculations. This is specifically true in the section in which the actual cost figures are developed. The previous URAR requested only reproduction costs. The current form allows the specification of reproduction or replacement costs. The form then requests the source of the data, the quality rating, and the effective date of the cost data. This information is sufficient to allow the calculations and data to be verified.

COST APPROACH TO VALUE (not required by Fannie Mae)					
Provide adequate information for the lender/client to replicate the below cost figures and calculations.					
Support for the opinion of site value (summary of comparable land sales or other methods for estimating site value)					
ESTIMATED ☐ REPRODUCTION OR ☐ REPLACEMENT COST NEW	OPINION OF SITE VALUE				= $
Source of cost data	Dwelling	Sq. Ft. @ $			=$
Quality rating from cost service Effective date of cost data		Sq. Ft. @ $			=$
Comments on Cost Approach (gross living area calculations, depreciation, etc.)					
	Garage/Carport	Sq. Ft. @ $			=$
	Total Estimate of Cost-New				= $
	Less Physical	Functional	External		
	Depreciation				=$( )
	Depreciated Cost of Improvements				=$
	"As-is" Value of Site Improvements				=$
Estimated Remaining Economic Life (HUD and VA only) Years	Indicated Value By Cost Approach				=$

Although the URAR states that the cost approach to value is not required by FNMA, USPAP requires any approach to value that is required for credible assignment results. Appraisers determine which approaches to value are appropriate when they evaluate their scope of work.

Site value is still the first line in the cost approach. In the form, the opinion of site value must be supported using one or more of the methods previously discussed. There are six possible methods of developing the site value with each requiring certain information. The method used and the data developed should be fully explained in this section of the form.

This form presupposes the use of the square foot method to develop costs of improvements. A per square foot number can be developed using any of the four techniques. If the square foot method is being used and data from a cost manual is the basis for that cost, then this form is perfect. The final estimate of cost-new can be placed in the line indicating the total estimate of cost new. It is appropriate to place an explanation of the method used and the actual calculations in the addendum. The "Comments" section on the lower left side of the form is where this information can be presented.

Depreciation is divided into physical, functional, and external with the final number a combination of those three. Many software programs allow automatic calculation of physical depreciation based on the straight-line age/life method. Use of a more detailed approach requires a full explanation and the placement of results in the proper boxes.

The final number to be developed is the "as is" value of site improvements. This is a one-line entry that may represent a more complex set of calculations. Again, a detailed discussion of the data sources and verification of techniques is required. The bottom line is simply the summation of all the developed values, which follows the cost approach formula.

COST APPROACH TO VALUE (not required by Fannie Mae)				
Provide adequate information for the lender/client to replicate the below cost figures and calculations.				
Support for the opinion of site value (summary of comparable land sales or other methods for estimating site value) The site value was obtained through the abstraction method applied to similar sites recently sold in the same neighborhood. Sites on which abstraction was developed were 1234 Good St. and 1432 Bad St.				
ESTIMATED ☐ REPRODUCTION OR ☒ REPLACEMENT COST NEW	OPINION OF SITE VALUE .... = $ 635,000			
Source of cost data building-cost.net	Dwelling 2,201 Sq. Ft. @ $ 87.50 .... =$ 192,588			
Quality rating from cost service Good Effective date of cost data 1/01/20xx	Pool. Spa. BBQ Sq. Ft. @ $ .... =$ 55,000			
Comments on Cost Approach (gross living area calculations, depreciation, etc.)				
Physical depreciation is based on the age/life method of calculating	Garage/Carport 420 Sq. Ft. @ $ 35.00 .... =$ 14,700			
straight line depreciation. Based on a total economic life of 70 years	Total Estimate of Cost-New .... = $ 262,288			
and an effective age of 25 years, a 36% physical depreciation estimate	Less 70 Physical	Functional	External	
was utilized. The remaining economic life is estimated to be 45 years.	Depreciation $94,424	$30,000		=$(124,424)
The land to value ratio is typical of the area. Functional obsolescence	Depreciated Cost of Improvements.............................. =$ 137,864			
represents the overadequacy of the pool/spa.	"As-is" Value of Site Improvements............................... =$ 7,500			
Estimated Remaining Economic Life (HUD and VA only) Years	Indicated Value By Cost Approach .... =$ 780,400			

The example above has a pool and spa which cost $55,000, but with a market value of only $25,000. This is an example of functional obsolescence resulting from overadequacy. As a result, the appraiser must manually input the value, $30,000, into the functional depreciation box. The cost of the dwelling was based on a per square foot calculation while the cost of the pool/spa/barbeque was a lump sum based on specific research or the owner's records. The form being used is supplied by an appraisal software suite, which automatically calculates the depreciation based on the effective age entered on page 1. The "as is" value of site improvements is entered as a single number. The comment section on the left side of the form allows the appraiser to detail the methods and calculations used. If the comment section is not sufficient for detailed explanations, most software programs allow comments that exceed the provided space to be placed automatically in the addendum. In addition, appraisers maintain the detailed analysis for site value in their workfiles. For the purposes of this example, the comments were restricted so they fit in the limited space.

The final indicated value also is rounded automatically by the software to the nearest $100. Rounding to the nearest $100 is a little optimistic and overstates the accuracy of the calculations performed. A more realistic approach would be to round the final value to the nearest $1,000.

FINAL OPINION OF VALUE

Applying all of the techniques presented in this text produces a verifiable result that can be replicated. Although the techniques are comprehensive and the results are trustworthy, that does not make the results perfectly accurate. The process requires that many estimates be made and each estimate presents an opportunity for error. It is incumbent upon the appraiser to know when an estimate is being made and what the potential for error is in that estimate.

There is potential for errors in an estimate.

Every method and technique presented in this text is a representation of real world situations. A significant amount of space has been allocated to discussing the strengths and weaknesses of each method. Most scientific measurements contain a range of accuracy. For example, if a wall were measured at 6 feet, the scientific approach would require that the measurement be presented as 6 feet +/– 3 inches. This provides the level of accuracy to which the measurement was completed.

Normally, appraisers do not present opinions with ranges of accuracy. There are good reasons for not including a range of accuracy. The most important reason is that measuring the range of accuracy is difficult and the final value is an opinion. This opinion of value includes subjective and objective data. Nonetheless, the appraiser should have a good idea of where and by how much the estimates could be in error. The example given above indicates that absolute accuracy is impossible even in measuring. In fact, the writer can usually obtain a measured GLA within 50 square feet of the public records, but not often the same number. The amount of error is small and of no relative importance to the final result, but it must be recognized as a possible source of error. The same goes for each step of the process.

USPAP even allows appraisers to make assumptions that, if wrong, could affect the appraiser's opinions and conclusions. It is imperative that the appraiser be knowledgeable enough to know when the estimates and assumptions affect the results. In these cases, the appraiser should state that an extraordinary assumption was made, state what the assumption is, and indicate the possible impact upon the final estimate of value if the assumption is proved incorrect. In this way, the reader is fully aware of the accuracy of the value estimate and understands the reasons for the assumptions. An extraordinary assumption can be used if it is needed to produce credible assignment results.

According to USPAP requirements, the report must not be misleading. It must be presented in a way that is logical enough for the client to know the appraisal's accuracy. The extensive efforts to present the weaknesses of each method and technique are all designed to prepare the appraiser to provide clients with reports that are as accurate as possible and to address fully any significant sources of error. Honesty and integrity are the foundation of the appraisal profession. Accurate reporting is essential to maintain the public trust.

CASE STUDY

It is time to apply theory to an actual case study. The case study is based on an actual appraisal assignment chosen to illustrate the variables that effect every appraisal.

The subject is a tract house. The research and analysis used are illustrated with supporting calculations. When estimates are made, they are discussed so that the reasoning becomes apparent. Many of the forms and research sites presented in the text are used here. This allows the reader to become familiar with the information and process.

Subject: 100 Any Street, Seaview, CA 90000

Date: January 15, 20xx

Assignment: Develop an opinion of value based on the cost approach.

Scope of Work: The scope of work is limited to the information presented in this case study. A site visit was made and the inspection checklists were completed. A cost evaluation was completed on both the subject and one comparable to allow the use of the abstraction method to obtain site value.

User: The hypothetical user is a lender.

Intended Use: Render an opinion of asset value, to assist the client with a mortgage-lending decision.

Procedure:

    a. Research the subject on both the public records database and the local multiple listing service.

    b. An exterior and interior inspection was completed of the subject.

    c. An exterior inspection was completed of the site comparable.

    d. A site valuation was made using the abstraction method.

    e. A cost estimate of the improvements for the site comparable was made.

    f. An estimate of physical, functional, and external depreciation was made for the site comparable.

    g. A cost estimate of the subject improvements was made.

    h. An estimate of physical, functional, and external depreciation was made for the subject.

    i. An estimate of "as is" site improvements was made for the subject.

    j. The final opinion of value is developed.

STEP 1: RESEARCH

Start with the research. Typically, a title company provides details of the property in a Property Detail Report, and also provides a plat map or parcel map from the county assessor's office.

The subject lot of the case study is circled on the photograph and it is located in Coastal County, California. The size of the lot is not available in public records, but the plat map does have dimensions so the lot size can be calculated. The property profile and plat map also provide some basic information necessary to the case study.

Comp House   More Street

Any Street   Subject Property

Property Detail Report

Land-SeaTitle.com

For Property Located At

100 Any St., Seaview, CA 90000

Owner Information:
Owner Name;
Mailing Address:
Phone Number: Vesting Codes: **HW / / JT**

Location Information:
Legal Description:	**N TR 12976 LOT 22**		
County:	**Coastal, CA**	APN:	**653-423-06**
Census Tract / Block:	**423.31 / 1**	Alternate APN:	
Township-Range-Sect:		Subdivision:	**12976**
Legal Book / Page:		Map Reference	**35-E5 / 951-G6**
Legal Lot:	**22**	Tract #:	**12976**
Legal Block:		School District:	**Coastal**
Market Area:		Munic/Township:	
Neighbor Code:			

Owner Transfer Information:
Recording/Sale Date	/	Deed Type:	
Sale Price:		1st Mtg Document #:	
Document #:			

Last Market Sale Information:
Recording/Sale Date:	**12/10/2003 / 10/23/2003**	1st Mtg Amount/Type:	**$322,700 / CONV**
Sale Price:	**$765,000**	1st Mtg Int. Rate/Type:	**/ FIXED**
Sale Type:	**FULL**	1st Mtg Document #:	**1469075**
Document #:	**1469074**	2nd Mtg Amount/Type:	**$142,300 / CONV**
Deed Type:	**GRANT DEED**	2nd Mtg Int. Rate/Type:	**/ FIXED**
Transfer Document #:		Price Per SqFt:	
New Construction:		Multi/Split Sale:	
Title Company:			
Lender:			
Seller Name:			

Prior Sale Information:
Prior Rec/Sale Date:	**12/15/2000 / 11/10/2000**	Prior Lender:	
Prior Sale Price:	**$459,000**	Prior 1st Mtg Amt/Type:	**$413,050 / CONV**
Prior Doc Number:	**681124**	Prior 1st Mtg Rate/Type:	**/**
Prior Deed Type:	**GRANT DEED**		

Property Characteristics:
Gross Area:		Parking Type:		Construction:	
Living Area:		Garage Area:		Heat Type:	
Tot Adj Area:		Garage Capacity:		Exterior wall:	
Above Grade:		Parking Spaces:		Porch Type:	
Total Rooms:		Basement Area:		Patio Type:	
Bedrooms:	**3**	Finish Bsmnt Area:		Pool:	
Bath (F/H)	**1 /**	Basement Type:		Air Cond:	**CENTRAL**
Year Built /Eff:	**1994 /**	Roof Type:		Style:	
Fireplace:		Foundation:		Quality:	
# of Stories		Roof Material:		Condition:	
Other Improvements:					

Site Information:
Zoning:		Acres:		County Use:	**SINGLE FAM RESIDENCE**
Flood Zone:	**X**	Lot Area:		State Use:	
Flood Panel:	**0607640439H**	Lot Width/Depth:	**x5880**	Site Influence:	
Flood Panel Date:	**02/18/2004**	Red/Comm Units:	**1**	Sewer Type:	**UNKNOWN**
Land Use:	**SFR**			Water Type:	**PUBLIC**

Tax Information:
Total Value:	**$795,906**	Assessed Year:	**2006**	Property Tax:	**$8,018.08**
Land Value:	**$574,865**	Improve %:	**028%**	Tax Area:	**29063**
Improvement Value:	**$221,041**	Tax Year:	**2006**	Tax Exemption:	**HOMEOWNER**
Total Taxable Value:	**$788,906**				

STEPS 2 & 3: PHYSICAL INSPECTION

Refer to the checklists that were completed during an inspection of the interior and exterior of the subject property. They provide the detailed information necessary to complete the cost approach.

Subject is the largest of three models in a housing tract. The exterior has been painted and the rear yard extensively remodeled. A custom pool with spa, rockscape, and water features has been added along with a balcony off the master bedroom. The balcony affords peek-a-boo views of the ocean 3 miles away. The owners indicated that they spent over $100,000 on the pool/BBQ/balcony improvements. The improvements to the rear yard are more than normal for the subject neighborhood and cause functional obsolescence through overadequacy. The subject backs to Niguel Road, a four-lane road, bordering subject's subdivision—a source of external depreciation.

The flooring is less than three years old and includes extensive use of marble in the living room and dining room. The kitchen and bathrooms are in original condition, with ceramic tile floors, countertops, and whitewashed oak cabinets in the kitchen. The kitchen has the original appliances, which include a downdraft range, built-in microwave, disposal, and center island. The refrigerator area is plumbed to include an icemaker. The bathrooms have paint grade cabinetry. There has been a small loft added over the dining room and a balcony added off the master suite with French doors.

The house is wood framed on a pre-stressed slab foundation, similar to all of the other homes in the housing tract. The roof is Spanish tile and the house has central air conditioning and forced air heating.

The home has one bedroom and one bathroom downstairs, with three bedrooms, a loft, and two bathrooms upstairs. The master suite has a walk-in closet. Electrical has been upgraded with a new larger panel to support the pool and spa. The plumbing is original and includes copper lines and plastic waste lines.

The appraiser now has enough information to prepare a cost analysis of the improvements using the website link to Building-Cost.net. The homes are in the same housing tract so most of the construction elements are the same, as are the highest and best uses of the subject and comparables. Differences in flooring, kitchens, bathrooms, and rear yards can be ascertained from review of the MLS listing (with confirmation from listing brokers) for the site being used. There are no vacant sites to use as site comparables so the abstraction method must be used, which requires the calculation of the depreciated cost of improvements.

DETAILED INSPECTION CHECKLIST

Due Date:	Lender:	Payment:	Lead From:	
Address:	*100 Any Street*	**City:** *Seaview*	**State:** *California*	**Zip:** *90000*
Ask About:		**Neighborhood Borders**		
Gross Living Area	*2143*			
Permits	*0*	**North:**	*Crown Valley*	
Dogs	*None*	**South:**	*Salt Creek Regional Park*	
Sales History for last 36 months	*12/10/2003*	**East:**	*Golden Lantern*	
Accesibility		**West:**	*Niguel Road*	
Parking				

SFR EXTERIOR CHECKLIST
(Circle Items as Noted or Enter Description)

SITE

Item	Circle/ Enter Description	Inspected	Item	Circle/ Enter Description	Inspected
# of Units		*one*	Alley	Public / Private / None	
# of Stories		*two*	Topography	Level / Sloping - How much?	
Type	Detached / Attached		Size	Average / Large / Small	
Corner Lot	Yes / No		Shape	Rectangular / Irregular	
Street	Asphalt / Gravel / Dirt / Other		Drainage	Adequate / Other	
Curb/Gutter	Yes / No		View	Mountains / Ocean / Other	
Sidewalks	Concrete / None		Landscaping	Average / Pro / None / Other	
Street Lights	Yes / No			*Rear - Professional*	

EXTERIOR DESCRIPTION

Item	Circle/ Enter Description	Inspected	Item	Circle/ Enter Description	Inspected
Foundation	Slab / Raised / Both		Sump Pump	Yes / No	
Exterior Walls	Stucco / Wood / Siding / Other		Dampness	Yes / No / None Observed	
Roof Surface	Shingle / Clay / Tile / Rock / Other		Settlement	Yes / No / None Observed	
Windows	Alum / Wood / Vinyl / Bars		Infestation	Yes / No / None Observed	
Mfg. Home	Yes / No				

BACKYARD AMENITIES

Item	Circle/ Enter Description	Inspected	Item	Circle/ Enter Description	Inspected
Patio	Concrete / Covered / Wood / Other		Pool	Pool / Spa / Both *	
Deck	Concrete / Covered / Wood / Other		BBQ	Built-in / Island / Firepit	
Porch	Concrete / Covered / Wood / Other		Fence	Blk / Wd / Chnlnk / Iron / Other	
Balcony	Concrete / Covered / Wood / Other			** and waterfall*	

VEHICLE STORAGE

Item	Circle/ Enter Description	Inspected	Item	Circle/ Enter Description	Inspected
Type	Garage / Carport / None		Driveway	Concrete / Asphalt / Gravel / Dirt	
Detached	Yes / No		RV Parking	Yes / No	
# of Cars		3	RV Parking		*None*
Driveway	Yes / No		Surface	Concrete / Asphalt / Gravel / Dirt	
# of Cars		3	RV Parking		

EXTERIOR AMENITIES AND OTHER SPECIAL/SIGNIFICANT ITEMS -

Pool /Spa/ Rockscape with waterfall and BBQ island - Balcony from Master w/peekaboo ocean view.

SFR INTERIOR CHECKLIST

Address:	100 Any Street	City:	Seaview	State:	California	Zip: 90000

SFR INTERIOR CHECKLIST
(Circle Items as Noted or Enter Description)

SITE

Item	Circle/ Enter Description	Inspected	Item	Circle/ Enter Description	Inspected
Flooring	Tile / Carpeting / HW / Lin		Living Room	FP / Bar: Wet / Dry	
Countertops	Granite / Laminate / Corian		Family Room	FP / Bar: Wet / Dry	
	Ceramic Tile / Other		Den	FP / Bar: Wet / Dry	
Walls	L&P / WB / Wood / Other	painted	Office	FP / Bar: Wet / Dry	
Doors	Flush / H.C. / Panel / French		Dining Room	Chandelier	
Stairs	Chandelier / Wood / Iron / Other		Laundry Room	Room / Area / Sink	
Lighting	Recessed / Chandelier / Other				
Heating	CTR - FAU / Wall / Other / None				
Cooling	CTR - FAU / Wall / Other / Evap				
Fireplace	Number	1 F/R			
	Brick / Marble / Tile / Other				
Attic	Scuttle / Stairs / Finished / None				
Basement	None / Finished				
	Entry: Outside / Inside				
Insulation	Adequate / Concealed				

KITCHEN

Item	Circle/ Enter Description	Inspected	Item	Circle/ Enter Description	Inspected
Flooring	Wood / Tile / Other	cer.tile	Appliances	Fan / Hood / Both	
Appliances	Refrigerator: Built-in / Personal			Microwave: Built-In / Personal	
	Range / Oven: Built-in / Personal				
	Disposal: Built-in / Personal				
	Dishwasher: Built-in / Personal				

BATHROOMS

Item	Circle/ Enter Description	Inspected	Item	Circle/ Enter Description	Inspected
Bathroom 1	Full / Half W/S, CT / Fg	shower	Bedroom 3	Fan / FP / Walk-In	✓
Bathroom 2	Full / Half W/S, CT / Fg	tub/shwr	Bedroom 4	Fan / FP / Walk-In	✓
Bathroom 3	Full / Half W/S, CT / Fg	tub/shwr	Other	Fan / FP / Walk-In	✓
Bathroom 4	Full / Half W/S, CT / Fg		Loft	Fan / FP / Walk-In	✓
Master Bedro	Fan / FP / Walk-In	✓			
Bedroom 2	Fan / FP / Walk-In	✓			

INTERIOR AMENITIES AND OTHER SPECIAL/SIGNIFICANT ITEMS

New flooring - marble and carpet downstairs - carpet upstairs.

Kitchen - original. Baths - original.

FINAL CHECKLIST

Address:	100 Any Street	City: Seaview	State: CA	Zip: 90000

Please make sure the following are completed

PICTURES

Front
Rear
Street
Interior

SFR MEASUREMENTS

Exterior:	2,143	2nd Story:	(included)	
Garage:	660	Attic: N/A		
Accessory Bldgs:	N/A			

HOMEOWNER'S ASSOCIATION

Project Name	CoastView	Units in Project	2,000	all sold
Fees	$ 102/mo	Litigation		
Units Rented	--	Guest Parking	Condo only	
Total Parking	Condo only	Subject's Floor	Condo	

Owner Parking	Garage / Carport / Underground / Street	# of Elevators		
	Owned / Assigned		Open Space:	
	Amount:		Pool / Spa -	both
	Space Number:	Common Area	Clubhouse:	large
			Gym:	
			Other: tennis/volleyball	

HOA Contact Information

Company: Coast Homeowners' Association			
Address: --	Phone: --	Fax: --	
Hours of Operation: --			

PERMITS REQUIRED

Zoning:		Legal/Non-Conforming:	
Additions:	Loft - permitted		
Other:	None		

STEP 4: SITE VALUATION

The top line of the cost approach in the Uniform Residential Appraisal Report form is site value. Subject is in a housing tract, completed 15 years ago in which there are no empty sites available for sale or properties recently sold. In this case, the sales comparison approach to site value cannot be used. Therefore, the next best technique for site valuation is abstraction. A suitable comparable site must be found and then the site value abstracted.

A recent sale in the neighborhood was found with a similar lot size. An exterior inspection from the curb was made of the comparable used in the site valuation. The MLS listing for the comparable is on the next page. It is important to review the MLS listing as well as public records as a verification source. This way it is less likely that any significant improvements will be missed. The **cost breakdown** is a detailed account of each individual cost to an improvement. The definitions for quality classes were presented in Unit 6 or they may be accessed at Building-Cost.net. The building cost breakdown (estimate) for the comparable property follows the MLS listing.

> This property is actually one street away from the subject, a slightly smaller model, but the lot is within 200 square feet. The sales price of the home was $699,999. The information from this listing was combined with the construction information observed during the inspection of the subject in order to develop a cost estimate for the improvements through www.building-cost.net. The cost new of the home according to the www.building-cost.net database is $232,737. In addition, the rear yard has an in-ground spa and BBQ island. Cost of these improvements is estimated at $10,000.

> The total improvement cost new is the sum of the improvement cost new and the rear yard improvements. From the building cost breakdown, we know the improvement cost new is $232,737. Add the rear yard improvements of $10,000 to get $242,737, which is the total improvement cost new.

An accurate cost breakdown allows for a more accurate calculation of depreciation. Depreciation must be calculated in these improvements. The age/life technique is applied to this example. This is the most often used approach because of its ease of application and the lack of specific information on the major components of the improvements. The estimated total economic life is 70 years and the effective age is estimated at 5 years.

Depreciation = Effective Age ÷ Total Economic Life

Depreciation = 5 ÷ 70

Depreciation = 0.0714 which rounds to 7% (0.07)

Depreciation = 0.07 x $242,737

Depreciation = $16,991 rounded to $17,000

Site Value = Sales Price − Depreciated Cost of Improvements

Site Value = $699,999 − ($242,737 − $17,000)

Site Value = $474,262 rounded to $475,000

Agent Report

For SFR Located At

AtoZ MLS

200 More St.
Seaview, CA 90000

Owner Information:

Owner Name;
Mailing Address:
Phone Number: Vesting Codes: **HW // JT**

Location Information:

Legal Description:	**N TR 12974 LOT 2**		
County:	**Coastal**	APN:	**653-423-06**
Census Tract / Block:	**423.2 / 1**	Alternate APN:	
Township-Range-Sect:		Subdivision:	**12974**
Legal Book / Page:		Map Reference	**35-E5 / 951-G6**
Legal Lot:	**2**	Tract #:	**12974**
Legal Block:		School District:	**Coastal**
Market Area:		Munic/Township:	
Neighbor Code:			

Owner Transfer Information:

Recording/Sale Date	**1/21/2007**	Deed Type:	**GRANT DEED**
Sale Price:	**$699,999**	1st Mtg Document #:	
Document #:	**TGNO 123A4**		

LOCATED IN THE COASTAL COMMUNITY OF SEAVIEW, THIS HOME FEATURES 4 BEDROOMS, 2.5 BATHS; UPGRADES INCLUDE EXTENSIVE USE OF FLAGSTONE HARDSCAPE WITH AN INGROUND SPA AND BUILT-IN BBQ. TRAVERTINE FLOORS IN LIVING AND DINING ROOMS, ENTRY, AND BATHROOMS, SLATE FLOORS IN FAMILY ROOM AND KITCHEN, GRANITE COUNTERS IN KITCHEN AND STAINLESS APPLIANCES. THE MASTER SUITE HAS A DRESSING AREA AND WALK-IN CLOSET AND THE MASTER BATHROOM HAS TRAVERTINE SHOWER, COUNTERS, AND FLOORING, SPA BATH HAS GRANITE COUNTERS, DESIGNER PAINT THROUGHOUT THE HOME.

Association Amenities:

Association Barbeque, Club Hse/Rec Facility, Pool, Tennis, Private and Association Spa.

Property Characteristics:

Gross Area:	**1943**	Parking Type:	**Attached**	Construction:	**/**
Living Area:	**1943**	Garage Area:	**/**	Heat Type:	**FORCED AIR**
Tot Adj Area:	**1943**	Garage Capacity:	**2**	Exterior wall:	**/**
Above Grade:	**1943**	Parking Spaces:	**/**	Porch Type:	**/**
Total Rooms:	**8**	Basement Area:	**/**	Patio Type:	**Slab / rock**
Bedrooms:	**4**	Finish Bsmnt Area:	**/**	Pool:	**Inground Spa**
Bath (F/H)	**2.5**	Basement Type	**/**	Air Cond:	**CENTRAL**
Year Built /Eff:	**1989**	Roof Type	**Sp Clay**	Style:	**/**
Fireplace:	**2**	Foundation:	**Slab**	Quality:	**/**
# of Stories	**2**	Roof Material:	**Tile**	Condition:	**/**
Other Improvements:					

Building Costs Estimate - Comparable Property
200 More St., Seaview, California 90000

Item Name	Material	Labor	Equip.	Total
Excavation	--	1,725	472	2,197
Foundation, Piers, Flatwork	3,908	5,844	959	10,711
Rough Hardware	531	795	131	1,457
Rough Carpentry	17,574	24,666	--	42,240
Insulation	3,291	2,139	--	5,430
Exterior Finish	9,356	5,312	690	15,358
Exterior Trim	634	949	156	1,739
Doors	1,399	1,116	--	2,515
Windows	2,409	1,557	--	3,966
Finish Hardware	233	186	--	419
Garage Door	660	256	--	916
Roofing, Flashing, Fascia	7,348	5,860	--	13,208
Finish Carpentry	849	4,068	--	4,917
Interior Wall Finish	4,077	5,986	--	10,063
Painting	2,436	5,407	--	7,843
Wiring	2,473	4,440	--	6,913
Lighting fixtures	1,854	555	--	2,409
Flooring	2,092	2,822	--	4,914
Carpeting	4,162	1,412	--	5,574
Bath Accessories	1,031	604	--	1,635
Shower and Tub Enclosure	658	525	--	1,183
Countertops	1,991	1,586	--	3,577
Cabinets	6,545	1,957	--	8,502
Built In Appliances	3,184	423	--	3,607
Plumbing Rough-in/Connection	2,988	6,900	432	10,320
Plumbing Fixtures	6,071	1,829	--	7,900
Heating and Cooling Systems	4,540	6,809	--	11,349
Unit Heating and Cooling	--	--	--	--
Fireplace and Chimney	1,020	1,530	--	2,550
Subtotal Direct Job Costs	**$93,314**	**$97,258**	**$2,840**	**$193,412**
Final Cleanup	--	884	--	884
Insurance	6,189	--	--	6,189
Permits and Utilities	3,758	--	--	3,758
Plans and Specifications	864	--	--	864
Subtotal Indirect Job Costs	**$10,811**	**$884**	**$0**	**$11,695**
Contractor Markup	27,630	--	--	27,630
TOTAL COST	**$131,755**	**$98,142**	**$2,840**	**$232,737**

STEP 5: COST ESTIMATE - SUBJECT IMPROVEMENTS

In Step 2, a physical interior and exterior inspection were made of the subject. During the inspection, the appraiser completed the inspection checklist. The information from that inspection was used to develop a cost estimate for subject using the Building-Cost.net website. In the cost breakdown, each item from the inspection was assigned to its appropriate line item and quality class. The following building cost breakdown (estimate) for the improvements of the subject was developed using www.Building-Cost.net.

The rear yard improvements were not included in the building cost breakdown. The costs of these improvements needed to be added. The appraiser obtained receipts from the owner supporting the $100,000 total cost for the pool, spa, waterfalls, rockscape, and BBQ island.

> The total improvement cost new is the sum of the improvement cost new and the rear yard improvements. From the building cost breakdown, we know the improvement cost new for the subject is $270,740. Add the rear yard improvements of $100,000 to get $370,740, which is the total improvement cost new. This number is rounded to $370,000.

Building Costs Estimate - Subject Property
100 Any Street, Seaview, California 90000

Item Name	Material	Labor	Equip.	Total
Excavation	--	2,050	561	2,611
Foundation, Piers, Flatwork	4,645	6,947	1,140	12,732
Rough Hardware	613	919	152	1,684
Rough Carpentry	20,316	28,515	--	48,831
Insulation	3,804	2,473	--	6,277
Exterior Finish	10,816	6,141	797	17,754
Exterior Trim	733	1,097	181	2,011
Doors	1,857	1,481	--	3,338
Windows	3,198	2,067	--	5,265
Finish Hardware	309	247	--	556
Garage Door	877	340	--	1,217
Roofing, Flashing, Fascia	8,495	6,775	--	15,270
Finish Carpentry	991	4,747	--	5,738
Interior Wall Finish	4,758	6,987	--	11,745
Painting	2,843	6,311	--	9,154
Wiring	2,887	5,182	--	8,069
Lighting Fixtures	2,164	647	--	2,811
Flooring	2,418	3,262	--	5,680
Carpeting	4,811	1,632	--	6,443
Bath Accessories	1,192	698	--	1,890
Shower & Tub Enclosure	761	607	--	1,368
Countertops	2,301	1,834	--	4,135
Cabinets	7,566	2,262	--	9,828
Built In Appliances	3,681	489	--	4,170
Plumbing Rough-in/Connection	3,455	7,977	499	11,931
Plumbing Fixtures	7,018	2,114	--	9,132
Heating/Cooling Systems	5,023	7,535	--	12,558
Unit Heating and Cooling	--	--	--	--
Fireplace and Chimney	1,020	1,530	--	2,550
Subtotal Direct Job Costs	**$108,552**	**$112,866**	**$3,330**	**$224,748**
Final Cleanup	--	1,034	--	1,034
Insurance	7,235	--	--	7,235
Permits & Utilities	4,392	--	--	4,392
Plans & Specs	1,034	--	--	1,034
Subtotal Indirect Job Costs	**$12,661**	**$1,034**	**--**	**$13,695**
Contractor Markup	32,297	--	--	32,297
Total Cost	**$153,510**	**$113,900**	**$3,330**	**$270,740**

STEP 6: SUBJECT DEPRECIATION

The next step is to evaluate the depreciation on the subject. Subject has all three types of depreciation: physical, functional, and external.

PHYSICAL DEPRECIATION

The age/life method is applied to calculate physical depreciation since no information on specific major components is available. Improvements deteriorate slowly at the beginning of their economic lives and physical depreciation accelerates over time.

> Subject was built in 1989 and normal maintenance has been completed, such as painting and repairs. None of the major components have been replaced. The kitchen and bathrooms are in original condition. The flooring has been replaced and upgraded. The electrical panel was upgraded to support the pool and spa. The subject is considered in good condition. Physical depreciation is normal or slightly below normal for the neighborhood. Subject has an actual age of 18 years and an estimated effective age of 8 years. Total economic life is estimated at 70 years.
>
> Physical Depreciation = (Effective Age ÷ Total Economic Life) x Cost New
>
> Physical Depreciation = (8 ÷ 70) x $370,000
>
> Physical Depreciation = $42,285 rounded to $42,300

FUNCTIONAL DEPRECIATION AND OBSOLESCENCE

As evidenced in the example below, functional depreciation and obsolescence can be a result of a poorly planned house or over-improving the property.

> Subject is a production home of good quality and average utility. The design and floor plan are adequate and the market has not reflected any discount with regard to the design. The improvements to the rear yard are not so fortunate. This subdivision is designed with small lots, a large clubhouse, pool, and open space that is maintained by a homeowners' association. This complex is a substitute for individual pools in the rear yards. This is due to the size of the lots. Subject is one of two homes in the tract with a pool. In this case, the pool is an over-improvement. The additions of the rockscape and water feature are more than reasonable for the neighborhood. Paired sales analysis at the time of the last sale of the subject suggests that the market valued the rear yard improvements at $65,000.

> Functional Obsolescence = Original Cost − Market Value
>
> Functional Obsolescence = $100,000 − $65,000
>
> Functional Obsolescence = $35,000

EXTERNAL DEPRECIATION OR OBSOLESCENCE

The close proximity of the subject to environmental forces over which the owner has little or no control is a good example of external depreciation.

> Subject is located on a single loaded street (houses on one side only) but it backs to a large four-lane street with moderate to heavy traffic resulting in noise and dirt. This is a good example of external obsolescence. The impact of this was calculated using paired sales analysis on two similar properties, one backing to Niguel Road and one on an interior lot. The analysis is maintained in the appraiser's workfile. The external obsolescence is $10,000.
>
> Total Depreciation = Physical Depreciation + Functional Obsolescence + External Depreciation
>
> Physical Depreciation   = $42,300
>
> Functional Obsolescence = $35,000
>
> External Obsolescence   = $10,000
>
> Total Depreciation = $42,300 + $35,000 + $10,000
>
> Total Depreciation = $87,300

STEP 7: "AS IS" VALUE OF SITE IMPROVEMENTS

The "as is" value of site improvements includes the hardscape, softscape, automatic sprinklers, fountains, fences, and other permanent improvements made to the site.

> The subject had extensive work completed in the rear yard, which has been incorporated in the cost estimate of the improvements. The site improvements being valued are the front landscape, sprinklers, hardscape including walkways and driveway, and ornamental fences. Subject has a block wall along the rear of the property, covered with stucco to match the theme of the development, and foam core wall, covered with stucco again to match the theme of the development.

> The analysis used to obtain the estimated "as is" value of site improvements is maintained in the appraiser's workfile. The estimated "as is" value of site improvements is $10,000.

STEP 8: FINAL ESTIMATE OF VALUE

The final estimate of value is obtained by summing the parts.

Site Value		**$475,000**
Reproduction or Replacement		
Cost of Improvements New	$370,000	
Less:		
Physical Depreciation	($ 42,300)	
Functional Depreciation	($ 35,000)	
External Obsolescence	($ 10,000)	
Reproduction or Replacement Cost		
of Improvements Less Depreciation		$282,700
"As is" Value of Site Improvements		$ 10,000
Final Estimate of Value		**$767,700**

Page three of the URAR contains the summary of the cost approach. An example of how it would appear completed for the above case is shown below.

COST APPROACH TO VALUE (not required by Fannie Mae)					
Provide adequate information for the lender/client to replicate the below cost figures and calculations.					
Support for the opinion of site value (summary of comparable land sales or other methods for estimating site value) The site value was obtained through the abstraction method applied to similar sites recently sold in the same neighborhood. Site on which abstraction was developed was 9 Cala Moreya, which sold for $699,999 within the past two months.					
ESTIMATED ☐ REPRODUCTION OR ☒ REPLACEMENT COST NEW	OPINION OF SITE VALUE .... = $ 475,000				
Source of cost data building-cost.net	Dwelling 2,201 Sq. Ft. @ $ .... =$ 270,000				
Quality rating from cost service Good Effective date of cost data 1/01/20xx	Pool, Spa, BBQ Sq. Ft. @ $ .... =$ 100,000				
Comments on Cost Approach (gross living area calculations, depreciation, etc.)					
Physical depreciation is based on the age/life method of calculating	Garage/Carport Included Sq. Ft. @ $ .... =$ 0				
straight line depreciation. Based on a total economic life of 70 years	Total Estimate of Cost-New .... = $ 370,000				
and an effective age of 8 years, a 11% physical depreciation estimate	Less 70 Physical	Functional	External		
was utilized. The remaining economic life is estimated to be 62 years.	Depreciation $42,300	$35,000	$10,000	=$(87,300)	
The land to value ratio is typical of the area. Functional obsolescence	Depreciated Cost of Improvements .... =$ 282,700				
represents the overadequacy of the pool/spa.	"As-is" Value of Site Improvements .... =$ 10,000				
Estimated Remaining Economic Life (HUD and VA only) 62 Years	Indicated Value By Cost Approach .... =$ 767,700				

The presentation on the URAR is straightforward. A lot of discussion has been directed toward understanding sources of error when completing the cost approach. The above case study used the age/life method of calculating physical depreciation, the abstraction method of arriving at site value, and a replacement estimate of the cost of improvements. All of these approaches must be applied carefully due to potential weaknesses, and the results reviewed for possible errors.

> Houses similar to the subject sold from $700,000 to $835,000, in the past 6 months. The home that sold at $835,000 was a former model home completely upgraded with renovated kitchen and bathrooms. According to market value, both of these items equal the full cost of the renovation.

The final estimate of value falls between the recent sales figures, which provide support for the final estimate.

SUMMARY

The unit dealt with the cost approach, also known as **summation**. All of the techniques and methods applied in the previous units result with the simple act of summation.

Appraisers must report the results of their appraisals in one of the three approved appraisal-reporting methods. The form that is widely used to outline the Summary Appraisal Report for residential property is the **Uniform Residential Appraisal Report (URAR)** form. The URAR is used to report the results of single-family residential appraisals. The **Federal National Mortgage Association (FNMA)** and the **Federal Home Loan Mortgage Corporation (FHLMC)** are responsible for creating the URAR form.

When using the cost approach, an appraiser must follow a series of steps in order to arrive at the final estimate of value. This was evidenced by the case study included in the unit. The first step is to research the subject on both the public records database and the local multiple listing service. After research, the appraiser must perform an inspection of the site comparable and obtain site value using the abstraction method. Next, a cost estimate of the improvements for the site comparable is made. Subsequently, an estimate of physical, functional, and external depreciation for the site comparable is necessary. Next, an estimate of "as is" site improvements was made for the subject property. Lastly, the final opinion of value is developed.

UNIT 8 REVIEW

MATCHING EXERCISE

Instructions: Write the letter of the matching term on the blank line before its definition.
Answers are in Appendix C.

Terms

A. cost breakdown

B. effective age

C. Federal Home Loan Mortgage
    Corporation (FHLMC)

D. Federal National Mortgage
    Association (FNMA)

E. mortgage-backed securities

F. summation

G. total economic life

Definitions

1. _____ The evaluation and reporting of information based on the cost approach to
develop an estimate of value

2. _____ A quasi-public agency converted into a private corporation whose primary
function is to buy and sell mortgages in the secondary market

3. _____ A detailed account of each individual cost to an improvement

4. _____ Investments with returns that are tied to pools of mortgage loans

5. _____ A federal agency whose primary function is to purchase residential
mortgages and sell them as mortgage-backed securities

MULTIPLE CHOICE QUESTIONS

Instructions: Circle your response and go to Appendix C to read the complete explanation for each question.

1. The URAR form is a type of:
    a. summary report.
    b. MLS report.
    c. cost estimate form.
    d. summary of costs report.

2. In the secondary market, the URAR form helps to facilitate:
    a. investments in foreign currencies.
    b. the sale of treasury bills.
    c. faster estimates of value.
    d. the sale of investments tied to pools of mortgage loans.

3. The main difference in the cost section for the current URAR form and previous forms is that:
    a. it only accounts for specification of reproduction costs.
    b. it only accounts for specification of replacement costs.
    c. it allows specification of reproduction and replacement costs.
    d. the cost approach is entirely eliminated from the report.

4. Why do appraisers refrain from offering accuracy ranges in their final opinion of value?
    a. Range of accuracy is relatively simple to calculate.
    b. Opinion of value does not include objective data.
    c. Opinion of value does not include subjective data.
    d. Measuring range of accuracy is complicated.

5. What is a first step in developing an opinion of value using the cost approach method?
    a. Perform a thorough physical inspection of the property
    b. Research the subject property
    c. Estimate the building costs of the property
    d. Utilize the abstraction method for site valuation

6. Other than performing extensive research, how can an appraiser obtain more detailed information regarding the subject property?

    a. Obtain more comparables
    b. Use the square foot method to obtain costs
    c. Perform an exterior and interior inspection
    d. Research the MLS

7. An appraiser is seeking to obtain the site value for a property located in a housing tract completed 12 years ago. There are no empty sites for sale or recently sold properties. What is the next logical step?

    a. Advise the client that an appraisal is not possible
    b. Use an income approach for the subject property
    c. Find suitable comparables using the sales comparison approach
    d. Use the abstraction method

8. When performing a cost analysis, it is important to review the:

    a. local subdivision laws where the subject property is located.
    b. multiple listing service for accurate depreciation calculation.
    c. effective age of other properties to calculate depreciation.
    d. purchase agreement for recently sold properties.

9. A subject property has a total economic life of 100 years and an effective age of 5 years. What is the depreciation calculation?

    a. 5%
    b. 7%
    c. 9%
    d. 10%

10. A property has a sales price of $500,000. Depreciation has been calculated at $12,000 and the cost of new improvements is $350,000. What is the site value using the abstraction method?

    a. $158,000
    b. $162,000
    c. $170,000
    d. $184,000

11. An appraiser obtains the site value of a property using the abstraction method. In order to continue with the cost approach, the next logical step is to:

   a. estimate the cost of improvements for a site comparable.

   b. reference the MLS for comparable properties.

   c. develop a final opinion of value.

   d. estimate external depreciation.

12. After obtaining the cost of improvements on a site comparable, what is the next step in the cost approach?

   a. Obtain physical depreciation

   b. Estimate functional depreciation

   c. Determine if external depreciation is present

   d. All of the above

13. What is the calculation for physical depreciation on a property that has an effective age of 10 years, a total economic life of 50 years, and costs $300,000 new?

   a. $50,000

   b. $60,000

   c. $65,000

   d. $72,000

14. A homeowner added two extra floors in a neighborhood dominated by one-story homes. The improvement cost the owner $200,000 and the market value of the property is $72,000. What is the cost of the functional obsolescence?

   a. $102,000

   b. $108,000

   c. $114,000

   d. $128,000

15. A property has a site value of $250,000 and a cost of improvements new of $300,000. Total depreciation was calculated at $50,000. What is the final estimate of value?

   a. $450,000

   b. $500,000

   c. $525,000

   d. $550,000

APPENDIX A:
UNIFORM RESIDENTIAL APPRAISAL REPORT

Uniform Residential Appraisal Report
File #

The purpose of this summary appraisal report is to provide the lender/client with an accurate, and adequately supported, opinion of the market value of the subject property.

SUBJECT

Property Address	City	State	Zip Code
Borrower	Owner of Public Record		County

Legal Description

Assessor's Parcel #	Tax Year	R.E. Taxes $
Neighborhood Name	Map Reference	Census Tract

Occupant ☐ Owner ☐ Tenant ☐ Vacant Special Assessments $ ☐ PUD HOA $ ☐ per year ☐ per month

Property Rights Appraised ☐ Fee Simple ☐ Leasehold ☐ Other (describe)

Assignment Type ☐ Purchase Transaction ☐ Refinance Transaction ☐ Other (describe)

Lender/Client Address

Is the subject property currently offered for sale or has it been offered for sale in the twelve months prior to the effective date of this appraisal? ☐ Yes ☐ No

Report data source(s) used, offering price(s), and date(s).

CONTRACT

I ☐ did ☐ did not analyze the contract for sale for the subject purchase transaction. Explain the results of the analysis of the contract for sale or why the analysis was not performed.

Contract Price $ Date of Contract Is the property seller the owner of public record? ☐ Yes ☐ No Data Source(s)

Is there any financial assistance (loan charges, sale concessions, gift or downpayment assistance, etc.) to be paid by any party on behalf of the borrower? ☐ Yes ☐ No
If Yes, report the total dollar amount and describe the items to be paid.

NEIGHBORHOOD

Note: Race and the racial composition of the neighborhood are not appraisal factors.

Neighborhood Characteristics	One-Unit Housing Trends	One-Unit Housing		Present Land Use %	
Location ☐ Urban ☐ Suburban ☐ Rural	Property Values ☐ Increasing ☐ Stable ☐ Declining	PRICE	AGE	One-Unit	%
Built-Up ☐ Over 75% ☐ 25–75% ☐ Under 25%	Demand/Supply ☐ Shortage ☐ In Balance ☐ Over Supply	$ (000)	(yrs)	2-4 Unit	%
Growth ☐ Rapid ☐ Stable ☐ Slow	Marketing Time ☐ Under 3 mths ☐ 3–6 mths ☐ Over 6 mths	Low		Multi-Family	%
Neighborhood Boundaries		High		Commercial	%
		Pred.		Other	%

Neighborhood Description

Market Conditions (including support for the above conclusions)

SITE

Dimensions	Area	Shape	View

Specific Zoning Classification Zoning Description

Zoning Compliance ☐ Legal ☐ Legal Nonconforming (Grandfathered Use) ☐ No Zoning ☐ Illegal (describe)

Is the highest and best use of the subject property as improved (or as proposed per plans and specifications) the present use? ☐ Yes ☐ No If No, describe

Utilities	Public	Other (describe)		Public	Other (describe)	Off-site Improvements—Type	Public	Private
Electricity	☐	☐	Water	☐	☐	Street	☐	☐
Gas	☐	☐	Sanitary Sewer	☐	☐	Alley	☐	☐

FEMA Special Flood Hazard Area ☐ Yes ☐ No FEMA Flood Zone FEMA Map # FEMA Map Date

Are the utilities and off-site improvements typical for the market area? ☐ Yes ☐ No If No, describe

Are there any adverse site conditions or external factors (easements, encroachments, environmental conditions, land uses, etc.)? ☐ Yes ☐ No If Yes, describe

IMPROVEMENTS

General Description	Foundation	Exterior Description materials/condition	Interior materials/condition
Units ☐ One ☐ One with Accessory Unit	☐ Concrete Slab ☐ Crawl Space	Foundation Walls	Floors
# of Stories	☐ Full Basement ☐ Partial Basement	Exterior Walls	Walls
Type ☐ Det. ☐ Att. ☐ S-Det./End Unit	Basement Area sq. ft.	Roof Surface	Trim/Finish
☐ Existing ☐ Proposed ☐ Under Const.	Basement Finish %	Gutters & Downspouts	Bath Floor
Design (Style)	☐ Outside Entry/Exit ☐ Sump Pump	Window Type	Bath Wainscot
Year Built	Evidence of ☐ Infestation	Storm Sash/Insulated	Car Storage ☐ None
Effective Age (Yrs)	☐ Dampness ☐ Settlement	Screens	☐ Driveway # of Cars
Attic ☐ None	Heating ☐ FWA ☐ HWBB ☐ Radiant	Amenities ☐ Woodstove(s) #	Driveway Surface
☐ Drop Stair ☐ Stairs	☐ Other Fuel	☐ Fireplace(s) # ☐ Fence	☐ Garage # of Cars
☐ Floor ☐ Scuttle	Cooling ☐ Central Air Conditioning	☐ Patio/Deck ☐ Porch	☐ Carport # of Cars
☐ Finished ☐ Heated	☐ Individual ☐ Other	☐ Pool ☐ Other	☐ Att. ☐ Det. ☐ Built-in

Appliances ☐ Refrigerator ☐ Range/Oven ☐ Dishwasher ☐ Disposal ☐ Microwave ☐ Washer/Dryer ☐ Other (describe)

Finished area **above** grade contains: Rooms Bedrooms Bath(s) Square Feet of Gross Living Area Above Grade

Additional features (special energy efficient items, etc.)

Describe the condition of the property (including needed repairs, deterioration, renovations, remodeling, etc.).

Are there any physical deficiencies or adverse conditions that affect the livability, soundness, or structural integrity of the property? ☐ Yes ☐ No If Yes, describe

Does the property generally conform to the neighborhood (functional utility, style, condition, use, construction, etc.)? ☐ Yes ☐ No If No, describe

Uniform Residential Appraisal Report

File #

There are	comparable properties currently offered for sale in the subject neighborhood ranging in price from $						to $	
There are	comparable sales in the subject neighborhood within the past twelve months ranging in sale price from $						to $	

FEATURE	SUBJECT	COMPARABLE SALE # 1		COMPARABLE SALE # 2		COMPARABLE SALE # 3	
Address							
Proximity to Subject							
Sale Price	$		$		$		$
Sale Price/Gross Liv. Area	$ sq. ft.	$ sq. ft.		$ sq. ft.		$ sq. ft.	
Data Source(s)							
Verification Source(s)							
VALUE ADJUSTMENTS	DESCRIPTION	DESCRIPTION	+(-) $ Adjustment	DESCRIPTION	+(-) $ Adjustment	DESCRIPTION	+(-) $ Adjustment
Sale or Financing Concessions							
Date of Sale/Time							
Location							
Leasehold/Fee Simple							
Site							
View							
Design (Style)							
Quality of Construction							
Actual Age							
Condition							
Above Grade	Total Bdrms. Baths	Total Bdrms. Baths		Total Bdrms. Baths		Total Bdrms. Baths	
Room Count							
Gross Living Area	sq. ft.	sq. ft.		sq. ft.		sq. ft.	
Basement & Finished Rooms Below Grade							
Functional Utility							
Heating/Cooling							
Energy Efficient Items							
Garage/Carport							
Porch/Patio/Deck							
Net Adjustment (Total)		☐ + ☐ -	$	☐ + ☐ -	$	☐ + ☐ -	$
Adjusted Sale Price of Comparables		Net Adj. % Gross Adj. %	$	Net Adj. % Gross Adj. %	$	Net Adj. % Gross Adj. %	$

I ☐ did ☐ did not research the sale or transfer history of the subject property and comparable sales. If not, explain

My research ☐ did ☐ did not reveal any prior sales or transfers of the subject property for the three years prior to the effective date of this appraisal.
Data source(s)
My research ☐ did ☐ did not reveal any prior sales or transfers of the comparable sales for the year prior to the date of sale of the comparable sale.
Data source(s)
Report the results of the research and analysis of the prior sale or transfer history of the subject property and comparable sales (report additional prior sales on page 3).

ITEM	SUBJECT	COMPARABLE SALE # 1	COMPARABLE SALE # 2	COMPARABLE SALE # 3
Date of Prior Sale/Transfer				
Price of Prior Sale/Transfer				
Data Source(s)				
Effective Date of Data Source(s)				

Analysis of prior sale or transfer history of the subject property and comparable sales

Summary of Sales Comparison Approach

Indicated Value by Sales Comparison Approach $

Indicated Value by: Sales Comparison Approach $ Cost Approach (if developed) $ Income Approach (if developed) $

This appraisal is made ☐ "as is", ☐ subject to completion per plans and specifications on the basis of a hypothetical condition that the improvements have been completed, ☐ subject to the following repairs or alterations on the basis of a hypothetical condition that the repairs or alterations have been completed, or ☐ subject to the following required inspection based on the extraordinary assumption that the condition or deficiency does not require alteration or repair:

Based on a complete visual inspection of the interior and exterior areas of the subject property, defined scope of work, statement of assumptions and limiting conditions, and appraiser's certification, my (our) opinion of the market value, as defined, of the real property that is the subject of this report is
$, as of   , which is the date of inspection and the effective date of this appraisal.

Uniform Residential Appraisal Report

File #

COST APPROACH TO VALUE (not required by Fannie Mae)

Provide adequate information for the lender/client to replicate the below cost figures and calculations.

Support for the opinion of site value (summary of comparable land sales or other methods for estimating site value)

ESTIMATED ☐ REPRODUCTION OR ☐ REPLACEMENT COST NEW	OPINION OF SITE VALUE .... = $
Source of cost data	Dwelling	Sq. Ft. @ $	.... =$
Quality rating from cost service Effective date of cost data		Sq. Ft. @ $	.... =$
Comments on Cost Approach (gross living area calculations, depreciation, etc.)		
	Garage/Carport	Sq. Ft. @ $	.... =$
	Total Estimate of Cost-New	.... = $
	Less Physical	Functional	External
	Depreciation		=$( )
	Depreciated Cost of Improvements... =$
	"As-is" Value of Site Improvements..................................... =$
Estimated Remaining Economic Life (HUD and VA only) Years	Indicated Value By Cost Approach .... =$

INCOME APPROACH TO VALUE (not required by Fannie Mae)

Estimated Monthly Market Rent $ X Gross Rent Multiplier   = $ Indicated Value by Income Approach

Summary of Income Approach (including support for market rent and GRM)

PROJECT INFORMATION FOR PUDs (if applicable)

Is the developer/builder in control of the Homeowners' Association (HOA)? ☐ Yes ☐ No Unit type(s) ☐ Detached ☐ Attached

Provide the following information for PUDs ONLY if the developer/builder is in control of the HOA and the subject property is an attached dwelling unit.

Legal name of project

Total number of phases   Total number of units   Total number of units sold

Total number of units rented   Total number of units for sale   Data source(s)

Was the project created by the conversion of an existing building(s) into a PUD? ☐ Yes ☐ No If Yes, date of conversion

Does the project contain any multi-dwelling units? ☐ Yes ☐ No Data source(s)

Are the units, common elements, and recreation facilities complete? ☐ Yes ☐ No If No, describe the status of completion.

Are the common elements leased to or by the Homeowners' Association? ☐ Yes ☐ No If Yes, describe the rental terms and options.

Describe common elements and recreational facilities

Uniform Residential Appraisal Report
File #

This report form is designed to report an appraisal of a one-unit property or a one-unit property with an accessory unit; including a unit in a planned unit development (PUD). This report form is not designed to report an appraisal of a manufactured home or a unit in a condominium or cooperative project.

This appraisal report is subject to the following scope of work, intended use, intended user, definition of market value, statement of assumptions and limiting conditions, and certifications. Modifications, additions, or deletions to the intended use, intended user, definition of market value, or assumptions and limiting conditions are not permitted. The appraiser may expand the scope of work to include any additional research or analysis necessary based on the complexity of this appraisal assignment. Modifications or deletions to the certifications are also not permitted. However, additional certifications that do not constitute material alterations to this appraisal report, such as those required by law or those related to the appraiser's continuing education or membership in an appraisal organization, are permitted.

SCOPE OF WORK: The scope of work for this appraisal is defined by the complexity of this appraisal assignment and the reporting requirements of this appraisal report form, including the following definition of market value, statement of assumptions and limiting conditions, and certifications. The appraiser must, at a minimum: (1) perform a complete visual inspection of the interior and exterior areas of the subject property, (2) inspect the neighborhood, (3) inspect each of the comparable sales from at least the street, (4) research, verify, and analyze data from reliable public and/or private sources, and (5) report his or her analysis, opinions, and conclusions in this appraisal report.

INTENDED USE: The intended use of this appraisal report is for the lender/client to evaluate the property that is the subject of this appraisal for a mortgage finance transaction.

INTENDED USER: The intended user of this appraisal report is the lender/client.

DEFINITION OF MARKET VALUE: The most probable price which a property should bring in a competitive and open market under all conditions requisite to a fair sale, the buyer and seller, each acting prudently, knowledgeably and assuming the price is not affected by undue stimulus. Implicit in this definition is the consummation of a sale as of a specified date and the passing of title from seller to buyer under conditions whereby: (1) buyer and seller are typically motivated; (2) both parties are well informed or well advised, and each acting in what he or she considers his or her own best interest; (3) a reasonable time is allowed for exposure in the open market; (4) payment is made in terms of cash in U. S. dollars or in terms of financial arrangements comparable thereto; and (5) the price represents the normal consideration for the property sold unaffected by special or creative financing or sales concessions* granted by anyone associated with the sale.

*Adjustments to the comparables must be made for special or creative financing or sales concessions. No adjustments are necessary for those costs which are normally paid by sellers as a result of tradition or law in a market area; these costs are readily identifiable since the seller pays these costs in virtually all sales transactions. Special or creative financing adjustments can be made to the comparable property by comparisons to financing terms offered by a third party institutional lender that is not already involved in the property or transaction. Any adjustment should not be calculated on a mechanical dollar for dollar cost of the financing or concession but the dollar amount of any adjustment should approximate the market's reaction to the financing or concessions based on the appraiser's judgment.

STATEMENT OF ASSUMPTIONS AND LIMITING CONDITIONS: The appraiser's certification in this report is subject to the following assumptions and limiting conditions:

1. The appraiser will not be responsible for matters of a legal nature that affect either the property being appraised or the title to it, except for information that he or she became aware of during the research involved in performing this appraisal. The appraiser assumes that the title is good and marketable and will not render any opinions about the title.

2. The appraiser has provided a sketch in this appraisal report to show the approximate dimensions of the improvements. The sketch is included only to assist the reader in visualizing the property and understanding the appraiser's determination of its size.

3. The appraiser has examined the available flood maps that are provided by the Federal Emergency Management Agency (or other data sources) and has noted in this appraisal report whether any portion of the subject site is located in an identified Special Flood Hazard Area. Because the appraiser is not a surveyor, he or she makes no guarantees, express or implied, regarding this determination.

4. The appraiser will not give testimony or appear in court because he or she made an appraisal of the property in question, unless specific arrangements to do so have been made beforehand, or as otherwise required by law.

5. The appraiser has noted in this appraisal report any adverse conditions (such as needed repairs, deterioration, the presence of hazardous wastes, toxic substances, etc.) observed during the inspection of the subject property or that he or she became aware of during the research involved in performing this appraisal. Unless otherwise stated in this appraisal report, the appraiser has no knowledge of any hidden or unapparent physical deficiencies or adverse conditions of the property (such as, but not limited to, needed repairs, deterioration, the presence of hazardous wastes, toxic substances, adverse environmental conditions, etc.) that would make the property less valuable, and has assumed that there are no such conditions and makes no guarantees or warranties, express or implied. The appraiser will not be responsible for any such conditions that do exist or for any engineering or testing that might be required to discover whether such conditions exist. Because the appraiser is not an expert in the field of environmental hazards, this appraisal report must not be considered as an environmental assessment of the property.

6. The appraiser has based his or her appraisal report and valuation conclusion for an appraisal that is subject to satisfactory completion, repairs, or alterations on the assumption that the completion, repairs, or alterations of the subject property will be performed in a professional manner.

Uniform Residential Appraisal Report
File #

APPRAISER'S CERTIFICATION: The Appraiser certifies and agrees that:

1. I have, at a minimum, developed and reported this appraisal in accordance with the scope of work requirements stated in this appraisal report.

2. I performed a complete visual inspection of the interior and exterior areas of the subject property. I reported the condition of the improvements in factual, specific terms. I identified and reported the physical deficiencies that could affect the livability, soundness, or structural integrity of the property.

3. I performed this appraisal in accordance with the requirements of the Uniform Standards of Professional Appraisal Practice that were adopted and promulgated by the Appraisal Standards Board of The Appraisal Foundation and that were in place at the time this appraisal report was prepared.

4. I developed my opinion of the market value of the real property that is the subject of this report based on the sales comparison approach to value. I have adequate comparable market data to develop a reliable sales comparison approach for this appraisal assignment. I further certify that I considered the cost and income approaches to value but did not develop them, unless otherwise indicated in this report.

5. I researched, verified, analyzed, and reported on any current agreement for sale for the subject property, any offering for sale of the subject property in the twelve months prior to the effective date of this appraisal, and the prior sales of the subject property for a minimum of three years prior to the effective date of this appraisal, unless otherwise indicated in this report.

6. I researched, verified, analyzed, and reported on the prior sales of the comparable sales for a minimum of one year prior to the date of sale of the comparable sale, unless otherwise indicated in this report.

7. I selected and used comparable sales that are locationally, physically, and functionally the most similar to the subject property.

8. I have not used comparable sales that were the result of combining a land sale with the contract purchase price of a home that has been built or will be built on the land.

9. I have reported adjustments to the comparable sales that reflect the market's reaction to the differences between the subject property and the comparable sales.

10. I verified, from a disinterested source, all information in this report that was provided by parties who have a financial interest in the sale or financing of the subject property.

11. I have knowledge and experience in appraising this type of property in this market area.

12. I am aware of, and have access to, the necessary and appropriate public and private data sources, such as multiple listing services, tax assessment records, public land records and other such data sources for the area in which the property is located.

13. I obtained the information, estimates, and opinions furnished by other parties and expressed in this appraisal report from reliable sources that I believe to be true and correct.

14. I have taken into consideration the factors that have an impact on value with respect to the subject neighborhood, subject property, and the proximity of the subject property to adverse influences in the development of my opinion of market value. I have noted in this appraisal report any adverse conditions (such as, but not limited to, needed repairs, deterioration, the presence of hazardous wastes, toxic substances, adverse environmental conditions, etc.) observed during the inspection of the subject property or that I became aware of during the research involved in performing this appraisal. I have considered these adverse conditions in my analysis of the property value, and have reported on the effect of the conditions on the value and marketability of the subject property.

15. I have not knowingly withheld any significant information from this appraisal report and, to the best of my knowledge, all statements and information in this appraisal report are true and correct.

16. I stated in this appraisal report my own personal, unbiased, and professional analysis, opinions, and conclusions, which are subject only to the assumptions and limiting conditions in this appraisal report.

17. I have no present or prospective interest in the property that is the subject of this report, and I have no present or prospective personal interest or bias with respect to the participants in the transaction. I did not base, either partially or completely, my analysis and/or opinion of market value in this appraisal report on the race, color, religion, sex, age, marital status, handicap, familial status, or national origin of either the prospective owners or occupants of the subject property or of the present owners or occupants of the properties in the vicinity of the subject property or on any other basis prohibited by law.

18. My employment and/or compensation for performing this appraisal or any future or anticipated appraisals was not conditioned on any agreement or understanding, written or otherwise, that I would report (or present analysis supporting) a predetermined specific value, a predetermined minimum value, a range or direction in value, a value that favors the cause of any party, or the attainment of a specific result or occurrence of a specific subsequent event (such as approval of a pending mortgage loan application).

19. I personally prepared all conclusions and opinions about the real estate that were set forth in this appraisal report. If I relied on significant real property appraisal assistance from any individual or individuals in the performance of this appraisal or the preparation of this appraisal report, I have named such individual(s) and disclosed the specific tasks performed in this appraisal report. I certify that any individual so named is qualified to perform the tasks. I have not authorized anyone to make a change to any item in this appraisal report; therefore, any change made to this appraisal is unauthorized and I will take no responsibility for it.

20. I identified the lender/client in this appraisal report who is the individual, organization, or agent for the organization that ordered and will receive this appraisal report.

Uniform Residential Appraisal Report   File

21. The lender/client may disclose or distribute this appraisal report to: the borrower; another lender at the request of the borrower; the mortgagee or its successors and assigns; mortgage insurers; government sponsored enterprises; other secondary market participants; data collection or reporting services; professional appraisal organizations; any department, agency, or instrumentality of the United States; and any state, the District of Columbia, or other jurisdictions; without having to obtain the appraiser's or supervisory appraiser's (if applicable) consent. Such consent must be obtained before this appraisal report may be disclosed or distributed to any other party (including, but not limited to, the public through advertising, public relations, news, sales, or other media).

22. I am aware that any disclosure or distribution of this appraisal report by me or the lender/client may be subject to certain laws and regulations. Further, I am also subject to the provisions of the Uniform Standards of Professional Appraisal Practice that pertain to disclosure or distribution by me.

23. The borrower, another lender at the request of the borrower, the mortgagee or its successors and assigns, mortgage insurers, government sponsored enterprises, and other secondary market participants may rely on this appraisal report as part of any mortgage finance transaction that involves any one or more of these parties.

24. If this appraisal report was transmitted as an "electronic record" containing my "electronic signature," as those terms are defined in applicable federal and/or state laws (excluding audio and video recordings), or a facsimile transmission of this appraisal report containing a copy or representation of my signature, the appraisal report shall be as effective, enforceable and valid as if a paper version of this appraisal report were delivered containing my original hand written signature.

25. Any intentional or negligent misrepresentation(s) contained in this appraisal report may result in civil liability and/or criminal penalties including, but not limited to, fine or imprisonment or both under the provisions of Title 18, United States Code, Section 1001, et seq., or similar state laws.

SUPERVISORY APPRAISER'S CERTIFICATION: The Supervisory Appraiser certifies and agrees that:

1. I directly supervised the appraiser for this appraisal assignment, have read the appraisal report, and agree with the appraiser's analysis, opinions, statements, conclusions, and the appraiser's certification.

2. I accept full responsibility for the contents of this appraisal report including, but not limited to, the appraiser's analysis, opinions, statements, conclusions, and the appraiser's certification.

3. The appraiser identified in this appraisal report is either a sub-contractor or an employee of the supervisory appraiser (or the appraisal firm), is qualified to perform this appraisal, and is acceptable to perform this appraisal under the applicable state law.

4. This appraisal report complies with the Uniform Standards of Professional Appraisal Practice that were adopted and promulgated by the Appraisal Standards Board of The Appraisal Foundation and that were in place at the time this appraisal report was prepared.

5. If this appraisal report was transmitted as an "electronic record" containing my "electronic signature," as those terms are defined in applicable federal and/or state laws (excluding audio and video recordings), or a facsimile transmission of this appraisal report containing a copy or representation of my signature, the appraisal report shall be as effective, enforceable and valid as if a paper version of this appraisal report were delivered containing my original hand written signature.

APPRAISER

Signature_____
Name _____
Company Name _____
Company Address _____
_____
Telephone Number _____
Email Address _____
Date of Signature and Report _____
Effective Date of Appraisal _____
State Certification # _____
or State License # _____
or Other (describe) _____ State # _____
State _____
Expiration Date of Certification or License _____

ADDRESS OF PROPERTY APPRAISED

_____
_____

APPRAISED VALUE OF SUBJECT PROPERTY $ _____

LENDER/CLIENT

Name _____
Company Name _____
Company Address _____
_____
Email Address _____

SUPERVISORY APPRAISER (ONLY IF REQUIRED)

Signature _____
Name _____
Company Name _____
Company Address _____
_____
Telephone Number _____
Email Address _____
Date of Signature _____
State Certification # _____
or State License # _____
State _____
Expiration Date of Certification or License _____

SUBJECT PROPERTY

☐ Did not inspect subject property
☐ Did inspect exterior of subject property from street
　Date of Inspection _____
☐ Did inspect interior and exterior of subject property
　Date of Inspection _____

COMPARABLE SALES

☐ Did not inspect exterior of comparable sales from street
☐ Did inspect exterior of comparable sales from street
　Date of Inspection _____

APPENDIX B:
DETAILED INSPECTION CHECKLIST

DETAILED INSPECTION CHECKLIST						
Due Date:	**Lender:**		**Payment:**		**Lead From:**	
Address:		**City:**		**State:**		**Zip:**
Ask About:			**Neighborhood Borders**			
Gross Living Area						
Permits			**North:**			
Dogs			**South:**			
Sales History for last 36 months			**East:**			
Accesibility			**West:**			
Parking						

SFR EXTERIOR CHECKLIST
(Circle Items as Noted or Enter Description)

SITE						
Item	**Circle/ Enter Description**	**Inspected**	**Item**	**Circle/ Enter Description**	**Inspected**	
# of Units			Alley	Public / Private / None		
# of Stories			Topography	Level / Sloping - How much?		
Type	Detached / Attached		Size	Average / Large / Small		
Corner Lot	Yes / No		Shape	Rectangular / Irregular		
Street	Asphalt / Gravel / Dirt / Other		Drainage	Adequate / Other		
Curb/Gutter	Yes / No		View	Mountains / Ocean / Other		
Sidewalks	Concrete / None		Landscaping	Average / Pro / None / Other		
Street Lights	Yes / No					

EXTERIOR DESCRIPTION						
Item	**Circle/ Enter Description**	**Inspected**	**Item**	**Circle/ Enter Description**	**Inspected**	
Foundation	Slab / Raised / Both		Sump Pump	Yes / No		
Exterior Walls	Stucco / Wood / Siding / Other		Dampness	Yes / No / None Observed		
Roof Surface	Shingle / Clay / Tile / Rock / Other		Settlement	Yes / No / None Observed		
Windows	Alum / Wood / Vinyl / Bars		Infestation	Yes / No / None Observed		
Mfg. Home	Yes / No					

BACKYARD AMENITIES						
Item	**Circle/ Enter Description**	**Inspected**	**Item**	**Circle/ Enter Description**	**Inspected**	
Patio	Concrete / Covered / Wood / Other		Pool	Pool / Spa / Both *		
Deck	Concrete / Covered / Wood / Other		BBQ	Built-in / Island / Firepit		
Porch	Concrete / Covered / Wood / Other		Fence	Blk / Wd / Chnlnk / Iron / Other		
Balcony	Concrete / Covered / Wood / Other					

VEHICLE STORAGE						
Item	**Circle/ Enter Description**	**Inspected**	**Item**	**Circle/ Enter Description**	**Inspected**	
Type	Garage / Carport / None		Driveway	Concrete / Asphalt / Gravel / Dirt		
Detached	Yes / No		RV Parking	Yes / No		
# of Cars			RV Parking			
Driveway	Yes / No		Surface	Concrete / Asphalt / Gravel / Dirt		
# of Cars			RV Parking			

EXTERIOR AMENITIES AND OTHER SPECIAL/SIGNIFICANT ITEMS -

SFR INTERIOR CHECKLIST

Address:	City:		State:		Zip:

SFR INTERIOR CHECKLIST
(Circle Items as Noted or Enter Description)

SITE

Item	Circle/ Enter Description	Inspected	Item	Circle/ Enter Description	Inspected
Flooring	Tile / Carpeting / HW / Lin		Living Room	FP / Bar: Wet / Dry	
Countertops	Granite / Laminate / Corian		Family Room	FP / Bar: Wet / Dry	
	Ceramic Tile / Other		Den	FP / Bar: Wet / Dry	
Walls	L&P / WB / Wood / Other		Office	FP / Bar: Wet / Dry	
Doors	Flush / H.C. / Panel / French		Dining Room	Chandelier	
Stairs	Chandelier / Wood / Iron / Other		Laundry Room	Room / Area / Sink	
Lighting	Recessed / Chandelier / Other				
Heating	CTR - FAU / Wall / Other / None				
Cooling	CTR - FAU / Wall / Other / Evap				
Fireplace	Number				
	Brick / Marble / Tile / Other				
Attic	Scuttle / Stairs / Finished / None				
Basement	None / Finished				
	Entry: Outside / Inside				
Insulation	Adequate / Concealed				

KITCHEN

Item	Circle/ Enter Description	Inspected	Item	Circle/ Enter Description	Inspected
Flooring	Wood / Tile / Other		Appliances	Fan / Hood / Both	
Appliances	Refrigerator: Built-in / Personal			Microwave: Built-In / Personal	
	Range / Oven: Built-in / Personal				
	Disposal: Built-in / Personal				
	Dishwasher: Built-in / Personal				

BATHROOMS

Item	Circle/ Enter Description	Inspected	Item	Circle/ Enter Description	Inspected
Bathroom 1	Full / Half W/S, CT / Fg		Bedroom 3	Fan / FP / Walk-In	
Bathroom 2	Full / Half W/S, CT / Fg		Bedroom 4	Fan / FP / Walk-In	
Bathroom 3	Full / Half W/S, CT / Fg		Other	Fan / FP / Walk-In	
Bathroom 4	Full / Half W/S, CT / Fg		Loft	Fan / FP / Walk-In	
Master Bedro	Fan / FP / Walk-In				
Bedroom 2	Fan / FP / Walk-In				

INTERIOR AMENITIES AND OTHER SPECIAL/SIGNIFICANT ITEMS

FINAL CHECKLIST

Address:		City:	State:	Zip:

Please make sure the following are completed

PICTURES

Front
Rear
Street
Interior

SFR MEASUREMENTS

Exterior:		2nd Story:		
Garage:		Attic:		
Accessory Bldgs:				

HOMEOWNER'S ASSOCIATION

Project Name		Units in Project		
Fees		Litigation		
Units Rented		Guest Parking		
Total Parking		Subject's Floor		
Owner Parking	Garage / Carport / Underground / Street	# of Elevators		
	Owned / Assigned	Common Area	Open Space:	
	Amount:		Pool / Spa -	
	Space Number:		Clubhouse:	
			Gym:	
			Other:	

HOA Contact Information

Company:			
Address: --		Phone: --	Fax: --
Hours of Operation: --			

PERMITS REQUIRED

Zoning:		Legal/Non-Conforming:		
Additions:				
Other:				

APPENDIX C: ANSWER KEY

Unit 1 – Fundamentals: Real Estate and Value

Answers Matching

1. U	6. Q	11. L	16. T
2. X	7. M	12. E	17. A
3. K	8. V	13. G	18. P
4. I	9. O	14. N	19. D
5. R	10. Y	15. F	20. S

Answers Multiple Choice

1. **(c)** Land is unique, indestructible, limited in supply, immovable, and useful. **Page 3**

2. **(b)** The full bundle of rights is associated with free and clear ownership of fee simple estates. **Page 5**

3. **(c)** The five tests of a fixture are method of attachment, adaptation, relationship of the parties, intention, and agreement of the parties. **Page 6**

4. **(c)** A piece of personal property installed by a tenant operating a business under a lease is considered a trade fixture. Trade fixtures are owned by the tenant and can be removed at the termination of the lease. **Page 8**

5. **(b)** Police power allows the government to make and enforce laws and regulations for the safety, health, and welfare of the public. Zoning regulations, building codes, and fire codes are all enacted under the government's police power. **Page 17**

6. **(d)** Escheat is the process by which private property reverts to the government when the owner dies without heirs and without a will (intestate). **Page 17**

7. **(b)** The four elements of value are demand, utility, scarcity, and transferability. **Page 21**

8. **(a)** The four basic factors that affect real estate are physical factors, economic conditions, political considerations, and social influences. **Page 22**

9. **(c)** The sales comparison method is similarly based upon the principle of substitution. In selecting comparable properties recently sold, the appraiser is substituting them for the subject. **Page 28**

10. **(b)** The present value of future benefits is exactly what the appraiser is calculating in the income approach. This is based on the principle of anticipation. **Page 28**

11. **(c)** Externalities are the countless influences outside the property that affect that property. **Page 29**

12. **(b)**   The principle of conformity states that maximum value results when properties in a defined area or neighborhood are similar in size, style, quality, use, or type. **Page 30**

13. **(b)**   Once a contribution has been made, the homeowner and the appraiser would like to know the market's response to that improvement. Analyzing the market's valuation of the contribution leads the appraiser and homeowner to evaluate whether the expense of the improvement generates a positive return or a negative return. **Page 31**

14. **(d)**   Surplus productivity is the income generated by a project after the four agents of production have been paid. **Page 32**

15. **(b)**   Capital covers the purchase of the land and the cost of improvements and equipment. Capital also includes the amortization of any loans to pay for capital expenditures, reserves for future depreciation, and insurance and tax expenses. **Page 33**

Unit 2 – Importance of the Appraisal Process

Answers Matching

1. B	6. F	11. E	16. O
2. D	7. H	12. A	17. N
3. R	8. S	13. I	18. C
4. G	9. L	14. U	19. W
5. V	10. X	15. Q	20. T

Answers Multiple Choice

1. **(b)**   The process begins exactly as one would expect it to begin—with the definition of the problem. **Page 40**

2. **(d)**   The scope of work establishes the type of information needed, the sources to be used, the approaches that add to the credibility of the appraisal, and the analysis necessary. **Page 45**

3. **(d)**   Firsthand data is data that has been observed personally by the appraiser. It requires the physical presence of the appraiser and usually includes the inspection of the subject and comparable properties. Physical observation is the most accurate means of verification. **Page 46**

4. **(b)**   The majority of the data used in appraisals is secondhand data. Every piece of secondhand data must be verified. The main issue with all secondhand data is its accuracy. **Page 47**

5. **(b)**   The life cycle is growth, equilibrium, decline, and revitalization. **Page 51**

6. **(a)** Equilibrium is the most stable part of the cycle while each of the other sections requires significant changes to be occurring. **Page 51**

7. **(b)** The appraiser identifies the property using the post office street address in the Letter of Transmittal in a summary report. **Page 52**

8. **(b)** The highest and best use is the one that is physically possible, legally permissible, and economically feasible that produces the best value. **Page 53**

9. **(d)** The best technique is always the sales comparison approach because it provides the most direct evidence of the market's valuation. However, sales comparisons are not always available for vacant land. **Page 54**

10. **(b)** USPAP requires the appraiser to use all approaches that add to the credibility of the appraisal. **Page 54**

11. **(c)** A good example of the use of the cost approach alone is for a single purpose building that has no income associated with it and no available comparable sales. **Page 55**

12. **(c)** Residential properties that are rented can be valued using the gross rent multiplier (GRM). **Page 57**

13. **(b)** The last step in the appraisal process is the final estimate of value. **Page 60**

14. **(a)** The choice of report type does not affect the amount of work done to complete the appraisal. The client needs determine the report type but the complete appraisal process must be completed prior to preparing the report. **Page 61**

15. **(c)** The three basic types of reports are the summary or form report, Self-Contained Appraisal Report or narrative report, and the Restricted-Use Appraisal Report. **Page 61**

Unit 3 – Depreciation

Answers Matching

1. I	6. S	11. U	16. C
2. B	7. G	12. O	17. F
3. K	8. R	13. M	18. D
4. A	9. H	14. L	19. P
5. J	10. N	15. V	20. T

Answers Multiple Choice

1. **(d)** Appraisers approach depreciation realistically with the goal of calculating actual depreciation from all sources. Depreciation is the loss in value of an improvement from any cause. **Page 70**

2. **(a)** The actual age of a property is the number of years elapsed since a structure's construction. **Page 71**

3. **(b)** Effective age takes into account a property's condition, maintenance, repair, renovation, and utility. A mathematical model for calculating effective age does not exist. **Page 72**

4. **(b)** Physical deterioration is a loss in value brought about by wear and tear, disintegration, use, and actions of the elements. Weather and deferred maintenance are examples of factors contributing to physical deterioration. **Page 74**

5. **(d)** The cost to cure is a method of estimating accrued depreciation based on the cost to cure or repair observed building defects. Establishing the cost to cure is part of that analysis process. **Page 75**

6. **(a)** The first type of functional obsolescence is caused by a deficiency in the plan or construction of the improvements. This can be the result of a deficient plan such as three bedrooms and one bathroom. **Page 76**

7. **(c)** Market extraction, age/life, observed condition, and the rent loss method are methods used by an appraiser to estimate depreciation. **Page 79**

8. **(a)** The age/life method or straight-line method is based on the passage of time, employs a simple model of depreciation, and its resulting calculations are basic. **Page 79**

9. **(d)** To calculate the depreciation percentage divide the effective age by the economic life. **Page 79**

10. **(b)** Straight-line depreciation is a method of measuring depreciation based on equal annual amounts during the remaining economic life of the asset or structure. Improvements depreciate an equal amount each year in the straight-line approach. **Page 79**

11. **(b)** Accrued depreciation using the straight-line method is equal to the depreciation percentage multiplied by the cost new of improvements ($200,000 x 20% = $40,000). **Page 80**

12. **(a)** Market extraction requires the appraiser to estimate accrued depreciation through the application of paired sales analysis and estimate the effective age of the subject property. **Page 84**

13. **(b)** Market extraction is often the best method as the results reflect the market's opinion of depreciation, not an objective, mathematical model of reality. **Page 84**

14. **(a)**   Competent application of the market extraction method requires that the two properties being compared are identical with the exception of that one item. If this is not the case, an advance statistical method called multivariable statistical analysis must be used to isolate the single differences. **Page 85**

15. **(d)**   The rent loss method estimates the total accrued depreciation of an income-producing property. **Page 85**

Unit 4 – Site Valuation: Theory

Answers Matching

1. F	4. O	7. Q	10. L
2. C	5. D	8. B	11. N
3. M	6. P	9. A	12. E

Answers Multiple Choice

1. **(b)**   One of the most significant principles underlying land valuations methods is that land can be valued apart from the improvements. **Page 96**

2. **(a)**   A developer, who understands assemblage and plottage, can purchase two or more contiguous lots. The developer may now build three units on the two lots and still comply with zoning. The value of the additional unit is the increase in value attributable to assemblage or plottage. **Page 98**

3. **(d)**   Important items to consider when researching comparables include location, size and shape, topography, utilities, accessibility, and zoning. **Pages 101-102**

4. **(b)**   The land would be valued at $200,000 (sales price – improvement value) since both the land and improvement constitute half of the sales price. **Page 103**

5. **(c)**   Ease of use is the primary strength of the allocation method. Once a reliable allocation has been developed, it can be easily used to calculate a land value. **Page 104**

6. **(b)**   Determining value through abstraction is obtained by deducting the depreciated costs of the improvements from the property's known sales price. The remaining value represents the value attributable to the land. **Page 104**

7. **(d)**   Lack of accuracy is the primary weakness of the abstraction method. Errors can occur in the dissimilarity of comparables, developing costs for improvement, and calculating depreciation. **Pages 105-106**

8. **(c)**   The subdivision method is a site valuation method used exclusively for finding lot value or land value in a pending subdivision. **Page 106**

9. **(a)**   Application requires some familiarity with construction, cost breakdowns, and the subdivision process. The appraiser must also have a basic understanding of the time value of money and the discounting process. **Page 107**

10. **(d)**   Ease of application is the primary strength of ground rent capitalization. Once the appraiser has identified the ground rent and the appropriate capitalization rate, the calculations are relatively easy. **Page 108**

11. **(d)**   The ground rent capitalization method is applicable to sites with income directly related or attributed to the land. This method is used when the land is leased to the owner of the improvements or the land is vacant and earns rent, such as a parking lot. **Page 109**

12. **(a)**   Establishing the residual income, calculating the income left over after determining the income attributable to the improvements, and capitalizing that income are all steps in the land residual technique. **Page 109**

13. **(c)**   In order to identify the income attributable to the land, the income attributable to the improvements must be calculated and subtracted from the total income in the land residual method. **Page 109**

14. **(d)**   The percentage that shows the rate of return derived from the amount of capital invested is the return on investment. **Page 110**

15. **(a)**   The land residual method can be applied to any improved income property and produce credible results. It is a bit complex for the beginning appraiser, but after a little practice, it can yield reliable valuations. **Page 110**

Unit 5 – Site Valuation: Practice

Answers Matching

1. N	5. D	9. A	13. H
2. C	6. P	10. Q	14. G
3. B	7. M	11. F	15. I
4. K	8. J	12. E	

Answers Multiple Choice

1. **(c)**   The sales comparison method is based on the principle of substitution. It consistently provides the most direct evidence of the market and is therefore the best approach to use, when good comparables are available. **Page 120**

2. **(a)**   The adjustment grid is a table or matrix of relevant data on comparable properties. **Page 120**

3. **(c)**   The actual adjustments are a dollar amount or percentage that is added to or subtracted from the sales price of a comparable property to account for a feature that differentiates it from the subject property. **Page 120**

4. **(b)**   Once all the adjustments have been made, the final opinion of value must be developed through reconciliation of the adjusted values of the comparable sales. **Page 120**

5. **(d)**   The allocation method is based upon the principle of balance as well as on the concept of contributory value. **Page 122**

6. **(c)**   Land value equals the percentage (expressed as a decimal) multiplied by the total property value. Therefore, $150,000 x .20 = $30,000. **Page 123**

7. **(b)**   To calculate land value using the abstraction method, the appraiser subtracts the value of the improvements today from the sales price. **Page 123**

8. **(a)**   In order to calculate depreciation, use the following equation: Depreciation = (Effective Age ÷ Economic Life) x RCT. As a result, (15 ÷ 100) x $350,000 = $52,500. **Page 124**

9. **(d)**   The land value is equal to the sales price subtracted by the value of improvements today. First, the value of improvements today needs to be calculated (VIT = RCT minus Depreciation). Therefore, VIT = $200,000 – $50,000 and is equal to $150,000. Then you find the land value (Land Value = Sales Price – Value Improvement Today) and obtain $270,000 ($420,000 – $150,000). **Page 124**

10. **(b)**   Direct costs include costs associated with the actual work completed to an improvement on-site. Examples of direct costs would be actual construction, wages for labor, supervision, and materials. **Page 125**

11. **(a)**   In order to find land value, you must subtract total costs from the total sales revenue. As a result, $1,500,000 – $500,000 = $1,000,000. **Page 126**

12. **(c)**   Land value is equal to the land income divided by the capitalization rate. In order to use this equation, the land income must first be calculated (Land Income = Total Income – Building Income). Therefore, land income is $75,000 ($175,000 – $100,000). The land income is then divided by the capitalization rate to obtain the land value ($75,000 ÷ .12 = $625,000). **Page 128**

13. **(d)**   Among the information required to apply the land residual technique is the building value today, its remaining economic life, and the market capitalization rate. **Page 128**

14. **(a)**   The recapture rate is equal to 1 ÷ by the remaining economic life. As a result, 1 ÷ 50 = .02 or 2%. **Page 128**

15. **(b)**   The value of a property is its income divided by the capitalization rate ($525,000 ÷ 0.07 = $7,500,000) **Page 129**

Unit 6 – Estimating Improvement Costs

Answers Matching

1. P	5. K	9. L	13. Q
2. O	6. B	10. G	14. R
3. F	7. H	11. N	15. M
4. J	8. C	12. E	

Answers Multiple Choice

1. **(d)** Estimating land value is straightforward. Land includes the ground itself and the rights inherent in the use of that ground. Estimating the value of improvements is a little more complex. Improvements are buildings or other structures that are permanently attached to the land. **Page 137**

2. **(a)** The most detailed approach to developing the cost of improvements is called reproduction. It is a complete replication of the improvements. **Page 138**

3. **(b)** Replacement cost, which is used most frequently, produces cost of improvements with equal utility. **Pages 138**

4. **(c)** When using the cost approach, the most important data to be collected by the appraiser is information on the building area and construction costs. **Page 140**

5. **(d)** Data sources of construction costs include Marshall & Swift, RSMeans, and Craftsman Book Company. **Page 141**

6. **(a)** Indirect costs are also known as soft costs. An easy way to distinguish between direct costs and indirect costs is that direct costs are those expenditures for labor and materials on site. **Pages 142-143**

7. **(a)** When the appraiser has all the necessary information to complete an accurate cost estimate, one of four different techniques can be used. These techniques or methods for estimating cost are the index method, square foot method, unit-in-place method, and quantity survey method. **Page 145**

8. **(c)** These four elements are the only information required: know the original cost of improvements, identify a relevant index, research the value of the index at the time of construction, and research the value of the index today. **Page 145**

9. **(b)** These four elements are the only information required: know the original cost of improvements, identify a relevant index, research the value of the index at the time of construction, and research the value of the index today. **Page 145**

10. **(c)** The quantity survey method is the most in-depth and detailed of the commonly used processes for estimating costs, but it also is the most time-consuming and arduous of the four. **Page 145**

11. **(a)**   Do not include the cost of the lot ($75,000). The index method formula is:
Today's Value = (Today's Index Value ÷ the Index Value at time of construction) x (the original Cost of the Improvements)
1. Today's Value = (387 ÷ 224) x $143,000 (original cost)
2. Today's Value = 1.73 x $143,000 (original cost)
3. Today's Value = $247,058.02
4. Today's Value (rounded off) = $247,058 **Page 147**

12. **(c)**   A regional multiplier is applied to the base cost to obtain a localized cost per square foot. **Page 148**

13. **(d)**   In the unit-in-place method, costs are calculated separately for various building components, component parts, and segments of the improvement. **Page 151**

14. **(b)**   The quantity survey method is the most thorough and accurate approach to estimating building costs or the cost of improvements. **Page 151**

15. **(a)**   Indirect costs include most of the work done off-site, including architecture, engineering, plan check, city fees, financing costs, and builder's overhead, which also may include accounting and legal fees. **Pages 142-143**

Unit 7 – Cost Approach: Application

Answers Matching

1. E	6. C	11. T	16. P
2. Q	7. U	12. L	17. D
3. I	8. J	13. G	18. F
4. M	9. A	14. V	19. B
5. O	10. H	15. K	20. S

Answers Multiple Choice

1. **(a)**   There are three basic approaches to developing an opinion of value used by appraisers: (1) the sales comparison approach, (2) the income approach, and (3) the cost approach. **Page 159**

2. **(a)**   If the footings and slab are poured at the same time, it is called a monolithic slab. **Page 161**

3. **(d)**   Brick and block construction is often used in the Eastern and Midwestern areas of the United States because of their insulation capacity and basic strength. However, these are not generally used in earthquake regions because they tend to crumble or split in an earthquake. **Page 161**

4. **(c)**   The strength of the electrical current going into the electrical box is rated in amperages or amps. In the 1950s, homes came with 50 to 100 amp panels. Today's homes require panels usually in the 150 to 200 amp range. **Page 163**

5. **(c)**   Significant finish items include windows, doors, appliances, countertops, cabinets, flooring, and molding. **Page 164**

6. **(b)**   Before going to the site for the inspection, the appraiser should have and be prepared to use these tools and files: camera, measuring device, blank or graph paper, and the appraisal file. **Page 166**

7. **(c)**   Observe the landscaping, both softscape—the plantings around the subject property that prevent erosion and improve aesthetic appearance, and hardscape—structures and features such as pathways, pools, and retaining walls. **Page 167**

8. **(d)**   GLA (gross living area) is defined as the area of the house, measured from the outside, less the garage, attic, and basement. Appraisers do not ignore the garage, attic, and basement, but these areas are not included in the area defined as GLA. **Page 168**

9. **(b)**   Property Value = Site Value + Cost New of Improvements – Depreciation of Improvements + "as is" value of the Site Improvements. **Page 170**

10. **(c)**   The careful observation of all three types of depreciation enables the appraiser to understand and account for any differences between cost and market value. **Page 170**

11. **(c)**   Four techniques that are used to obtain the cost of the improvements today are the index method, the square foot method (the most frequently used and part of the URAR form), the unit-in-place method, and the quantity survey method. **Page 172**

12. **(b)**   Entrepreneurial profit is required to compensate the entrepreneur (developer) for both the coordination of the project and the risk associated with the project. **Page 172**

13. **(d)**   The value of the site improvements as used in the URAR is the value "as is", which is after depreciation. **Page 174**

14. **(d)**   The type of appraisal for which the cost approach is the primary approach is any appraisal in which research determines that there are few similar comparables and the property does not generate income. Replacement cost is sufficient to determine functional utility. Reproduction cost is not necessary for this assignment. **Page 175**

15. **(a)**   The cost approach is the primary approach in any appraisal in which research determines that there are few similar comparables and the property does not generate income (i.e. unique or one-of-a-kind buildings, government-owned properties, properties that are significantly overbuilt for the neighborhood, and single or special use properties). Appraisals that do not lend themselves to the use of the cost approach include land without improvement. **Page 175**

Unit 8 – Cost Approach: Summation

Answers Matching

1. F
2. D
3. A

4. E
5. C

Answers Multiple Choice

1. **(a)**   Appraisers report the results of their appraisals in one of the three approved appraisal reports discussed in Unit 2. Most appraisers use the URAR, which is a summary report. **Page 184**

2. **(d)**   The form helps to facilitate the sale and trading of mortgage-backed securities in the secondary market. Mortgage-backed securities are investments with returns that are tied to pools of mortgage loans. **Page 184**

3. **(c)**   The previous URAR form requested only reproduction costs. The current form allows the specification of reproduction or replacement. **Page 184**

4. **(d)**   The most important reason appraisers do not present opinions with ranges of value is because measuring the range of accuracy is difficult and the final value is an opinion. This opinion of value includes subjective and objective data. **Page 187**

5. **(b)**   The first step is to research the subject on both the public records database and the local multiple listing service (MLS). **Page 189**

6. **(c)**   After research is completed, more detailed information is necessary to complete the cost approach and must be obtained through an interior and exterior inspection of the subject. **Page 191**

7. **(d)**   A subject property in a housing tract with no empty sites available for sale or properties recently sold cannot use the sales comparable approach to site value. Therefore, the next best technique for site valuation is abstraction. **Page 195**

8. **(b)**   It is important to review the MLS listing as well as public records so that the cost analysis includes any significant improvements. This allows for a more accurate calculation of depreciation. **Page 195**

9. **(a)**   The depreciation calculation is the effective age divided by the total economic life: $5 \div 100 = 0.05$ which rounds to 5%. **Pages 195-196**

10. **(b)**   In the abstraction method, site value is equal to sales price – (depreciated cost of improvements). Therefore, $500,000 – ($350,000 – $12,000) = $162,000. **Page 196**

11. **(a)**   A cost estimate of the improvements for the site comparable is made after obtaining site valuation using the abstraction method. **Page 199**

12. **(d)**   The next step after obtaining the cost of improvements for a site comparable is to evaluate the depreciation on the subject based on physical, functional, and external factors. **Page 201**

13. **(b)**   Physical depreciation = (effective age ÷ total economic life) x cost new. Therefore, physical depreciation = $(10 \div 50)$ x $300,000 = $60,000 **Page 201**

14. **(d)**   Functional obsolescence = original cost – market value. Therefore, $200,000 – $72,000 = $128,000. **Page 202**

15. **(b)**   The final estimate of value is obtained by calculating the sum of the site value and the cost of improvements new less depreciation. As a result, ($250,000 + $300,000) – $50,000 = $500,000. **Page 203**

GLOSSARY

absorption analysis
A study of the number of units of residential or nonresidential property that can be sold or leased over a given period of time in a defined location.

absorption period
The estimated time period required to sell, lease, place in use, or trade the subject property in its marketing area at prevailing prices or rental rates.

abstraction method
See extraction method.

abut
To border on, touch, as contiguous lots along a border or with a projecting part.

abutter's rights
The reasonable right to light, air, and visibility that a property enjoys from another.

access right
The right of an owner to have ingress to and egress from owner's property over adjoining property.

accession
An addition to property through the efforts of man or by natural forces.

accessory building
A building separate from the main structure on a property.

accretion
Accession by natural forces, e.g., alluvium.

accrued depreciation
Depreciation that has already occurred. It is the difference between the cost to replace the property and the property's current market value.

acquisition appraisal
A market value appraisal of property condemned or otherwise acquired for public use, to establish the compensation to be paid to the owner.

actual age
The number of years elapsed since a structure's construction. Also called physical age, real age, or chronological age.

actual depreciation
The depreciation occurring as a result of physical, functional, or economic forces, causing loss in value to a building.

adjacent
Lying near, close, contiguous, neighboring, bordering, or juxtaposed.

adjoining
In contact with, abutting on, or lying next to, especially in actual contact along a line.

adjustment
In the sales comparison approach, a dollar or percentage amount that is added to or subtracted from the sale price of a comparable property, to account for a feature that the property has or does not have which differentiates it from the subject property.

adjustment grid
Lists important items affecting value such as site area, location, design and appeal, quality, condition, gross building area, basement area, room count, view, age, amenities, etc. Also known as a matrix.

adjustment guidelines
Per Fannie Mae, state that a single line item adjustment should not exceed 10% of the sales price of the comparable.

administration expense
The cost of direct management and services related to the management of property.

Advisory Opinions
The Appraisal Standards Board (ASB) issues Advisory Opinions to illustrate the applicability of USPAP in specific situations and offers advice for the resolution of appraisal issues and problems.

aesthetic value
Relating to beauty, rather than to functional considerations.

aesthetic zoning
Regulates the appearance of buildings in the area.

A-frame roof
A roof whose two sides slope upward at a steep pitch and meet at the top.

age/life method
A method of computing accrued depreciation in which the cost of a building is depreciated at a fixed annual percentage rate. This is the method most frequently used by residential appraisers. Also known as the straight-line method.

agents of production
Land, labor, capital, and management. See principle of increasing and decreasing returns and principle of surplus productivity.

air rights
The rights in real property for the reasonable use of the air space above the surface of the land.

airspace
The interior area which an apartment, office, or condominium occupies. Airspace is considered real property to a reasonable height. For example, an owner or developer of condominiums may sell the airspace as real property.

allocation method
The allocation of the appraised total value between land and improvements. Allocation may be made using a ratio comparing building value to the total price (or value).

allowance for vacancy and collection losses
The percentage of potential gross income that will be lost due to vacant units, collection losses, or both.

amenities
Features that add value to a property.

amenity value
That value, difficult to measure in monetary terms, that is attributable to a property because of pleasant surroundings, such as a pretty view, quiet area, or ideal climate.

annuity method
A method of capitalization that treats income from real property as a fixed, regular return on an investment. For the annuity method to be applied the lessee must be reliable and the lease must be long term.

appraisal
An unbiased estimate or opinion of the property value on a given date.

appraisal process
An orderly systematic method to arrive at an estimate of value.

appraisal report
A written statement in which an appraiser gives his or her opinion of value.

appraisal review
The review of an appraiser's analysis, research, and conclusions by another appraiser.

Appraisal Standards Board (ASB)
Part of The Appraisal Foundation, the ASB develops, interprets, and amends USPAP.

appraised value
An appraiser's estimate of the amount of a particular value, such as assessed value, insurable value, or market value, based on the particular assignment.

appraiser
A person qualified by education, training, and experience who is hired to estimate the value of real and personal property based on experience, judgment, facts, and use of formal appraisal processes.

Appraiser Qualification Board (AQB)
Part of The Appraisal Foundation and responsible for establishing minimum requirements for licensed and certified appraisers and for licensing and certifying examinations.

appreciation
An increase in the worth or value of property over time.

approaches to value
Any of the following three methods used to estimate the value of real estate: sales comparison approach, cost approach, and income capitalization approach.

area
The space or size of a surface that is defined by a set of boundaries.

arm's-length transaction
A transaction, such as a sale of property, in which all parties involved are acting in their own self-interest and are under no undue influence or pressure from other parties.

aseptic system
The clean water system.

assemblage
The process of putting several smaller, less valuable lots together under a single ownership.

assessed value
Value placed on land and buildings by a public tax assessor as a basis for use in levying annual real estate taxes.

assessment roll
A list of all taxable property showing the assessed value of each parcel, establishing the tax base.

assessor
The official who has the responsibility of determining assessed values.

association agreement
Set of conditions and restrictions applying to all properties in a planned unit development, condominium, or other community project.

attached housing
Any number of houses or other dwellings, which are physically attached to one another.

automated valuation models (AVM)
Computer software programs that analyze data using automated systems, such as regression analysis and/or so-called artificial intelligence.

average deviation
In statistics, the measure of how far the average variate differs from the mean of all variates.

avigation easement
An easement over private property near an airport that limits the height of structures and trees in order to keep the take off and landing paths of airports clear.

avulsion
A sudden and perceptible loss of land by the action of water, as by a sudden change in the course of a river.

band of investment technique
Method of estimating interest and capitalization rates, based on a weighted average of the mortgage interest rate (or other cost of borrowed funds) and the rate of return on equity required.

bargain and sale deed
Any deed that recites a consideration and purports to convey the real estate.

baseline
A survey line running east and west, used as a reference when mapping land.

basement
A building's lowest story, which is partially or entirely below ground.

bearing wall
A wall or partition that supports a part of a building, usually a roof or floor above.

benchmark
Definite identification characteristics familiar to the appraiser and relied upon in his or her further analysis of a property. A location indicated on a durable marker by surveyors.

betterment
The enhanced value of real property from improvements.

bias
A preference or inclination that precludes an appraiser's impartiality, independence, or objectivity in an assignment.

blighted area
A district affected by extensive or numerous detrimental influences that have caused real property values to seriously decline.

blockbusting
The unscrupulous practice of inducing panic selling of homes at prices below market value, particularly by exploiting neighborhoods in which the racial makeup is or appears to be changing.

book depreciation
An accounting concept referring to an allowance taken to provide for recovery of invested capital.

book value
The current value, for accounting purposes, of an asset expressed as original cost plus capital additions minus accumulated depreciation.

bracketing
When using the sales comparison approach, selection of market data so that the subject is contained within a range of data.

breakdown method
A method of computing depreciation in which the appraiser estimates the loss in value for each type of depreciation separately. Also known as observed condition method.

breezeway
A covered porch or passage, open on two sides and connecting house and garage or two parts of the house.

brownfield
An abandoned commercial or industrial site or under-utilized neighborhood where redevelopment is complicated by actual or perceived contamination.

buffer zone
A segment of land between two disparate municipal zones acting as a shield to keep one zone from encroaching upon the other. Often used to separate residential districts from commercial areas.

building components
Parts of a building.

building capitalization rate
The sum of the discount and capital recapture rates for a building.

building code
Municipal ordinance that regulates the type and quality of building materials and methods of construction permitted.

building residual technique
Technique of income capitalization in which the net income to the building (after deducting the income required for the land) is capitalized into an estimated value for the building.

building restrictions
Restrictions that limit the way a property can be used. They may appear in building codes or title documents.

built-ins
Cabinets or similar features built as part of the house.

bulk zoning
Controls density and prevents overcrowding. Bulk zoning regulates setbacks, building height, and percentage of open area.

buyer's market
A market containing more supply than demand.

capital
Money and/or property owned or used by a person or business to acquire goods or services.

capital assets
Assets of a permanent nature used in the production of an income, such as land, buildings, machinery, and equipment. Under income tax law, these are usually distinguished from inventory, which are assets held for sale to customers in the ordinary course of the taxpayer's trade or business.

capital gain
At resale of a capital item, the amount by which the net sale proceeds exceed the adjusted cost basis (book value).

capital improvement
Any permanent improvement made to real estate for the purpose of increasing the useful life of the property or increasing the property's value.

capital recapture
The return of an investment.

capitalization
The process that can be employed to convert income to value.

capitalization method
See income capitalization method.

capitalization rate
The rate of interest, which is considered a reasonable return on the investment, and used in the process of determining value, based upon net income. It may also be described as the yield rate that is necessary to attract the money of the average investor to a particular type of investment.

carport
A roofed space having at least one side open to the weather.

cash equivalency technique
Method of adjusting a sales price downward to reflect the increase in price due to assumption or procurement by buyers of a loan at an interest rate lower than the prevailing market rate.

central tendency
The numeric value that is suggested as a typical value in a statistical sample.

certification
A signed and dated statement included in an appraisal report that the appraiser has performed an appraisal in an unbiased and professional manner and that all assumptions and limiting conditions are set forth in the report.

Certified General Appraiser
An individual who has met specific education, experience, and examination requirements. May appraise any property.

Certified Residential Appraiser
An individual who has met specific education, experience, and examination requirements. May appraise any 1-4 unit residential properties without regard to complexity.

characteristics
Distinguishing features of a property.

chronological age
The number of years elapsed since a structure was built. Also known as actual or physical age.

client
The person who employs an agent to perform a service for a fee.

closing costs
The numerous expenses buyers and sellers normally incur in the transfer of ownership of real property.

cloud on title
A claim, encumbrance, or condition that impairs the title to real property until disproved or eliminated as, for example, through a quitclaim deed or a quiet title legal action.

code of ethics

A set of rules and principles expressing a standard of accepted conduct for a professional group and governing the relationship of members to each other and to the organization.

collateral

(1) The property subject to the security interest. (2) Anything of value a borrower pledges as security.

collection loss

A loss incurred if tenants do not pay their agreed-upon rents.

collusion

An agreement between two or more persons to defraud another of rights by the forms of law or to obtain an object forbidden by law.

color of title

That which appears to be good title but is not title in fact.

Comments

Extensions of USPAP DEFINITIONS, Rules, and Standards Rules that provide interpretation, and establish context and conditions for application.

common area

An entire common interest subdivision except the separate interests therein.

common interest development (CID)

A common-interest development combining the individual ownership of private dwellings with the shared ownership of common facilities of the entire project. The common areas are usually governed by a homeowners' association. Also known as common interest subdivision.

community

Part of a metropolitan area, a number of neighborhoods that tend toward common interests and problems.

community property

All property acquired by a husband and wife during a valid marriage (excluding certain separate property).

comparable sales (comps)

Sales that have similar characteristics to the subject property and are used for analysis in the appraisal process. Commonly called "comps", they are recently sold properties similarly situated in a similar market.

comparative market analysis (CMA)

A comparison analysis that real estate brokers use, while working with a seller, to determine an appropriate listing price for the seller's house.

comparative unit method

A method for estimating reproduction or replacement cost, using typical per unit costs for the type of construction being estimated. See square-foot method.

comparison approach

A real estate appraisal method, which compares a given property with similar or comparable surrounding properties. Also known as sales comparison approach or market comparison approach.

COMPETENCY RULE

Per USPAP, identifies requirements for experience and knowledge both when completing an appraisal and prior to accepting an appraisal assignment.

complete appraisal

The act or process of estimating value or an estimate of value, performed without invoking the Departure Rule of the Uniform Standards of Professional Appraisal Practice.

component

One of the features making up the whole property.

composite rate

A capitalization rate composed of interest and recapture in separately determined amounts.

comps

See comparable sales.

concessions

Additional value granted by a buyer or seller to entice another party to complete a transaction.

conclusion

(1) The final estimate of value, realized from facts, data, experience, and judgment, set out in an appraisal. (2) An appraiser's certified conclusion.

condemnation

The process to exercise the power of the government to take private property from an owner for the public good, paying fair market value.

conditional use

A use that does not meet the current use requirements but may be allowed by obtaining a special permit.

conditions of sale

Circumstances of the sale such as exposure time, marketing process, and buyer motivation. Unusual conditions may affect the final purchase price of a comparable sale and cause the sales price to reflect the market improperly.

condominium

A housing unit consisting of a separate fee interest in a particular specific space, plus an undivided interest in all common or public areas of the development. Each unit owner has a deed, separate financing and pays the property taxes for the unit.

Conduct

The section of the USPAP ETHICS RULE that identifies issues regarding appraisers' conduct.

Confidentiality

Per USPAP, the section of the ETHICS RULE which states that the appraiser must protect the confidential nature of the appraiser-client relationship and is obligated to obey all confidentiality and privacy laws.

conforming loans

Loans which conform to Fannie Mae guidelines, which set loan limits to a certain amount.

construction classification

A system that rates fireproofing of structures according to the relative fire resistance of the structures, taking into account the type of frame, walls, and roof. Class A is the most fireproof, descending to Class D, the least fire resistant.

contiguous

In actual contact, touching.

contingent

Conditional, uncertain, conditioned upon the occurrence or nonoccurrence of some future event.

contingent valuation methodology (CVM)

A method used to identify how a particular feature affects the value of a property by asking those who are knowledgeable about that market (other appraisers and agents) when no sales data is available.

contour

The surface configuration of land. Shown on maps as a line through points of equal elevation.

contract rent

The rent established by agreement or contract.

contributory value

Value given by appraisers to site improvements after identifying them.

conventional loan

Any loan made by lenders without any governmental guarantees (FHA-insured or VA-guaranteed).

conversion

Change from one character or use to another, as converting an apartment building to condominium use.

cooperative (co-op)

(1) A form of legal ownership with each owner holding a stated ownership percentage in the cooperative association. The association owns the land and buildings, and grants each owner the permanent right to occupy the specific dwelling unit, as well as the right to the joint use of the common areas. (2) A residential multifamily building.

coordination

As an agent of production, it is management.

corner influence

The effect on a property's value due to its location on or near a corner.

corner lot

A lot at the confluence or convergence of two streets.

cost

The expenses in money, labor, material, or sacrifices in acquiring or producing something.

cost approach

An approach to value in which a value estimate of a property is derived by estimating the replacement cost of the improvements, deducting the estimated accrued depreciation, and then adding the market value of the land. Also known as the summation method.

cost basis

Original price paid for a property.

cost index

Figure representing construction cost at a particular time in relation to construction cost at an earlier time, prepared by a cost reporting or indexing service.

cost multiplier

Regional or local factor used in adjusting published construction cost figures to estimate local costs.

cost services

Companies who collect and provide information regarding cost trends.

cost-to-cure method of depreciation

Method of estimating accrued depreciation based on the cost to cure or repair observed building defects.

courtyard home

A zero-lot-line home.

crawlspace

An unfinished accessible space below the first floor of a building with no basement.

credible

Something worthy of belief.

credit

A bookkeeping entry on the right side of an account, recording the reduction or elimination of an asset or an expense or the creation of or addition to a liability or item of equity or revenue.

cubic-foot method

Similar to the square-foot method, except that it takes height as well as area into consideration. The cubic contents of buildings are compared instead of just the square footage.

cul-de-sac lot

A lot situated at the end of a dead-end street that has a turn-around area.

cumulative zoning

Zoning laws that allow so-called higher uses (residential) to exist in lower use zones (industrial), but not vice versa.

curable depreciation

Items of physical deterioration and functional obsolescence which are economically feasible to repair or replace.

curb appeal

A phrase implying an informal valuation of a property based on observation and experience.

cut

The level building site or the space created in areas of sloping land when earth is removed. Unlike fill material, which can be unstable, a building site from a cut is generally a more solid base for structures.

cyclical movement

The sequential and recurring changes in economic activity of a business cycle, moving from prosperity through recession, depression, recovery, and back again to prosperity.

data

Information pertinent to a specific appraisal assignment. Data may be general (relating to the economic background and the region), local (relating to the city and the neighborhood), or specific (relating to the subject property and comparable properties in the market).

data services

The numerous companies engaged in the business of selling data to real estate appraisers.

data sources

Any of a variety of sources used by appraisers when collecting general, local, and specific information.

date of appraisal

The specific point in time when an appraiser designates the value of a home. Often stipulated as the date of inspection.

debit

A bookkeeping entry on the left side of an account, recording the creation of or addition to an asset or an expense or the reduction or elimination of a liability or item of equity or revenue.

debt capital

The amount borrowed by the buyer to purchase a property.

decline phase

Third phase in the cycle of a neighborhood, generally marked by delayed repairs and deterioration of buildings.

deed

A formal legal document used to transfer title from one person to another.

deed in lieu of foreclosure

A deed to real property accepted by a lender from a defaulting borrower to avoid the necessity of foreclosure proceedings by the lender.

deed of reconveyance

Document used to transfer legal title from the trustee back to the borrower after a debt secured by a trust deed has been paid to the lender.

deed of trust

A security instrument that conveys naked legal title of real property.

deed restrictions

Limitations in the deed to a property that dictate certain uses that may or may not be made of the property.

deferred maintenance

Building maintenance that has been postponed or neglected. A type of physical deterioration.

define the problem

Part of the appraisal process, includes identifying the client and other intended users, the intended use of the appraiser's opinions and conclusions, the type and definition of the value sought, and the effective date of the appraiser's opinions and conclusions.

DEFINITIONS section

The first section of USPAP containing definitions of terms specific to USPAP.

demand
The desire to possess plus the ability to buy.

demographic profile
A profile of a specific area that contains general demographic information such as employment, education, average age, average salary ranges, gender, occupation, number of children, etc.

demographics
The statistical characteristics of human population studies.

Department of Housing and Urban Development (HUD)
A federal department active in national housing programs, including but not limited to urban renewal, public housing, and FHA subsidy programs. HUD oversees FHA, FNMA, GNMA, and FMIC, among others.

Department of Veteran Affairs (VA)
Functions to guarantee loans to purchase and construct homes for eligible veterans and their spouses.

DEPARTURE RULE
This USPAP rule allows appraisers to "depart" from certain Standards Rules in particular situations. Replaced by the SCOPE OF WORK RULE in 2006 USPAP.

depreciated cost method
Method for adjusting comparable sales in which adjustments are calculated from an analysis of the depreciated replacement cost for each differentiating feature.

depreciation
(1) In appraisal, a loss in value from any cause. (2) A tax advantage of ownership of income property.

depreciation rate
The degree of lessening in value of an object or property, usually applied on an annual scale.

depression
A phase of the business cycle marked by industrial and commercial stagnation, scarcity of goods and money, low prices, and mass unemployment.

depth
Distance from the front lot line to the rear lot line.

depth table
A statistical table that may be used to estimate the value of the added depth of a lot.

detached house
A house surrounded by permanent open spaces.

deterioration
A worsening, impairment, or degeneration.

development method (land development method)
Method of vacant land valuation in which development costs and developer's profits are subtracted from estimated gross sales, resulting in a raw land value estimate.

development phase
First phase of the life cycle of a neighborhood, consisting of initial construction of improvements on vacant land.

diminished utility
A loss in the usefulness of a property resulting in a loss in property value.

direct capitalization method
Income capitalization technique in which value is estimated by dividing net operating income by the overall capitalization rate.

direct costs
All of the costs directly involved with the construction of a structure, including labor, materials, equipment, design and engineering, and subcontractors' fees.

direct lender
Lends their own funds and handles the entire loan process from origination to funding.

direct market comparison approach
See sales comparison approach.

discount rate
The interest rate that is charged by the Federal Reserve Bank to its member banks for loans.

discounted cash flow
Estimated future investment returns mathematically discounted to their present value.

distressed property
Property foreclosed on by the lender.

documents
Legal instruments, such as mortgages, contracts, deeds, options, wills, and bills of sale.

downzoning
A zone change from a high-density use to a lower density use. For example, a commercial zone to a light industrial zone.

drainage
The removal of excess surface water or groundwater from land by means of ditches or drains.

dry rot
A wood fungus that thrives in damp conditions and turns wood fibers into powder.

duress
The use of force to get agreement in accepting a contract.

easement
A non-possessory right to enter or use someone else's land for a specified purpose.

easement appurtenant
An easement that is connected to a particular property and is transferred along with that property. Each easement appurtenant involves two properties—the servient tenement and the dominant tenement.

easement in gross
An easement that is not appurtenant to any one parcel. For example, public utilities to install power lines.

ecology
The relationship between organisms and their environment.

economic age
Estimated age of a building based on its condition and usefulness.

economically feasible
Financially possible, reasonable, or likely. One of the tests of highest and best use.

economic base
The companies that provide jobs for a community or defined geographic area.

economic life
The estimated period over which a building may be profitably used. Also known as useful life.

economic obsolescence
Depreciation caused by changes in the economy that negatively affects the subject property's value.

economic rent
What a leased property would be expected to rent for under current market conditions if the property were vacant and available for rent. Also known as market rent.

economics
The science that studies the production, distribution, and consumption of wealth.

economic trend
Pattern of related changes in some aspect of the economy.

effective age
The age of a building based on its condition and usefulness. The apparent age based on the condition of the structure, instead of the chronological age.

effective date
The specific day the conclusion of value applies whether it is a present, past, or future date.

effective demand
Demand or desire coupled with purchasing power.

effective gross income (EGI)
The amount of income that remains after vacancy and credit losses are deducted from gross income.

egress
A way to exit a property.

element of comparison
Any aspect of a real estate transaction or any characteristic of the property that may affect the property's sales price.

elements of value
Four prerequisites that must be present for an object to have value: demand, utility, scarcity, and transferability.

elevation sheet
A labeled diagram or cutaway of a home detailing its features and building components, both interior and exterior.

Ellwood technique
A mortgage/equity method of capitalization, expressed in tables.

eminent domain
The right of the government to take private property from an owner, for the public good, paying fair market value.

encroachment
The unauthorized placement of permanent improvements that intrude on adjacent property owned by another.

encumbrance
An interest in real property that is held by someone who is not the property owner.

entrepreneur
One who assumes the risk and management of business.

entrepreneurial profit
A market-derived figure that represents the compensation the owner or developer expects to gain from developing the property.

entry-level home
A type of home for first-time buyers.

environment surroundings
All the external conditions and influences affecting the life and development of an organism, for example, human behavior, society.

Environmental Impact Report (EIR)
A formal report assessing the results or impact of a proposed activity or development upon the environment.

environmental obsolescence
See economic obsolescence.

equity
The difference between the market value of a home and the loan amount.

equity build-up
The gradual increase of the borrower's equity in a property caused by amortization of loan principal.

equity capital
The amount a buyer invests into a property.

equity capitalization rate
(1) Factor used to estimate the value of the equity in the band of investment method of capitalization and other mortgage and equity techniques. (2) The equity cash flow divided by the equity value.

equity investors
Investors using venture capital to take an unsecured and thus relatively risky part in an investment.

erosion
The gradual wearing away of land by natural processes.

escrow
A small and short-lived trust arrangement used to close real estate transactions.

estate
The ownership interest or claim a person has in real property. It defines the nature, degree, extent, and duration of a person's ownership in land.

estate at sufferance
A tenancy created when one is in wrongful possession of real estate even though the original possession may have been legal.

estate at will
A tenancy that may be ended by the unilateral decision of either party. There is no agreed-upon termination date, and either party must give 30 days notice before ending the tenancy.

estate for years
A leasehold estate with a definite end date. The lease must be renegotiated.

estate from period to period
A leasehold estate that does not need to be renegotiated upon each renewal.

estimate
(1) A preliminary opinion of value. (2) To appraise or determine value.

estimated remaining life
The period of time (years) it takes for improvements to become valueless.

ETHICS RULE
Per USPAP, identifies the requirements for "integrity, impartiality, objectivity, independent judgment, and ethical conduct".

evaluation
An analysis of a property and/or its attributes in which a value estimate is not required.

excess land
Surplus land beyond that which is needed to support the property's highest and best use.

excess rent
The amount by which the total contract rent exceeds market rent.

execute
(1) To perform or complete. (2) To sign.

execution sale
The forced sale of a property to satisfy a money judgment.

expansible house
Home designed for further expansion and additions in the future.

expenditures
Money laid out, disbursed, or expended.

expense ratio
See operating expense ratio.

expenses
The costs incurred in an enterprise. In appraisal, expenses are estimated on an annual basis regardless of the period in which they are incurred or paid.

expert testimony
Testimony given in a court trial by a person qualified by the court as an expert on a particular subject, for example, as an expert witness on real estate values.

expert witness
One qualified to give expert testimony in a court of law on a particular subject, such as medicine, engineering, or real estate appraising.

external obsolescence
A type of depreciation occurring because of negative influences outside of the specific property site (i.e. an airport flight pattern). See economic obsolescence.

externalities

Outside influences that may have a positive or negative effect on property value.

extraction method

A method of determining the land value of a comparable property by deducting the depreciated costs of the improvements on that property from the property's known sale price. The remaining value represents value attributable to the land. This method is a variation on the allocation method and is based on the same principles. Also known as abstraction method.

extraordinary assumption

Per USPAP, "an assumption, directly related to a specific assignment, which, if found to be false, could alter the appraiser's opinions or conclusions."

facade

The face of a building, especially the front face.

factory-built housing

Housing built in a factory instead of on site. Includes manufactured, modular, panelized, and precut homes.

fair market value

See market value.

fair rental value

See rent, economic.

feasibility study

An analysis of a proposed subject or property with emphasis on the attainable income, probable expenses, and most advantageous use and design. The purpose of such a study is to ascertain the probable success or failure of the project under consideration. A study of the cost-benefit relationship of an economic endeavor.

Federal Emergency Management Agency (FEMA)

A government agency involved with all the different aspects of emergency management from preparation to recovery and prevention.

Federal Housing Administration (FHA)

A government agency that insures private mortgage loans for financing of homes and home repairs.

federally related transaction

Any real estate transaction involving federal insurance or assistance.

fee simple absolute

An estate in fee with no restrictions on its use. It is the largest, most complete ownership recognized by law.

fee simple estate

The most complete form of ownership of real property, which can be passed by descent or by will after the owner's death. Also known as estate of inheritance or estate in fee.

fiduciary duty

The duty owed by an agent to act in the highest good faith toward the principal and not to obtain any advantage over the latter by the slightest misrepresentation, concealment, duress, or pressure.

fill

(1) Earth used to raise the existing ground level. (2) In residential real estate, base material that is borrowed from another source and is not generally as stable as a cut.

filtering

The process whereby higher priced properties become available to lower income buyers.

final value estimate

The appraiser's estimate of the defined value of the subject property, arrived at by reconciling the estimates of value, derived from the sales comparison, cost, and income approaches.

Financial Institutions Reform, Recovery, and Enforcement Act (FIRREA)

A federal law passed in 1989 to provide guidelines for the regulation of financial institutions. One part of the law requires a state license or certification for the performance of federally related real estate transactions (with de minimus exceptions).

finished area

The enclosed area in a home that is suitable for year-round use.

fire door

A door of fire-resistant material to prevent or retard the spread of fire.

firewall

A wall of fire-resistant material to prevent or retard the spread of fire.

FIRREA

See Financial Institutions Reform, Recovery, and Enforcement Act.

fiscal year

A 12-month accounting period not related to the actual calendar year.

fixed expenses

Operating costs that are more or less permanent and that vary little from year to year regardless of occupancy.

fixity of location
The physical characteristic of real estate that subjects it to the influence of its surroundings.

fixture
Personal property that has become affixed to real estate.

flag lot
A lot located so that access can be had only at the side of another lot.

flipping
Buying a property at one price and quickly selling it to another at an inflated price.

flood plain
An area that is adjacent to a river or watercourse and is subject to periodic flooding.

floor plan
A depiction of the floor layout including each room's size and connection with other rooms.

foreclosure
The legal procedure by which mortgaged property is sold to satisfy a debt when the borrower has defaulted on the loan.

form report
Written appraisal report, presented on a standardized form or checklist.

fraud
An act meant to deceive in order to get someone to part with something of value.

freehold estate
An estate in real property which continues for an indefinite period of time. It differs from a leasehold estate, which allows possession for a limited time.

frequency distribution
The arrangement of data into groups according to the frequency with which they appear in the data set.

front foot
Measurement in feet of the width of a property on the side facing the street.

frontage
The width of a property on the side facing a street.

frostline
The depth of frost penetration in the soil. Varies in different parts of the country. Footings should be placed below this depth to prevent movement.

fully amortized note
The most common type of loan with institutional lenders. Interest is charged on the outstanding principal balance at the rate and term agreed upon by the lender and borrower in a loan.

functional obsolescence
A type of depreciation stemming from poor architectural design, lack of modern facilities, out-of-date equipment, changes in styles of construction or in utility demand.

functional utility
The combined factors of usefulness with desirability.

future benefits
The anticipated benefits the present owner will receive from the property in the future.

future interest
An interest in real property that will take effect at a future time.

future value
The estimated lump-sum value of money or property at a date in the future.

gable roof
A roof with two sides sloping upward and meeting at the top.

gambrel roof
A curb roof, having a steep lower slope with a flatter upper slope above.

garage
A building or enclosure primarily designed or used for motor vehicles.

general warranty deed
A deed which conveys not only all the grantor's interests in and title to the property to the grantee, but also warrants that if the title is defective or has a cloud, the grantee may hold the grantor liable.

gentrification
A form of revitalization that occurs when run down properties are renovated or rehabilitated.

geodetic survey
A U.S. government survey generally used in identifying government lands and coastal areas.

gift deed
Used to make a gift of property to a grantee, usually a close friend or relative.

going concern value

The value existing in an established business property compared with the value of selling the real estate and other assets of a concern whose business is not yet established. The term takes into account the goodwill and earning capacity of a business.

goodwill

An intangible, but salable, asset of a business derived from the expectation of continued public patronage.

Government National Mortgage Association (GNMA)

An agency of HUD, called Ginnie Mae, that functions in the secondary mortgage market.

government survey system

See rectangular survey system.

grade

Ground level at the perimeter of the building.

grading

A process used when the level or elevation of the ground has to be changed or altered using bladed machines that scrape the earth.

graduated lease

A long-term lease that provides for adjustments in the rental rate on the basis of some future determination.

graphic analysis

A technique used to identify and measure adjustments to the sale prices of comparable properties.

grandfather clause

A legal clause that keeps a law from being retroactive. For example, a grandfather clause in a zoning law would allow the continuation of a previously legal use even if the new zoning law does not permit such use.

grant deed

A deed in which the grantor warrants that he or she has not previously conveyed the property being granted, has not encumbered the property except as disclosed, and will convey to the grantee any title he or she may acquire afterwards.

gross building area (GBA)

All enclosed floor areas, as measured along a building's outside perimeter.

gross income

Total income from property before any expenses are deducted.

gross income multiplier (GIM)

A figure which, when multiplied by the annual gross income, will equal the property's market value. The amount of the GIM must be obtained from recent comparable sales since it varies with specific properties and areas.

gross leasable area

Total space designed for occupancy and exclusive use of tenants, measured from outside wall surfaces to the center of shared interior walls.

gross lease

A lease agreement in which the tenant pays an agreed-upon sum as rent and the landlord pays any other expenses such as taxes, maintenance, or insurance. Also known as a flat, fixed, or straight lease.

gross living area (GLA)

The total finished, habitable, above-grade space, measured along the building's outside perimeter. This generally excludes garages and screened patios or porches ("Florida rooms").

gross rent

Income (calculated annually or monthly) received from rental units before any expenses are deducted.

gross rent multiplier (GRM)

A figure which, when multiplied by the monthly rental income, will equal the property's market value. The amount of the GRM must be obtained from recent comparable sales since it varies with specific properties and areas.

ground lease

A lease of land only on which the lessee usually owns the building or is required to build as specified by the lease. Such leases are usually long-term net leases.

ground rent

Earnings of improved property credited to earnings of the ground itself after allowance has been made for earnings of improvements.

hidden amenities

Assets of a property that contribute to its value, but are not readily apparent. Examples might include upgraded or premium building materials.

highest and best use (HBU)

The use, from among reasonably probable and adequately supported alternative uses, that is physically possible, legally permitted, economically feasible, and maximally productive. This is the starting point for appraisal.

hip roof

A roof with four sides sloping upward to meet at a ridge.

historic cost

Cost of a property at the time it was constructed or purchased.

holding period
The length of time the property will be used as an investment.

homogeneous
Of the same kind or nature.

house
A single-family detached residence.

houseboat
Essentially a barge designed and equipped for use as a dwelling.

HUD
See Department of Housing and Urban Development.

HUD-1 Statement
A standardized, itemized list, published by the U.S. Department of Housing and Urban Development (HUD), of all anticipated CLOSING COSTS connected with a particular property purchase.

hypothetical condition
Defined in USPAP as "that which is contrary to what exists but is supposed for the purpose of analysis".

improved value
A value placed upon a property when proposed improvements have been completed.

improvements
Additions made to property to enhance value or extend useful life. This term is typically used to refer to buildings and other structures that are permanently attached to the land.

incentive zoning
Allows a developer to exceed the limitations set by a zoning law if the developer agrees to fulfill conditions specified in the law.

income approach
An appraisal method that estimates the present worth of future benefits from ownership of a property to determine that property's value. Also known as income capitalization approach.

income capitalization method
Method for estimating depreciation by comparing the subject's capitalized value to its replacement cost new or by determining loss in rental income attributable to a depreciated item and applying a gross rent multiplier to that figure.

income forecast
Gross or net income estimate.

income property
Property that is purchased for its income-producing capabilities.

income stream
Actual or estimated flow of net earnings over time.

increment
An increase. Most frequently used to refer to the increase of value of land that accompanies population growth and increasing wealth in the community. The term unearned increment is used in this connection, since values are supposed to have increased without effort on the part of the owner.

incurable depreciation
Building defects or problems that would cost more to repair than the anticipated value increase from such repair.

index method
Method for estimating construction costs that adjusts the original costs to the current cost level by a multiplier obtained from a published cost index.

indicated value
Value estimate calculated or produced by an appraisal approach.

indirect costs
All of the time and money costs involved in a construction project that are not directly involved with construction itself. Examples are loan fees, interest, legal fees, and marketing costs.

industrial property
Land and/or improvements adapted for industrial use.

inflation
The increase in the general price level of goods and services.

inspection
The examination of a property, its buildings or other amenities.

instrument
A formal legal document such as a contract, deed, or will.

insurable value
The highest reasonable value that can be placed on property for insurance purposes.

intangible property
Property that lacks a physical form.

intangible value
That value attributable to a property that is difficult to determine precisely.

intellectual property (IP)
A general term for various legal rights, which attach to certain types of information, ideas, or other intangibles.

intended users
Per USPAP, parties intending to use an appraisal.

interest
(1) The charge for the use of money. (2) A legal share of ownership in property.

interest rate
The percentage of interest charged on the principal.

interim use
A short-term and temporary use of a property until it is ready for a more productive highest and best use. Occurs when the highest and best use is expected to change.

interior lot
A lot situated so that its boundaries touch no more than five lots. Generally, it is surrounded by three lots.

internal rate of return
The rate of return generated by an investment over the holding period, considering all future benefits, and discounting them to equal the present value.

intrinsic value
The value inherent in the property itself.

inverse condemnation
An action brought by a private party to force the government to pay just compensation for diminishing the value or use of his or her property.

investment property
Property purchased for expected future return.

investment value
The value of a particular property to a particular investor.

joint appraisal
An appraisal made by two or more appraisers working together.

joint tenancy
A type of ownership interest in which two or more parties own real property as co-owners, with the right of survivorship.

jumbo loans
Loans that exceed the maximum loan limit set by Fannie Mae and Freddie Mac.

junior mortgage
A mortgage recorded subsequently to another mortgage on the same property or made subordinate by agreement to a later-recorded mortgage.

jurisdiction
(1) The authority by which judicial officers take cognizance of and decide causes. (2) The power to hear and determine a cause.

JURISDICTIONAL EXCEPTION RULE
Part of USPAP, preserves the remainder of USPAP if one portion is contrary to a jurisdiction's law or public policy.

just compensation
Fair and reasonable payment due to a private property owner when his or her property is condemned under eminent domain.

key lot
A lot situated so that it is surrounded by the backyards of other lots.

labor
As an agent of production, it is the cost of all operating expenses and wages except management costs.

land
The surface of the earth including airspace, surface rights, mineral rights, and water rights.

land capitalization rate
The rate of return in investment and return of investment for the land only.

land residual technique
Income capitalization technique in which the net income remaining to the land (after income attributable to the building has been deducted) is capitalized into an estimate of value for the land.

landlocked
Property surrounded by other property with no access to a public road or street.

landlord
One who rents property to another. The lessor under a lease.

landscaping
The art of arranging plants, rocks, and lumber around the outside of a property for aesthetic or practical purposes, such as to prevent erosion or provide parking areas.

latent defects
Any defect in a property which is not readily apparent, but which has an impact on the value. Structural damage or termite infestation would be examples of latent defects.

lateral support
The support the soil of an adjoining owner gives to a neighbor's land.

lean-to
A temporary structure for protection from the elements.

lease
A contract between landlord (owner/lessor) and tenant (lessee) which gives the tenant an interest in the property. Also known as a rental agreement.

leased-fee estate
The property owner's interest in the leased property.

leasehold estate
The tenant's interest in the leased property during the term of the lease. This type of estate only has value if the agreed-on rent is less than the market rent. Also known as a less-than-freehold estate.

leasehold value
Market value of the excess of economic rent over contract rent

legal description
A land description recognized by law which can be used to locate a particular piece of property. Lot, block, and tract, government survey, and metes and bounds are types of legal descriptions.

legally permitted
Land uses that are allowed under current zoning and other land use regulations. One of the tests of highest and best use.

lender pressure
A lender directly or indirectly pressuring an appraiser to estimate a property's value at a certain amount.

lessee
Tenant or renter.

lessor
The person (landlord or property owner) who signs the lease to give possession and use to the tenant.

less-than-freehold estate
See leasehold estate.

lien
A claim on the property of another for the payment of a debt. A type of encumbrance.

life estate
An estate that is limited in duration to the life of its owner or the life of another designated person.

limited appraisal
An appraisal developed under and resulting from invoking USPAP's Departure Rule.

linear regression
Statistical technique used to calculate adjustment value or estimate sales price.

liquid assets
Assets that can be promptly converted into cash.

liquidation value
The value that can be received from the marketplace when the property has to be sold immediately.

liquidity
Holdings in or the ability to convert assets to cash or its equivalent. The ease with which a person is able to pay maturing obligations.

littoral
Land bordering a lake, ocean, or sea—as opposed to land bordering a stream or river (running water).

living units
A house or portion thereof providing complete living facilities for one family, including provisions for living, sleeping, eating, cooking, and sanitation.

loan closing
When all conditions have been met, the loan officer authorizes the recording of the trust deed or mortgage.

loan-to-value ratio (LTV)
The ratio of debt to the value of the property.

location
The site, setting, or position of a property or object in relation to other properties or objects.

locational obsolescence
Depreciation caused by the physical location of the subject property and its proximity to a negative influence. See external obsolescence.

long-lived
Structural components that need replacement infrequently, and sometimes never.

lot
A plot of ground.

lot, block, and tract system
A type of legal description that is created when developers divide parcels of land into lots. Each lot in a subdivision is indentified by number, as is the block in which it is located, and each lot and block is in a referenced tract. Also known as lot and block system, subdivision system, or recorded map system.

maintenance expenses
Costs incurred for day-to-day-upkeep, such as management, employee wages and benefits, fuel, utility services, decorating, and repairs.

management
The section of USPAP that discusses the disclosure of certain fees and commissions, identifies prohibited compensation arrangements, and discusses certain prohibited advertising and solicitation issues.

mansard roof
A roof with four sides sloping upward but stopping short of meeting, so that the top of the roof is flat.

margin of security
The difference between the amount of the mortgage loan(s) and the appraised value of the property.

manufactured home
A home built in a factory after June 15, 1976 which must conform to the U.S. government's Manufactured Home Construction and Safety Standards.

marginal land
Land whose value has been diminished due to some internal defect or external condition. In most cases, the cost to correct the flaw or condition is as much or more than the expected return from the property.

marital property
A general term for property owned by married people. Forms of ownership vary from state-to-state.

market
A place or condition suitable for selling and buying.

marketable title
Title that a reasonable purchaser, informed as to the facts and their legal importance and acting with reasonable care, would be willing, and ought, to accept.

market analysis
To identify, research, and analyze the particular market in which the appraised property operates.

market area
A geographic area in which similar property types compete for potential buyers or customers.

market exposure
Making a reasonable number of potential buyers of a property aware that the property is available.

market extraction
(1) General term for collecting information from the market. (2) Method of estimating depreciation in which building values abstracted from sales are compared to current costs new.

market price
The price paid regardless of pressures, motives, or intelligence.

market rent
The rent a property should bring in the open market as determined by current rents on comparable properties.

market segmentation
The process of identifying and analyzing submarkets within larger markets.

market value
The price a property would bring if freely offered on the open market, with both a willing buyer and a willing seller. Also known as objective value or value in exchange.

mass appraisal
Appraising more than one property using standard computerized techniques (statistical analysis, regression, automated valuation models, etc.).

master plan
A city or county's overall plan for physical development.

matched pair method
See paired sales method.

matrix
See adjustment grid.

mature phase
Second phase in the cycle of a neighborhood, marked by the stability of the existing buildings and occupants.

maximally productive
The property use that produces the greatest return on investment. One of the tests of highest and best use.

mean
A measure of central tendency which is calculated by adding the average prices or numeric values of a statistical sample and dividing that by the number of values in the sample. Also known as the average.

median
A measure of central tendency that equals the middle value in a statistical sample. The middle value in a statistical sample.

metes and bounds
A type of legal description that delineates boundaries and measures distances between landmarks to identify property.

mile

A linear measurement of distance. Equals 5,280 feet.

mill

Equals one-thousandth of a dollar and is numerically expressed as $0.001

millage rate

Expresses the property tax rate in terms of tenths of a cent per dollar of property value. The rate varies from district to district and county to county.

mineral rights

The legal interest in the valuable items found below the surface of a property (i.e., gold and coal).

minimum rent

The fixed minimum rent amount paid under a percentage lease. Also known as base rent.

minor

All persons under 18 years of age.

misplaced improvements

Improvements on land that do not conform to the most profitable use of the site.

mobile home

A factory-built home manufactured prior to June 15, 1976, constructed on a chassis and wheels, and designed for permanent or semi-attachment to land.

mode

A measure of central tendency that equals the most frequently occurring price or value in a statistical sample.

modified age/life method

A method of calculating depreciation. Curable physical and functional items of accrued depreciation are identified. The cost to cure all these items is deducted from the reproduction or replacement cost of the improvements. The ratio derived from the age/life method is then multiplied by the remaining cost to arrive at an estimate of accrued depreciation from all other causes.

modified gross lease

Tenant and landlord share expenses in accordance to the provisions of the lease.

modular home

Building composed of modules constructed on an assembly line in a factory.

monument

A fixed landmark used in a metes and bounds land description.

moratorium

The temporary suspension, usually by statute, of the enforcement of liability of debt.

mortgage

A legal document used as security for a debt. The mortgage is the instrument which secures the promissory note.

mortgage constant or mortgage capitalization rate (RM)

The capitalization rate of the debt. It is the ratio of annual debt service to the principal amount of the mortgage loan.

mortgage yield

The amount received or returned from an investment expressed as a percentage.

multiple listing service (MLS)

A cooperative listing service conducted by a group of brokers (usually members of a real estate association) to provide an inventory of all available properties in an area.

multiple regression analysis

A statistical technique for estimating a particular variable, such as probable sales price, using more than one other known variable.

multiplier

A number that, when multiplied by the income, gives an estimate of value. Also known as gross income multiplier or gross rent multiplier.

narrative appraisal report

A detailed, formal written report of the appraisal and the value conclusion.

negative cash flow

When monies will flow from the investor toward the investment.

negative easement

Prohibits a property owner from doing something on his or her estate because of the effect it would have on the dominant estate.

neighborhood

An area whose occupants and users share some common ties or characteristics. A neighborhood may be defined by physical boundaries, a change in land use, or intangible factors like school district boundaries.

neighborhood life-cycle

The process of neighborhood change, including four phases of change: development, maturity, decline, and renaissance.

net income
Gross annual income, less income lost due to vacancies and uncollectible rents, less all operating expenses.

net income ratio (NIR)
Net income divided by the effective gross income.

net lease
The tenant pays an agreed-upon sum as rent, plus certain agreed upon expenses per month (e.g., taxes and insurance).

net operating income (NOI)
The income remaining after deducting operating expenses from effective gross income.

net operating income ratio
The ratio between the net operating income of a property and its effective gross income (EGI).

net worth
The surplus of assets over liabilities.

non-conforming building
An existing building that does not conform to the latest building or zoning codes.

non-conforming loan
A loan that does not meet the standards of Fannie Mae and Freddie Mac. Jumbo loans and sub-prime loans are types of non-conforming loans.

non-conforming use
Legal use of property that was established and maintained at the time of its original construction but no longer conforms to the current zoning law.

non-economic highest and best use
A type of highest and best use that focuses on contribution to the community and community developmental goals rather than income-production.

nuisance value
The value reflected in the price that a buyer would be willing to pay to eliminate an objectionable situation.

observed condition method
See breakdown method.

observed conditions
The condition of a property, determined by observation.

obsolescence
Loss in value due to reduced desirability and usefulness of a structure because its design and construction became obsolete or due to factors outside the property itself. May be functional or economic.

occupancy
An act of taking or holding possession of an owned thing.

occupancy rate
The percentage of total rental units occupied and producing income.

off-site improvements
Improvements not directly on the site that add to the site's utility.

off-street parking
Designated parking spaces associated with a particular building or other structure that are not located on public streets.

on-site improvements
Buildings, structures or other amenities that are erected on a property and contribute to its value.

open housing law
A law passed by Congress in April 1968 that prohibits discrimination in the sale of real estate because of race, color, or religion of buyers.

operating expense ratio
Relationship of a property's expenses to income, found by dividing total operating expenses by effective gross income.

operating expenses
Expenses required to run a property (i.e., to maintain its income). Includes fixed, variable, and reserves for replacement.

operating statement
Written record of a property's gross income, expenses, and resultant net income for a given period of time.

optimum use
See highest and best use.

oral report
An appraisal report that is communicated to the client verbally, rather than in writing.

orientation
The placement of a building on its lot in relation to exposure to sun, prevailing wind, traffic, and accessibility from the street.

overage rent
The amount paid over and above the base rent, under a percentage lease.

overall rate
A capitalization rate that measures income attributable to both land and improvements, that is, to the whole property.

over-improvement

An improvement which is not the highest and best use for the site on which it is placed by reason of excess size or cost. Also called superadequacy.

ownership

(1) The right of one or more persons to possess and use property to the exclusion of all others. (2) A collection of rights to the use and enjoyment of property.

ownership in severalty

Property owned by one person or entity.

paired sales analysis

A method of estimating the amount of adjustment for the presence or absence of any feature by pairing the sales prices of otherwise identical properties with and without that feature. Also known as paired data set analysis, matched pairs analysis, and direct market method.

panelized home

A type of factory-built housing. A panelized home arrives at the construction site in small units, usually as completed walls with all the wiring and plumbing intact.

par value

Market value, nominal value.

parameter

A statistical term for a single number or attribute of the individual things, persons, or other entities in a population.

parcel

(1) A tract or an extended area of land. (2) A part, as in a certain piece of land is part and parcel of another piece.

parcel map

Map showing a parcel of land that will be subdivided into less than five parcels or units, and shows land boundaries, streets, and parcel numbers.

partial interest

An interest in real estate that represents less than the fee simple estate (i.e., a leased fee or leasehold estate).

partial taking

The process by which a governmental agency acquires only a portion of a property through condemnation.

partition action

A court action to divide a property held by co-owners.

party wall

A wall erected on the line between two adjoining properties that are under different ownership, for the use at both properties.

percentage adjustment

Type of sales adjustment in which the estimated difference between the comparable sale and the subject is first calculated as a percentage of the sale price of the comparable, and then applied as an upward or downward adjustment to the price.

percentage lease

A type of lease in which the tenant pays a percentage of gross monthly receipts in addition to a base rent.

percolation

The draining or permeating of water through soil.

personal property

Anything movable that is not real property.

physical deterioration

Depreciation that comes from wear and tear, negligent care, damage by dry rot or termites, or severe changes in temperature. Also known as deferred maintenance.

physical life

The length of time a structure can be considered habitable, without regard to its economic use.

physically possible

A use for the property that is not prevented by any physical issues such as poor access, steep topography, or unusable soil. The first test for highest and best use.

planned development

A planning and zoning term describing land not subject to conventional zoning to permit clustering of residences or other characteristics of the project which differ from normal zoning.

planning commission

An agency of local government charged with planning the development, redevelopment, or preservation of an area.

plat

An illustration, plan, or map of a plot of ground or a town site.

plat map

Map of a subdivision indicating the location and boundaries of individual lots.

plottage

The value added by combining two or more parcels together into one large parcel.

plottage increment

The appreciation in unit value created by joining smaller ownerships into one large single ownership.

plottage value
The increase in value brought about by the combining of two or more parcels of land with the result that the total value of the combined parcels in the "after" situation exceeds the value of the sum of the individual parcels in the "before" situation.

point of beginning
Starting place for a legal description of land using the metes and bounds method.

point estimate of value
The final value indication reported as a single dollar amount.

police power
The power of the state to enact laws within constitutional limits to promote the order, safety, health, morals, and general welfare of our society.

population
(1) The total number of people inhabiting a specific area. (2) In statistics, the entire set of data from which a statistical sample is drawn.

positive cash flow
When income generated by the property flows toward the owner.

potential gross income
A property's total potential income from all sources during a specified period of time.

potential value
The value that can reasonably be foreseen in the future.

precut home
A type of factory-built housing. A precut home is like a house in a box. All the materials are delivered to the construction site unassembled, but precut to fit exactly in place.

prefabricated
Any building or portion thereof, which is manufactured and assembled off site, then erected on a property.

pride of ownership
The pride of the owner in his or her property, reflected in the care and maintenance of the property.

primary mortgage market
The term for the market made up of lenders who make mortgage loans by lending directly to borrowers.

prime rate
The rate the bank charges its strongest customers (those with the highest credit ratings), is heavily influenced by the discount rate.

principal
(1) In a real estate transaction, the one who hires the broker to represent him or her in the sale of the property. (2) The amount of money borrowed.

principal meridian
One of 35 north and south survey lines established and defined as part of the U.S. government survey system.

principle(s) of:
anticipation
States that value is created by the anticipation of benefits derived in the future.

balance
States that the greatest value of a property will occur when the type and size of the improvements are proportional to each other as well as to the land.

change
Holds that it is the future, not the past, which is of prime importance in estimating value. Real estate values are constantly changed by environmental, economic, political, and social forces.

competition
States that real estate values are affected by supply and demand because of competition. Typically follows three steps: (1) market demand generates profits, (2) profits generate competition, and (3) competition stabilizes profits.

conformity
States that maximum value results when properties in a neighborhood are relatively similar in size, style, quality, use, and/or type.

consistent use
Requires that land and improvements be appraised on the basis of the same use.

contribution
Calculates the worth of a particular component in terms of its contribution to the value of the whole property, or an item's worth is calculated as the amount that its absence would detract from the value of the whole.

increasing and decreasing returns
The idea that income and other benefits available from real estate may be increased by adding capital improvements only up to the point of balance in the agents of production, beyond which the increase in value tends to be less than the increase in costs. Also known as law of increasing and decreasing returns.

opportunity cost

The economic principle that recognizes competing investments, usually in different industries, that may have a greater return.

progression

States that the worth of a lesser valued residence tends to be enhanced by association with higher valued residences in the same area.

regression

States that higher-valued properties tend to suffer when placed in close proximity with lower-valued properties.

substitution

Affirms that the maximum value of a property tends to be set by the cost of acquiring an equally desirable and valuable substitute property, assuming no cost delay is encountered in making the substitution. The foundation for the appraisal process.

supply and demand

States that market value is affected by the intersection of supply and demand forces in the market as of the appraisal date. Prices and rent levels tend to increase when demand is greater than supply and tend to decrease when supply exceeds demand.

surplus productivity

States that the net income that remains after the ownership expenses of labor, capital, and management have been paid is surplus income that is attributable to the land. This is also known as land rent and is used as the basis for the residual land valuation techniques.

private restrictions

Created at the time of sale or in the general plan of a subdivision.

pro rata

According to a certain percentage or proportion of a whole.

profits

The excess of returns over expenditures in a given transaction or series of transactions. Also, the excess of income over expenditure, as in a business, during a given period of time.

progress payments

Scheduled, periodic, and partial payment of construction loan funds to a builder as each construction stage is completed.

promissory note

The evidence of the debt, which states the amount of the money borrowed and the terms of repayment.

property

Anything that may be owned and gained lawfully.

property residual technique

A method of value estimation by capitalizing the income to the whole property.

proprietary lease

The lease used in co-op apartment buildings.

proration

Adjustments of interest, taxes, and insurance, etc., on a pro rata basis as of the closing or an agreed-upon date.

public record

A document disclosing all-important facts about the property.

qualitative analysis

Compares data on properties to obtain relative comparisons between properties in the same market.

quantitative analysis

Compares data on properties to obtain results that are then applied to other properties in the same market.

quantity survey method

The most in-depth and detailed method used to estimate reproduction or replacement cost. This method requires a detailed estimate of all labor and materials used in the components of a building. Items such as overhead, insurance, and contractor's profit are added to direct costs of building. This method is time consuming but very accurate.

quitclaim deed

Transfers any interest the grantor may have at the time the deed is signed with no warranties of clear title.

radon

Colorless, odorless, gas that is a carcinogen detected by a spectrometer.

range of value

The difference between the highest and lowest variant.

rate

(1) A fixed ratio, proportion. (2) A charge, payment, or price fixed according to a ratio, scale, or standard. (3) To appraise or assess value for tax assessment purposes.

ratio

Fixed or approximate relation, as between things, in number, quantity, degree, rate, or proportion.

ratio capitalization

Describes any capitalization method that uses the typical ratio of income to value to convert projected income into a value estimate for the property (or property component) under appraisal. Includes direct capitalization, as well as land, building, and equity residual capitalization methods when sales price-income ratios are used.

real estate

An identified parcel or tract of land, including any improvements.

Real Estate Settlement Procedures Act (RESPA)

A federal law requiring the disclosure to borrowers of settlement (closing) procedures and costs by means of a pamphlet and forms prescribed by the United States Department of Housing and Urban Development.

real property

Land (air, surface, mineral, water rights), appurtenances, and anything attached, and immovable by law. Also included are the interests, benefits, and rights inherent in owning real estate, i.e., the "bundle of rights". Current usage makes the term real property synonymous with real estate.

recapture

The recovery by an owner of money invested. Known as return of investment, not to be confused with interest, which is a return on investment. Also known as capital recapture.

reconciliation

The adjustment process of weighing results of all three appraisal methods to arrive at a final estimate of the subject property's market value. Also known as correlation.

reconstructed operating statement

One that eliminates the inapplicable expense items for appraisal purposes and adjusts the remaining valid expenses, if necessary.

Record Keeping

Per USPAP, this section of the ETHICS RULE identifies the record keeping requirements appraisers must follow.

rectangular survey system

A method of specifying the location of a parcel of land using prime meridians, base lines, standard parallels, guide meridians, townships, and sections. Also known as the rectangular survey system, or the U.S. Government Section and Township Survey.

redlining

An illegal lending policy, which denies real estate loans on properties in older, changing urban areas, usually with large minority populations, because of alleged higher lending risks and without due consideration being given by the lending institution to the creditworthiness of the individual loan applicant.

refinancing

The paying-off of an existing obligation and assuming a new obligation in its place. To finance anew, or to extend or renew existing financing.

region

Generally a segment of the nation set apart from other areas by geographical boundaries.

regression analysis

Statistical technique for calculating sales price or adjustments, or for estimating probable sales prices or other variables.

rehabilitation

The restoration of a property to its former or improved condition without changing the basic design or plan.

remainder depreciation

The possible future loss in value of an improvement to real property.

remaining economic life

The number of years between the structure's estimated economic life and its effective age.

remodel

An activity designed to improve the value or desirability of a property through rebuilding, refurbishing, redecorating or adding on to it.

renaissance

Fourth phase in the cycle of a neighborhood. The transition to a new cycle through the demolition, relocation, or major renovation of existing buildings.

renovation

Renewal, repair, or restoration to life.

rent

Payment for the use of a property, generally under a lease agreement.

rent roll

Total of all scheduled rental amounts for tenant space, services, and parking.

rental income

The total of the economic, or fair, rent for each of the units.

rental survey
An analysis of competitive rents used to identify the amount of income the subject property might generate.

replacement cost
Cost of constructing a building or structure that would have a similar utility to the subject improvement, but constructed with modern materials and according to current standards, design, and layout.

replacement reserves
Funds set aside by the property owner to pay for the replacement of certain building components and fixtures that periodically wear out. Also known as reserves for replacement.

replacement value
The amount of money required to replace any improvements that have been lost to fire, flood, wind, or other natural disasters.

reproduction cost
The current cost of building a replica of the subject structure, using similar quality materials.

residential lease
A lease used for single-family homes and duplexes.

RESPA
See Real Estate Settlement Procedures Act.

Restricted Use Appraisal Report
This is the briefest presentation of an appraisal and contains the least detail. Also known as restricted-use because the client is the only intended user of the report.

restriction
A limitation placed on the use of property. A restriction may be placed by a private owner, a developer, or the government.

retaining walls
Walls constructed to hold back soil and prevent erosion.

retrospective appraisal
An appraisal that looks at the value of a property at a point of time in the past.

return of investment
Recapture or conversion of the investment in real estate to cash or other valuable assets.

return on investment
The interest earned by an investor on an investment. Also known as return or yield.

reversion
The right to future possession or enjoyment by a person, or the person's heirs, creating the proceeding estate.

reversionary interest
A future interest. For example, the right of a landlord to reclaim the property at the end of the lease.

right-of-way
A right of passage on, over, or under another person's land.

riparian rights
The rights of a landowner whose land is next to a natural watercourse to reasonable use of whatever water flows past the property.

risk analysis
A study made, usually by a lender, of the various factors that might affect the repayment of a loan.

risk rating
A process used by the lender to decide on the soundness of making a loan and to reduce all the various factors affecting the repayment of the loan to a qualified rating of some kind.

room
Space that is enclosed or set apart by a partition.

rounding
Expressing an amount as an approximate number.

row house
A single-family residence, much like a townhouse, with sidewalls that are common with adjoining row houses. Differs from a townhouse in that the tandem garage and utility area usually occupy the ground floor or basement level and there are generally no common areas of ownership.

RULES
The rules in USPAP: the ETHICS RULE, the COMPETENCY RULE, the DEPARTURE RULE (or SCOPE OF WORK RULE), and the JURISDICTIONAL EXCEPTION RULE.

rural
An area outside of an established urban area or metropolitan district.

R-value
A rating that measures how well insulation resists heat.

sale-leaseback-buyback
A sale and leaseback transaction in which the leaseholder has the option to buy back the original property after a specified period of time.

sale-resale analysis

A method for determining adjustment or depreciation amounts that is useful when a property sells and is resold in a relatively short period of time. Assuming both sales are arm's-length, open market transactions, and assuming that there have been no significant changes to the property during the time between the two sales, the difference in price could be a basis for a time adjustment.

sales price

The actual price that a buyer pays for a property.

salvage value

(1) For income tax purposes, the anticipated fair market value of the property at the end of its useful life. (2) The value imputable to a house, structure, or object if it were to be moved to another location.

sample

A defined group within the whole that appraisers work with when analyzing statistical data.

sandwich lease

A lease agreement in which a tenant sublets the property to another person, thus creating a sublessor-sublessee relationship.

scarcity

A lack of supply of some type of real property resulting in increased value when demand exceeds supply.

scheduled rent

Rent paid by agreement between lessor and lessee. Also known as contract rent.

scope of work

The type and extent of research done and the type and extent of analysis applied.

scrap value

The value imputable to components of a structure, such as lumber, copper, roofing materials, or bricks, if they are removed from the existing premises for use elsewhere.

secondary mortgage market

The market involved in the buying and selling of existing mortgage loans from the primary mortgage market or from each other.

section

An area of land that is one square mile, 640 acres, or 1/36 of a township.

Self-Contained Appraisal Report

Contains the most detailed information. Self-contained means that everything the user of the report needs to fully understand it is contained within the report.

seller's market

The market condition in which demand exceeds supply.

semi-detached house

A house with one side a party or lot-line wall.

sentimental value

The value imputable to a property because of a close personal interest or relationship by the owner or potential owner.

separate property

Property owned by a married person in his or her own right outside of the community interest including property acquired by the spouse before marriage or by gift or inheritance.

septic system

The waste removal system.

septic tank

A watertight sewage-settling tank designed to accommodate liquid and solid waste.

service income

Includes receipts from laundry facilities, vending machines, and selling of utility services to tenants.

setback

The distance a building must be set back from the lot line. It is usually a front, back, or side setback.

setback line

A line set by an ordinance that determines how close to a property line a structure can be erected or installed.

setback ordinance

An ordinance requiring improvements built on property to be a specified distance from the property line, street, or curb.

severance damage

In eminent domain actions, the damage to the remainder of a property resulting from a part take of the whole property and the construction of the improvements as proposed.

shed roof

A lean-to type roof with one sloping side and one vertical side meeting at a ridge.

shopping center, regional

A large shopping center with 250,000 to 1,000,000 square feet of store area and serving 200,000 or more people.

short-lived

Structural components that are expected to be replaced or repaired on a consistent basis throughout the life of the structure.

significant digits
Those that go from the first numeral on the left over to the last numeral on the right that is not a zero.

single-family residence
Any improvement used as a dwelling for one related family group.

sinking fund
A fund set aside from a property's income which, with accrued interest, will eventually pay for replacement of the improvements.

site
(1) Land that has been prepared for use with grading, utilities, and access. (2) The position, situation, or location of a piece of land in a neighborhood.

skylight
An opaque window in the roof.

slab-on-grade
A type of foundation in which the structure sits directly on the ground. Monolithic slabs, floating slabs, screeded slabs, and post-tensioned slabs are all types of slab-on-grade foundations.

slum area
An area of generally run-down, overcrowded residences, usually multiple-family, whose inhabitants are usually economically deprived.

solar panels
Gather the sun's heat for use in a solar water heater, solar heating system, and even as a source of electricity in the residence.

special flood hazard area
Flood-prone area identified by FEMA. If the subject property is within a flood hazard zone, it needs to be noted in the appraisal report.

special warranty deed
A deed in which the grantor warrants or guarantees the title only against defects arising during the grantor's ownership of the property and not against defects existing before the time of the grantor's ownership.

special-purpose property
Property that has unique usage requirements, such as a church or a museum, making it difficult to convert to other uses.

square foot cost
The cost per square foot of area of land or a building found by dividing the number of square feet of area into the total cost of the structure or land.

special-use permit
See conditional-use permit.

square-foot method
A method for calculating reproduction or replacement cost by multiplying the cost per square foot by the building's area in square feet. The most common method used by appraisers and real estate agents to estimate the cost of construction.

squatter's rights
The right of use and enjoyment by reason of a long and uncontested possession of a parcel of real property.

stable phase
Second phase in the cycle a neighborhood, marked by stability of the existing buildings and occupants.

standard depth
The most typical lot depth in the neighborhood.

standard deviation
A measure of the extent of variability in a sample, that is, whether the observations are clustered near the mean or scattered throughout the range.

Standards Rules
A series of rules within USPAP that specify what the appraiser must do.

Statements on Appraisal Standards
Part of USPAP, they clarify, interpret, explain, or elaborate on a Rule or Standard.

statistics
The science of collecting, classifying, and interpreting information based on the number of things.

stigmatized property
Property which buyers or tenants may avoid for reasons which are unrelated to its physical conditions or features. Also known as psychologically impacted property.

straight lease
Lease agreement in which rent is a fixed amount that stays the same over the entire lease term.

straight-line method
See economic age/life method.

structure
Anything constructed or erected from an assembly of materials (for example, a house or garage).

subdivision
A tract of land divided by the owner into building lots and streets by a recorded subdivision plat.

subdivision development method
A method of valuing land used for subdivision development. Also known as the land development method.

subdivision system

See lot, block, and tract system.

subject property

The property that is being appraised.

subjective value

Value based on personal reasons.

sublease

A lease given by a lessee.

sub-marginal land

Land from which the return or income falls short of paying all expenses.

subprime loans

loans that do not meet the borrower credit requirements of Fannie Mae and Freddie Mac. Also known as "B" and "C" paper loans as opposed to "A" paper conforming loans.

substructure

Refers to all the below grade improvements.

subsurface

That which lies below the surface.

subsurface rights

Rights in property (oil, water, minerals) found below the surface.

Summary Appraisal Report

The most commonly used report option. It fulfills the minimum requirements for lenders to process their loans.

summation method

Establishes a safe rate for an investment and adds or subtracts from this basic rate according to the proper interest rate for the subject property. Another name for the cost approach to estimating value.

superadequacy

A feature that is too large or of a higher quality than needed for a property. Also known as an over-improvement.

superstructure

Refers to all the above-grade improvements.

supply

The total amount of a given type of property for sale or lease, at various prices, at any given point in time.

surface rights

The rights to use the surface of land, including the right to drill or mine through the surface when subsurface rights are involved.

survey

The process by which a parcel of land is measured and its area is ascertained.

tangible property

Property that has a physical form. Physical objects and/or the rights thereto.

tax rate

The ratio of the tax to the tax base. The rate to be applied to assessed value of real property, which determines the amount of ad valorem tax to be paid.

tenancy by the entirety

The joint ownership, recognized in some states, of property acquired by husband and wife during marriage. On the death of one spouse the survivor becomes the owner of the property.

tenancy in common

When two or more persons, whose interests are not necessarily equal, are owners of undivided interests in a single estate.

tenancy in partnership

Ownership by two or more persons who form a partnership for business purposes.

tenant

The party who has legal possession and use of real property belonging to another.

The Appraisal Foundation

An entity created by the appraisal profession to regulate its own industry. Empowered by the Financial Institutions Reform, Recovery, and Enforcement Act of 1989 to set minimum standards and qualifications for performing appraisals in federally related financial transactions.

tidelands

Lands that are covered and uncovered by the ebb and flow of the tide.

time adjustment

A term usually applied to adjustments made because of changing market conditions.

time value of money

The financial principle that a dollar in the present is worth more than a promised dollar in the future because of the present dollar's interest earning capability.

time-share

A real estate development in which a buyer can purchase the exclusive right to occupy a unit for a specified period each year.

T-intersection lot
A lot that is fronted head-on by a street.

title
Evidence that the owner of land is in lawful possession.

title plant
The storage facility of a title company in which it has accumulated complete title records of properties in its area.

topography
Nature of the surface of land.

townhouse
One of a row of houses usually of the same or similar design with common side walls or with a very narrow space between adjacent side walls. Also known as a row house.

township
Used in the government survey system, an area six miles by six miles (36 square miles) described by its location relative to the intersection of the baseline and meridian.

tract
A piece of land in an unimproved state – it does not have utilities, sewer lines, etc.

trade fixture
An item of personal property, such as a shelf, cash register, room partition or wall mirror, used to conduct a business.

Trainee License
In some states, this is the beginning level of appraisal license. The education, experience, and exam requirements to obtain a trainee license vary widely by state. Trainees must be supervised.

transferability
The ability to transfer ownership of an item from one person or entity to another.

transition
Change in use, such as farm to residential to commercial.

trend
A particular direction of movement.

trend analysis
Analysis that uses an arrangement of statistical data in accordance with its time of occurrence, usually over a period of years.

trust deed
See deed of trust.

turnkey costs
Costs that include all of the charges to the consumer, not just the costs to the developer or builder.

under-improvement
An improvement which, because of a deficiency in size or cost, is not the highest and best use of the site.

underwriting
Insuring something against loss.

unearned increment
An increase in real estate value that comes about from forces outside the control of the owner(s), such as a favorable shift in population.

unfinished areas
The areas of a home that do not have flooring, insulation, etc., that is similar to the rest of the house.

Uniform Residential Appraisal Report (URAR)
An example of a summary report. It is probably the most widely used form.

Uniform Standards of Professional Appraisal Practice (USPAP)
A set of standards and ethics, originally developed by nine appraisal associations to guide members in the development and reporting of appraisals. Now developed, published, interpreted, and amended by the Appraisal Standards Board of the Appraisal Foundation.

unimproved
Not improved, as not used, tilled, cultivated, or built upon.

unit
(1) A single object. (2) A standard of measure by which other quantities are evaluated.

unit cost
The cost in money of a standard quantity (for example, a square foot or a cubic yard) of a particular item.

unit-in-place method
A method of determining reproduction or replacement cost. Also known as the segregated cost method.

unit-of-comparison adjustment
Sales analysis tool, wherein the sales prices of the comparables are converted to price per physical or economic unit that is found to be closely related to selling price or value.

unit of measurement
The particular measurement being used. The two most commonly used are square foot (area) and cubic foot (volume).

urban property
City property.

urban sprawl
The unplanned and often haphazard growth of an urban area into adjoining areas.

usable area
That portion of the gross area of a site that can be built on or developed. Also known as useful area.

useful life
See economic life.

utility
The ability of a property to satisfy a need or desire, such as for shelter or income.

vacancy factor
The percentage of a building's space that is unrented over a given period.

vacancy loss
Loss of potential income because of a vacant unit.

vacant land
Land or site that is unimproved and that does not have any structures.

valuation
The process of estimating value.

value
The present and future anticipated enjoyment or profit from the ownership of property. Also known as worth.

value conclusion
See final value estimate.

value in exchange
See market value.

value-in-use
(1) The subjective value of an item or object to a particular user. (2) The value of a property under a given use. Also known as use value.

variable expenses
Operating expenses that vary with occupancy level or intensity of use of a property (e.g., utility costs and maintenance).

variance
An exception granted to existing zoning regulations for special reasons.

verification
An inquiry into the circumstances surrounding and affecting a sale.

warranty deed
A deed used to transfer title to property, guaranteeing that the title is clear and the grantor has the right to transfer it.

waste
The destruction, or material alteration of, or injury to, premises by a tenant.

water rights
(1) The right to draw water from a water course. (2) The right to use water, as water on a lake, for recreation.

water table
The depth below the land surface at which water is found.

wear and tear
Depreciation of an asset due to ordinary usage.

workfile
Appraiser's records that contain all the documentation necessary to support the appraiser's analyses, opinions, and conclusions conveyed in the appraisal report.

xeriscape
A patented name for landscaping that conserves water by using a wide variety of plants appropriate for the natural environment.

yield
The interest earned by an investor on an investment (or by a bank on the money it has loaned). Also known as return or profit.

yield capitalization
A method that discounts future benefits at appropriate yield rates, producing a value that reflects the income pattern, value change, and yield-rate characteristics of the investment.

yield rate
The yield expressed as a percentage of the total investment. Also known as rate of return.

zero lot line
A municipal zoning category wherein a building or other fixture may abut the property line.

zeroscaping

The use of rock and hardscape with only a few sparse plants to create low water landscaping.

zone

An area subject to certain restrictions or restraints.

zoning

The regulation of structures and uses of property within selected districts.

zoning law

Type of law used to execute master plans and control the mix of properties in a particular area.

zoning variance

An exemption from a zoning ordinance or regulation permitting a structure or use that would not otherwise be allowed.

INDEX

absorption analysis 107
abstraction method 104, 123
accessibility 102
accrued depreciation 71
actual age 71
adaptability 6
adjustment grid 120
adjustments 120
ad valorem taxes 17
adverse easement 15
age/life method 79
agents (factors) of production 32
air rights 3
allocation method 103, 122
amps 163
analysis 50
annuity 83
annuity method 83
appraisal 40
appraisal file 166
appraisal process 40
appraisal report 60
appurtenant 4
arm's-length relationship 7
assemblage 98
assessed value (APN) 97
Assessor's Parcel Number 53

balance 27
balloon framing 162
band of investment technique 111
breakdown method 87
bundle of rights 5

capital 33
capitalization rate 58
CC&Rs 18
client 42
community property 12

comparable property 41
component depreciation 81
concurrent ownership 11
condominium 8
conforming neighborhood 30
construction costs 141
consumer price index (CPI) 146
contribution 30, 170
contributory value 122
cost approach 55, 159, 170
cost breakdown 195
cost databases 148
cost to cure 75
curable depreciation 74

data sources 46, 140
date of the appraisal 43
Declaration of Restrictions 18
decreasing return 31
deed restrictions 4, 17
definition of the problem 41
demand 21
depreciation 70, 71, 106
direct capitalization 58
direct costs 125, 142
dominant tenement 15
drywall 162

easement 8, 15
easement in gross 16
economic factors 23
economic life 72
economic obsolescence 78
economic principles 25
economically feasible 25
effective age 72
effective demand 21
electrical 162
eminent domain 17
encumber 5
encumbrance 13
enjoyment 5

easement 8, 15
easement in gross 16
economic factors 23
economic life 72
economic obsolescence 78
economic principles 24
economically feasible 25
effective age 72
effective demand 21
electrical 162
eminent domain 17
encumber 5
encumbrance 13
enjoyment 5
entrepreneurial profit 172
equal utility 138
equilibrium 51
escheat 17
estate in remainder 10
estate in reversion 10
excess land 167
exterior inspection 167
external obsolescence 78
externalities 29
extraordinary assumption 44

Federal Home Loan Mortgage Corporation (FHLMC) 184
Federal National Mortgage Association (FNMA) 184
fee simple 8
fee simple estate 8
financial encumbrances 14
finish (interior/exterior) 164
finish plumbing 162
fire-rated door 165
firsthand data 46
fixture 6
floating slab 161
forecast absorption 124
foundations 160
framing 161
functional obsolescence 74, 76

galvanized steel pipes 162
general data 46
grant 6

gross income multiplier (GIM) 57
gross living area (GLA) 47, 168
gross rent multiplier (GRM) 57
ground rent capitalization 108, 127
ground rent method 108, 109

hard costs 142
hardscape 167
heating and air conditioning 163
highest and best use 25-26, 41, 53
hypothetical condition 45

improvements 4
income approach 57
income capitalization 85
increasing return 31
incurable depreciation 74
index 146
index method 145
indirect costs 125, 143
inspection process 166
insurance value 97
intended use 42
intended user 42
intention 7
interest 8, 83
interim use 26
intestate 17
involuntary liens 14

joint tenancy 12
judgment lien 14

labor 32
land 2, 33
land-to-improvement ratio 122
land/site value opinion 41
land residual method 109, 127

---

lath and plaster 162
leased fee 9
leasehold estate 8
leasehold interest 8
legal description 53
legally permitted 25
lessee 8
lessor 8
lien 14
life cycle 51
life estate 9
loan constant 111
location 101
locational obsolescence 78
long-lived items 76

management 32
market data 41
market extraction 84
market value 19
maximally productive 25
measuring device 166
method of attachment 6
monolithic slab 161
mortgage-backed securities 184
multiple listing service 48
multivariable statistical analysis 85

neighborhood 51
non-conforming neighborhood 30
non-financial encumbrances 14

observed condition method 87
opinion 40
opinion of value 40
ownership 11
ownership in severalty 11

paired sales analysis 56, 120
partial interest 8
personal property 6

physical deterioration 74
physical factors 22
physical observation 46
physically possible 25
pier and beam foundation 160
pitch 164
platform 162
plottage 98
plumbing 162
police power 17
political factors 23
possession 5
price 19
principle of
    anticipation 28
    balance 32
    change 29
    conformity 30
    contribution 30
    highest and best use 24
    substitution 27, 101, 170
    supply and demand 26
private restrictions 18
producer price index (PPI) 146
profit-à-prendre 16
projected gross sales 124
property 4, 44
property rights 44
public restrictions 17

quantity survey method 145, 151
quiet enjoyment 6

raised foundation 160
range of value 56
ratio 122
real estate 2
real property 5
reconciliation 58
regional multiplier 148
regression 77
remaining economic life 73
rent loss method 85
replacement cost 138
reproduction cost 138, 139

residual 109
Restricted-Use Appraisal Report 62
retail price index (RPI) 146
return of investment 110
return on investment 110
reversionary interest 9
right of survivorship 12
roofing 164, 165
rough plumbing 162

sales analysis 107
sales comparison approach 55
sales comparison method 101, 120
scarcity 21
scope of work 45
secondhand data 47
Self-Contained Appraisal Report 61
servient tenement 15
short-lived items 75
significant digits 59
site improvements 174
site value 54
situs 52
size and shape 101
social factors 24
soft costs 143
softscape 167
sole ownership 11
specific data 46
square foot method 105, 145, 147
straight-line depreciation 79, 105
straight-line method 79
street address 52
stucco 162
subdivision 99
subdivision method 106, 124
subject property 41
subsurface rights 3
Summary Appraisal Report 61
summation 183
superadequacy 76, 77
surplus land 167
surplus productivity 32, 122

taxation 17
tenancy 11
tenancy by the entirety 12
tenancy in common 11
tenancy in severalty 11
title 11
topography 102
trade fixture 8
transfer 5
transferability 21

undivided interest 11
Uniform Residential Appraisal Report (URAR) 61
unit-in-place method 145, 151
use 5
useful life 73
USPAP 60
utilities 102
utility 21

value 18
value in exchange 19
value of improvements today 123
verify 49
voluntary liens 14

wall systems 161
will 17
workfile 48

zoned system 163
zoning 102